Drugs and the FDA

# Drugs and the FDA

Safety, Efficacy, and the Public's Trust

Mikkael A. Sekeres

**The MIT Press**

Cambridge, Massachusetts | London, England

The MIT Press would like to thank the anonymous peer reviewers who provided comments on drafts of this book. The generous work of academic experts is essential for establishing the authority and quality of our publications. We acknowledge with gratitude the contributions of these otherwise uncredited readers.

This book was set in Stone Serif and Stone Sans by Westchester Publishing Services. Printed and bound in the United States of America.

Library of Congress Cataloging-in-Publication Data

Names: Sekeres, Mikkael A., author.
Title: Drugs and the FDA : safety, efficacy, and the public's trust / Mikkael A. Sekeres.
Description: Cambridge, Massachusetts : The MIT Press, [2022] | Includes bibliographical references and index.
Identifiers: LCCN 2021051380 | ISBN 9780262047319 (hardcover)
Subjects: MESH: United States. Food and Drug Administration. | Drug Approval | United States Government Agencies | Bevacizumab—therapeutic use | Breast Neoplasms—drug therapy | Antibodies, Monoclonal, Humanized—therapeutic use. | United States
Classification: LCC HV5825 | NLM QV 771 | DDC 362.290973—dc23/eng/20211228
LC record available at https://lccn.loc.gov/2021051380

10  9  8  7  6  5  4  3  2  1

To my wife, Jennifer, and children, Gabriel, Samantha, and Silas, the centers of my world; for my parents, my brother, Art and Pat Long, and my teachers, you made me who I am; and always for my patients, who teach me how to live a life, and remind me every day to cherish it

# Contents

# Preface

The United States Food and Drug Administration—the FDA—is the most trusted regulatory body in the world. Because of the confidence we place in the agency, we have the luxury of ignoring (or casually tossing out) the complicated labels and package inserts it writes for our medications, or of muting the television commercials that urge us to consult a physician if we experience "the following side effects." But no matter how we look at it, the FDA's responsibility—and thus its effect on our lives—is enormous. That was made crystal clear through its emergency-use authorization, and eventual approval, of vaccines to combat COVID-19.

The FDA protects the public health in myriad ways: by ensuring the safety, efficacy, and security of human and veterinary drugs, biological products, and medical devices; and by ensuring the safety of our nation's food supply, cosmetics, and products that emit radiation. It helps to speed innovations that make medical products more effective, safer, and more affordable, and it helps the public get the accurate, science-based information they need to use medical products and foods to maintain and improve their health.

The FDA also regulates more than $1 trillion worth of products each year. Because of the FDA, as a doctor I can comfortably prescribe medications knowing their potential risks and benefits, and as a patient and consumer I can take medications with the same confidence. Frankly, because of the FDA, my patients and I are living far longer and much better than if we had been born a century earlier.

The legislation that led to its birth, though, resulted from tragedy. And this history, along with how the FDA has evolved in response to public pressure, informs the decisions it makes about drug approvals today.

Prior to the twentieth century, drug manufacturers could hawk any potion, claim treatment of any ailment, and hail efficacy or potency on a bottle's label to any extent that they wanted, all in the name of increasing sales.

After all, no agency had authority to rein them in, or to ensure that their manufacturing processes and distribution plans were consistent and safe.

But then, dozens of children were given poisoned vaccines for smallpox and diphtheria, and many died. This is particularly poignant as we have debated the safety of vaccines sanctioned under an emergency-use authorization for the treatment of that other infection, COVID-19, and whether we should trust the FDA's assessment of their safety.

Soon after, the first federal regulations of biologic products were put into place.

Then, it took the deaths of dozens of children and adults, all prescribed an antibiotic by their trusted family doctors, before the FDA was empowered to actually require that drugs be *safe* for ingestion or injection.

But the clout to demand whether drugs actually work—to demand they be *effective*? That took thousands of children from around the world being born terribly disfigured, without arms, sometimes without legs or ears, and sometimes with just the ghostly suggestion of any of these appendages.

Because of its unholy birth, the FDA is cautious before it approves drugs for marketing in the United States. Embedded in its very DNA, first and foremost, is its mission to ensure a drug's safety, safety, safety. As a result, medicines given marketing approval in the United States are considered the safest in the world.

But for people with life-threatening illnesses who see their own mortality staring at them starkly at preternaturally young ages—like the patient James Petrarcha portrayed in this book, a composite of people I have cared for—the FDA can be maddeningly deliberate and slow to get medicines approved. When confronting a deadly scourge of unknown cause and undiscovered cure, be it AIDS or COVID-19—particularly with a cold and uncaring government in power—a community faced with just such a health crisis revolts, protesting loudly enough to be heard, to provoke change.

And once again, the FDA did change. It introduced accelerated approval, a formal process to get drugs to the patients who really, really need them sooner—a mechanism that, sure enough, gets new drugs to patients desperate to treat serious, life-threatening conditions *fast* (well, fast by FDA standards). Many of these drugs have in fact revolutionized the treatment of conditions like cancer, making hundreds of thousands, if not millions of people's lives better. Some have not been as transformative, though, and their rush to market may have violated the FDA's own DNA to ensure the safety of the public.

*Drugs and the FDA: Safety, Efficacy, and the Public's Trust* tracks the FDA's progress, beginning with the agency's genesis more than a hundred years ago (see the FDA timeline in figure 0.1). The story unfolds against the backdrop of the Avastin hearing, an unprecedented trial that took place in 2011 involving a wunderkind breast cancer drug that pit the drug's manufacturer—Genentech—against the FDA itself. Avastin was one of the dozens of drugs brought to market during the past two to three decades under the FDA's accelerated-approval mechanism.

At this trial, I and five other cancer specialists served as the jury (see the trial's cast of characters in table 0.1). Charged with deciding the fate of this drug taken by tens of thousands of women with

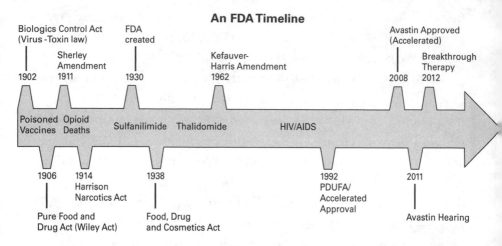

Highlights from FDA history, showing major events relevant to the Avastin trial and beyond.

breast cancer around the world, we would vote to recommend to either keep it on the market or remove it.

At this trial, dozens of brave women with breast cancer played witness to Avastin's ability to keep them alive for years, hearty and hale enough to testify before us; yet dozens of other women with breast cancer, also treated with Avastin, were no longer alive to testify.

At this trial, we saw how studies of cancer drugs can be "built to win," to gain regulatory approval, without necessarily benefiting patients. We witnessed the tension in the FDA's mission to balance a drug's safety and efficacy with promoting innovation and rapidly meeting the needs of sick and dying patients.

The Avastin hearing would put to the test not only the FDA's century-long evolution, but also the trust the public holds in this federal agency to safeguard our health in treating cancer, cardiovascular disease, AIDS, or COVID-19. And the FDA's decision about whether to maintain Avastin's breast cancer approval, or revoke it, would be the ultimate demonstration of how the agency's system of checks and balances really works. Or, in how it doesn't.

M.A.S.

**Table 0.1**
The Avastin Hearing Cast of Characters

| FDA | Genentech |
| --- | --- |
| Margaret Hamburg, MD—commissioner | Hal Barron, MD—chief medical officer |
| Richard Pazdur, MD—director, Office of Oncology Drug Products | Sandra Horning, MD—global head of clinical development, hematology and oncology |
| Karen Midthun, MD—presiding officer | Paul Schmidt, Esq.—general counsel |
| Patricia Keegan, MD—director, Division of Biologic Oncology Products | Jeff Helterbrand, PhD—global head of biostatistics |
| John Jenkins, MD—director, Office of New Drugs | Michael Labson, Esq.—attorney specializing in food and drug regulation |
| Rajeshwari Sridhara, PhD—statistician | |
| Abigail Brandel, Esq.—Office of Chief Counsel | Joyce O'Shaughnessy, MD—breast cancer oncologist |

ODAC Members and 2011 Affiliations

Frank Balis, MD—Children's Hospital of Philadelphia
Natalie Compagni-Portis, PsyD—patient representative
Ralph Freedman, MD, PhD—MD Anderson Cancer Center
Brent Logan, PhD—Medical College of Wisconsin
Wyndham Wilson, MD, PhD—National Cancer Institute (ODAC chairperson)
Gregory Curt, MD—AstraZeneca (non-voting industry representative)
Me—Cleveland Clinic

# 1

# This Little Drug Came to Market . . .

I have known hours when death for me would be a welcome relief.

—A. S. Calhoun, MD, Tulsa, Oklahoma, 1937

The 130-acre White Oak campus of the US Food and Drug Administration is located one mile north of the Capital Beltway in Montgomery County, Maryland, making it convenient to get to by car. Its fragmented buildings house the Office of the Commissioner, the Office of Regulatory Affairs, the Center for Drug Evaluation and Research, the Center for Devices and Radiologic Health, the Center for Biologics Evaluation and Research, and offices for the Center for Veterinary Medicine.[1]

The site, acquired by the US Department of the Navy in 1944, originally housed the Dahlgren Division of the Naval Surface Warfare Center, White Oak Detachment, which developed and tested ballistics, torpedoes, mines, and other explosives. In 1993, the Navy moved its operations and transferred the site to the General Services Administration; the FDA then occupied the campus in 2009.[2] True to its military origins, the main ingress to the FDA—Building

1—resembles a fortress, and still has *Naval Ordnance Laboratory* etched in stone on its frontispiece.

The quarter-mile-long Mahan Road, named for the nineteenth-century naval strategist Alfred Thayer Mahan, leads from New Hampshire Avenue and ends with a circular driveway in front of the building. The low-slung glass entrance, accessible only by navigating a row of cement pillar barricades, fronts a four-story, imposing red-brick building with long, vertical windows, opaque when viewed from the outside. On the inside, TSA-level security awaits visitors, who must also wear black-and-white photo identification stickers while on the premises. At any given time taxis or Uber or Lyft vehicles line the drive, along with the occasional catering service delivery car or corporate limousine.

But early in the morning on June 28, 2011, seven police cruisers bearing the insignia of the Department of Homeland Security Federal Protective Service and the Montgomery County Police Department blocked the campus entrance from casual visitors.[3] A crowd had started to form on New Hampshire Avenue. Many people wore pink T-shirts with a white ribbon on the front and the words "Avastin Works! Let Doctors and Patients Decide!" on the back. Some carried home-made signs with pictures of families and messages of "Breast Cancer Patients are NOT Statistics!" and "It's MY cancer! It should be MY decision!"

On this day the FDA would hold a hearing to decide whether to withdraw its previous approval of the drug bevacizumab (brand name Avastin)—the anti-angiogenesis wunderkind born from studies conducted by the Harvard researcher Judah Folkman—for the treatment of metastatic breast cancer. Studies from his laboratory showed that killing the blood vessel growth and, thus, the blood supply to tumors could eliminate the tumors themselves. Representatives of the FDA would face off against the attorneys and leadership of Avastin's manufacturer, Genentech, who desperately wanted to keep their blockbuster drug on the market for breast cancer.

Protest organizer Terry Kalley from Troy, Michigan, whose wife Arlene had battled breast cancer for over 30 years and eventually was treated with Avastin herself when the cancer became metastatic, stood in front of a crowd. Wearing one of the pink T-shirts, he held up a white megaphone to speak to those gathered, using language more commonly invoked at abortion rights rallies, pitting a woman's choice—in this case, to have access to Avastin—against a government agency's proposed restrictions to that choice.

"Today, it's Avastin for women with breast cancer. Tomorrow, it's the next drug that you or a loved one may need. . . . This is a national disgrace," Kalley shouted.[4]

A folk singer, Andrew Katz, sported one of the same pink T-shirts along with dark shades as he strummed a guitar and played the harmonica, singing the Bob Dylanesque "Avastin Protest Anthem":

Now I tell this story and I tell it right,
Tell about women in a hell of a fight.
Mothers, sisters, daughters too,
Americans just like me and you,
17,500 of 'em—
Cancer in their breast.
Tell you what son, boy, dad, pops, Mr. President
It's a hell of a test.[5]

These sorts of issues—a government agency's regulatory reach; patient autonomy and access to drugs for life-threatening conditions; testimonials from patients and doctors; assessment of drug safety and efficacy; and the precedent set by preventing the sales and marketing of a drug—were not new to the FDA, and in fact had both colored and informed its authority for over a century.

But it begged the question: Had the FDA made a mistake in approving the drug in the first place?

One hundred and twenty years earlier, therapeutic options for breast cancer were far more limited, and a regulatory body that had the authority to review safety and efficacy data for a drug and allow its marketing for a specific medical indication had not yet been created.

Imagine, back then, that you'd noticed a lump growing in your breast. You go to see the only doctor in your small town, who may even have confirmed that it was likely a cancer but isn't able to perform the disfiguring surgery that William Stewart Halsted, MD, a professor of surgery at Johns Hopkins University, would first describe in 1894—removing the breast tissue, underlying muscles, and lymph nodes—that could cure some women. This surgical approach had only become possible because of the rapid improvements in anesthesia and in aseptic technique that occurred in medicine during the latter part of the nineteenth century.[6]

In fact, Halsted's radical surgery would remain the standard treatment for breast cancer for more than 80 years until Bernard Fisher, MD, a surgeon from the University of Pittsburgh, bucked fierce opposition from his colleagues in demonstrating that a modified surgical approach was far less debilitating and worked just as well. Fisher was one of the first doctors to question traditional medical decision-making, which was often based on anecdotes, personal experiences, testimonials, and opinions. He once famously told a reporter, "In God we trust. All others [must] have data."[7]

Breast cancer has been documented in written records for more than 4,000 years.[8] Centuries before modern imaging techniques (like CT scans and MRIs) or autopsies revealed the inner mysteries of the human body, it was easier to detect than many other cancers because it wasn't hidden somewhere in the abdomen or the chest. But even though it arose close to the body's surface, breast cancer often wasn't recognized until it had started eating through the skin covering the breast, and in those cases was hidden from friends and even close family members, out of shame.

Back in the town doctor's office, he shakes his head, pitying you and frustrated at the limits of medicine, particularly in rural parts of the country. He tells you that some cancers grow slowly,

**Figure 1.1**
Hamlin's Wizard Oil, a patent medicine for ailments ranging from toothache, rheumatism, lame back, hydrophobia, and pneumonia, all the way to cancer. "There is no sore it will not heal, no pain it will not subdue." *Source*: US Library of Congress, from a print by Hughes Lithographers, Chicago, https://www.flickr.com/photos /trialsanderrors/3449228921/, public domain, https://commons.wikimedia.org/w /index.php?curid=7892703.

so maybe you'll be one of the lucky few, then instructs you on ways to hide the lump and mask the rancid smell of the ulcer expanding over it.

The following month, a traveling medicine show with a performance troupe comes to town, advertising Hamlin's Wizard Oil, a patent medicine and wondrous cure for ailments that range from toothache, rheumatism, lame back, hydrophobia, and pneumonia, all the way to cancer (see figure 1.1). Its cocksure slogan brags, "There is no sore it will not heal, no pain it will not subdue."[9] The oil works so well, the advertisement claims, that it can be used topically—as a liniment—or ingested. It is said to contain alcohol, camphor, sassafras oil, clove oil, turpentine, ammonia, and chloroform— ingredients that seem more appropriate for a potent wallpaper remover than a medicinal cure-all.[10]

Frankly, you don't have any other treatment options, so you hand 35 cents to the barker who stands near a case of this wondrous oil. In reality, the actual formula for this batch probably varies to include, aside from alcohol, whatever the manufacturers had on hand at the time. You swallow your first dose of the solution that night. Weeks go by, but despite your taking the nostrum religiously, the mass in your breast continues to worsen, and now you've developed a gastric ulcer, which prevents you from taking in a decent meal. You lose weight, get weaker, and six months from the time the medicine show came to town, you die, either from complications of breast cancer, or from the side effects of Hamlin's liniment.

Throughout the nineteenth century, entrepreneurs in the United States had absolute freedom to manufacture and market any food or drug in any way and for any purpose.

It wasn't until 1902 that progress toward regulation of food and drugs began. Dr. Harvey Washington Wiley, chief chemist of the Bureau of Chemistry of the US Department of Agriculture (figure 1.2), started assessing drug ingredients in nostrums like the one manufactured by Hamlin and discovered that many were either misbranded or completely adulterated.[11]

He was not alone: a crusade of lobbyists, including the Woman's Christian Temperance Movement and the general federation of Women's Clubs, led by the activist Alice Lakey, also feared for their safety and the safety of their families, and started pushing for a bill to move through Congress that would more formally regulate drugs.[12]

While it may not have been a complete surprise that patent medicines such as Benjamin Brandreth's Vegetable Universal Pill—a cathartic so well known it was even mentioned in Herman Melville's *Moby-Dick*—were not the medicinal panaceas they claimed to be, this was the first time the nostrums were called out officially, by a government agency.

**Figure 1.2**
Harvey Washington Wiley, MD, chief chemist in the US Department of Agriculture and architect of the Pure Food and Drugs Act of 1902. *Source*: https://www.fda.gov /about-fda/fda-leadership-1907-today/harvey-wiley.

But the bill didn't get far until tragedy struck. Around the same time, at the dawn of the twentieth century, a diphtheria outbreak occurred in St. Louis, and a smallpox outbreak arose in Camden, New Jersey.

Diphtheria antitoxin was made by inoculating horses with increasingly concentrated doses of diphtheria toxin (so that the horses' immune systems would produce antibodies to attack the toxin) and then bleeding the animals to obtain their serum—and more importantly the antibodies contained in the serum. When this antitoxin was then injected into a patient suffering from diphtheria, the antibodies in the horse serum neutralized the patient's toxin, enabling the patient to survive the infection.[13]

This approach to treating infection was similar in theory to the antibody therapy used to treat COVID-19 infections starting in 2020.

Smallpox vaccine, on the other hand, was often produced on the skin of calves. Both production methods, both uncontrolled and without formal regulation, were prone to errors.

Diphtheria antitoxin and smallpox vaccines were manufactured and then shipped to the sick people in St. Louis and Camden to treat their life-threatening infections. But in a horrible irony, both were contaminated during the manufacturing process with another deadly toxin—tetanus. Twenty-two children inoculated with the tainted vaccines died—not from diphtheria or smallpox, but from tetanus. In response, Congress passed the Biologics Control Act of 1902, also known as the Virus-Toxin Law after it was signed by Theodore Roosevelt on July 1 of that year.[14] It was the first law that instituted federal regulations of biologic products, in which a board that included the Surgeons General of the US Army, Navy, and Marine Hospital Service had the power to issue, suspend, and revoke licenses to produce products such as vaccines. Laboratories could be inspected, and fines or even prison sentences issued for violations.

Perhaps more importantly, the Biologics Control Act started a crusade for a law that would cover more than just biologics, but all drugs, and food.

At around 7:30 a.m. on that hot June day in 2011, many of the pro-Avastin protestors drifted toward the entrance of Building 1. After passing the many police cars, barricades, the formidable building's entrance, and the security checkpoint, they walked by a small historical display of some of the FDA's accomplishments, headed down a hallway, and then exited through a small courtyard to reach Building 31, where the hearing on Avastin would take place in the Room 1503, known as the Great Room.

The white shuttle bus bringing me and the six other members of the Oncologic Drugs Advisory Committee (ODAC) of the FDA took an alternate route from the Hilton Hotel in Silver Spring, Maryland, where we had spent the night. It drove past the protestors and our usual destination at FDA Building 1, depositing us instead at the entrance to the nondescript Building 32 to receive our temporary badges and run the gauntlet through a smaller security area before heading to the hearing.

Our job as ODAC members was typically to evaluate data concerning the safety and efficacy of marketed and investigational drugs for use in the treatment of cancer, and then to make recommendations to the FDA commissioner. But that day we would serve as the hearing's "jury." A member of the FDA itself had already informed us that it might be helpful to think of this debate—between the FDA's Center for Drug Evaluation and Research (CDER, the arm of the FDA that regulates over-the-counter and prescription drugs) and Genentech—as a trial.

Both the agency and the company would present witnesses who would try to make the case for their respective positions—for Genentech, that Avastin should remain on the market, retaining its breast cancer indication; and for the FDA, that the breast cancer indication should be withdrawn. The opposing party would then question those witnesses. We would then have an opportunity to question those witnesses, as would the presiding officer for the FDA, Karen Midthun, MD. Finally, the party presenting the witnesses would have a chance to ask clarifying questions of its own witnesses.

We would have a busy couple of days ahead of us: reviewing the evidence supporting Avastin's safety and efficacy track record across multiple clinical trials; then hearing the testimonies of physician experts and individual patients who have taken the drug (the women I would consider to be particular experts about the drug's side effects and its impact on beating back breast cancer); and, finally, asking questions of the people making presentations at the hearing. We would then provide advice and recommendations to the FDA: advice on whether it should continue to allow the company to market Avastin to the tens of thousands of women with metastatic breast cancer who had few other treatment options (Genentech's contention), or whether the toxicities of the drug outweighed its potential benefit and it should therefore be withdrawn from the market (FDA's position). We would vote publicly, for all to see in real time, whether we were for or against Avastin. The FDA Commissioner would then make the final decision on whether or not to withdraw Avastin's label for metastatic breast cancer.

Throughout the latter part of the nineteenth century and into the twentieth, concern over toxicities from drugs that were wantonly being pedaled grew along with worry over the safety of a much more basic human need: food.

With the Industrial Revolution, food production occurred on a large scale in the United States, and inventions like canning allowed food to be shipped around the country on the vast railway network that had also been built. But some nefarious manufacturers used spices or other additives to mask the taste of expired meat or other substandard ingredients that they packaged in the cans, and food poisoning outbreaks occurred frequently right up to the dawn of the twentieth century. In an attempt to introduce standards and regulate these products, a national pure food and drugs bill had actually passed the House twice, but both times without Senate action.

A final push to move a bill through Congress occurred with the help of two writers. In 1906, Upton Sinclair (figure 1.3) published his novel *The Jungle*, the main purpose of which was to highlight the harsh working conditions of immigrants in Chicago and other industrialized cities. It was supposed to be a socialist polemic. Sinclair, a journalist, spent seven weeks in 1904 working undercover in a meatpacking plant in the Chicago stockyards to get material for a series of articles he wrote for a socialist newspaper in 1905, as well as for his book.

**Figure 1.3**
Upton Sinclair, author of *The Jungle* (1906), a novel about unsanitary conditions in meatpacking plants. *Source*: Bain News Service, publisher. Public domain, https://commons.wikimedia.org/w/index.php?curid=89345430.

Rather than heed the socialist message Sinclair was trying to promote, many readers focused instead on sections of the book describing the unsanitary practices and health violations that occurred in the plant: how diseased, rotten, and contaminated meats were processed, doctored by chemicals, and mislabeled for sale to the public, and how, after hours, when no meat inspectors were around, workers processed dead and injured animals that were not supposed to be sold for human consumption. *The Jungle* became the most popular book in the country, leading Sinclair to quip, "I aimed at the public's heart, and by accident I hit it in the stomach."[15]

Also in 1905, the journalist Samuel Hopkins Adams published a 12-part series on the fraudulence and dangers of the patent medicine industry in *Collier's* magazine.[16] Adams, who could be considered the Michael Moore of his day, was an American muckraker from the Progressive Era who exposed institutions or leaders as being corrupt.[17] The term was popularized in a speech given by Theodore Roosevelt in 1906, in which he conceded, "the men with the muck rakes are often indispensable to the well-being of society; but only if they know when to stop raking the muck." His comment alluded to a muckrake-wielding character in Paul Bunyan's 1678 classic *Pilgrim's Progress* who could look no way but downward, his interest only in raking filth.[18]

Adams had a huge impact on the public perception of so-called cure-alls. His *Collier's* series was a damning exposé of medical charlatanry in which he called out fake practitioners by name, revealed the alcohol and narcotic content of specific nostrums, and made clear the profitable codependence of patent medicine advertisers and publishers. In one such description, of the drug Peruna, he wrote:

> Any one wishing to make Peruna for home consumption may do so by mixing half a pint of cologne spirits, 190 proof, with a pint and a half of water, adding thereto a little cubebs for flavor and a little burned sugar for color. Manufactured in bulk, so a former Peruna agent estimates, its cost, including bottle and wrapper, is between fifteen and eighteen cents a bottle. Its price is $1.00.[19]

Concerns about profiteering from high drug costs, which can far outstrip research and development expenses, is not just a modern-century phenomenon.

The series of articles would be collected in an edition called *The Great American Fraud*, reprinted by the American Medical Association, which sold 500,000 copies at 50 cents per copy.[20] Partly as a result, the AMA established the Council on Pharmacy and Chemistry, an in-house lab that analyzed the contents of patent medicines and determined which products were worthy of being granted permission to advertise in the *Journal of the American Medical Association*.[21]

This was at a time when medical journals and magazines vetted the advertisements included in their pages as they might have done for scientific articles, viewing them as a tacit endorsement of the product advertised. *The Great American Fraud* opened with the sobering warning:

> Gullible America will spend this year some seventy-five millions of dollars in the purchase of patent medicines. In consideration of this sum it will swallow huge quantities of alcohol, an appalling amount of opiates and narcotics, a wide assortment of varied drugs ranging from powerful and dangerous heart depressants to insidious liver stimulants; and, in excess of all other ingredients, undiluted fraud.[22]

All of this—the widely read articles and books, the grass-roots advocacy, the death of children from contaminated anti-toxins and vaccines, the pure and unabashed greed and charlatanry, and most of all the lack of safety checks on products people were consuming—could finally be ignored no longer. Members of Congress who had stonewalled previous pure food and drug bills were replaced by representatives and senators who rode Teddy Roosevelt's coattails into office in 1904. In 1905, in his State of the Union address, Roosevelt requested "that a law be enacted to regulate inter-state commerce in misbranded and adulterated foods, drinks, and drugs."[23]

In response, Weldon Brinton Heyburn, a senator from Idaho, introduced just such a bill. Lobbyists representing the canning, drug and whiskey, and proprietary medicine interests, got to work trying to prevent the bill's passage, claiming its provisions were "too harsh, and in fact insane."[24]

Yet, Roosevelt had asked for an independent investigation of the meat packing industry, and it essentially corroborated reports from Sinclair and others of the dirt, disease, and negligence in the poorly ventilated factories, poor health conditions of workers, and "extraneous materials" in the food products.

The report from the investigation was disclosed to the public in May 1906, and that same month the Pure Food and Drug Act was passed by the Senate. In June the House passed a similar bill with a vote of 241 to 17, and on June 30, 1906, it was signed into law by President Roosevelt.

The first major step leading to the creation of the FDA had been taken.

But the Wiley Act, as it was also known, was limited in its scope, focusing on interstate commerce of food and drugs, and truth in their labeling. Enforcement was assigned to the Bureau of Chemistry in the US Department of Agriculture.

What mas meant by "truth" on a label, though, was open to wide interpretation. Some, such as the inventor of Dr. Johnson's Mild Combination Treatment for Cancer, felt that the act referred just to the ingredients of a drug, and that it was therefore permissible to have a label claim that the drug was a "cure-all for cancer" as long as a manufacturer accurately represented the bottle's ingredients of, say, "spirits, water, cubebs, and sugar."

In 1911 the Supreme Court, in *United States v. Johnson*, actually upheld this narrow interpretation.[25] In response, Congressman Joseph Swagger Sherley, a Democrat from Kentucky, proposed an amendment to the Pure Food and Drug Act in 1912 that would make such deceptive claims illegal. It included the following clause:

> The phrase "false and fraudulent" must be taken with its accepted legal meaning, and thus it must be found that the statement regarding the curative or therapeutic effect of the article was made with actual intent to deceive—an *intent* which may be derived from facts and circumstances, but which must be established.[26]

The Sherley Amendment passed, but its fatal flaw would prove to be the difficulty in demonstrating *intent*.

Two years later, the Harrison Narcotics Act of 1914, introduced by Representative Francis Burton Harrison of New York, required prescriptions for products exceeding the allowable limit of narcotics and mandated increased record keeping for physicians and pharmacists who dispensed narcotics. This regulation responded to concerns over rising opium and cocaine consumption, and it was used as a method to arrest and imprison doctors.[27]

Amazing how, precisely 100 years later, history managed to repeat itself, with an opioid crisis hitting the United States like a scourge: doctors and pharmacists (and manufacturers like Purdue Pharma) being vilified for the amount of narcotics they prescribe, dispense, and market; and opioid overdoses having been identified as a leading factor causing life expectancies in the United States among younger adults to dip, for the first time in decades, starting in 2014.

The next major event leading to the birth of the FDA occurred in 1927, when the Bureau of Chemistry was reorganized into two separate entities: the US Bureau of Chemistry and Soils, and the US Food, Drug, and Insecticide Administration. Three years later, the bugs won (or lost, depending on how you look at it). "Insecticide" was dropped from the name, and the FDA came into existence.

I had never seen the Great Room—Room 1503 in the FDA's Building 31 (figure 1.4)—and the building's vestibule that served as its antechamber, so crowded.

A few times each year, the FDA holds a public hearing and calls together our committee, ODAC, to consider a cancer drug's safety and efficacy data in making a recommendation for approving, or not approving, that drug. And a few times a year, a line maybe four or five people deep waits in front of a folding table to sign in before being allowed to enter into the rear of the Great Room. On June 28, 2011, however, a line of people 25 or 30 long snaked around the vestibule, disrupting another line of 20 people waiting in front of the small snack bar that typically struggled for business.

## Typical Setup of ODAC Meetings in the Great Room at the FDA

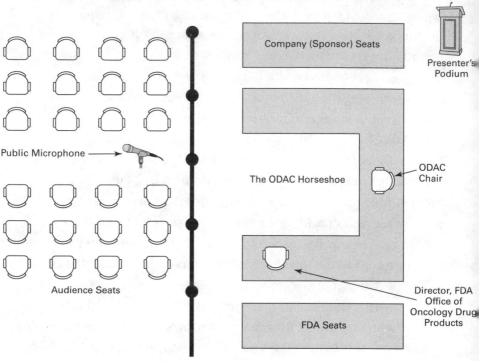

**Figure 1.4**
Typical setup of ODAC meetings in the Great Room at the FDA.

Usually, these open hearing were attended by those required to be there—maybe 50 to 75 people comprising FDA representatives, pharmaceutical company employees, and members of ODAC, along with other FDA personnel who may have been part of the team evaluating the drug's application documents, other company staff, a few employees from other pharmaceutical companies who may have an upcoming ODAC meeting and are preparing themselves for what to expect, some reporters, and a lot of representatives from financial investment firms.

Financial investment firms? That's because drugs are big business.

They are such big business—and an ODAC recommendation is so impactful on a pharmaceutical manufacturer's bottom line—that trading of a company's stocks on Wall Street is suspended during a public hearing because swings in stock prices can became too volatile, depending on positive or negative comments made by individual members of ODAC, in real time.

On that unusual day in June 2011, hundreds of people packed the room that appeared, not so much "Great," but just the right size for the number of attendees.

I walked down a side hallway that runs the length of the room, passing television cameras and encamped cameramen, and reporters from local and network news stations jockeying for position near an open door. Another door at the far end of the hallway was marked "ODAC Members Only." I swung it open and walked in.

Chaos.

The seats were already three-quarters filled. A cacophony of heated conversation filled the room, where usually it was respectfully quiet before hearings began. A scrum of cameramen sat, knelt, or stood, like encroaching jackals surrounding fresh kill, near the table where I would sit.

At a typical ODAC proceeding, the tables at the front of the hall are arranged in a horseshoe (see figure 1.4). The ODAC chairperson sits at the horseshoe's fulcrum, facing the audience, who are separated from the horseshoe of tables by rope cordons. Other members of ODAC flank the chairperson, and senior members of the FDA occupy seats along the far-left horseshoe arm, close to the audience. A couple of rows of chairs behind the left horseshoe arm are reserved for other FDA staff, while two rows of chairs behind the right arm seat pharmaceutical company employees.

This was different; the chairs were set up like a courtroom, with those of us on this special ODAC assigned to the jury's seats. The FDA personnel sat with their backs to the audience in a row closest to us, and Genentech employees were gathered, some sitting and some standing, by a row of seats farther away. Enormous screens, on which slides would be projected, hung from the front and sides of the room.

I glanced at the other six members of this special ODAC. They stood there, staring wide eyed at this spectacle, just as I had done upon entering. Were they, too, debating the wisdom of participating in this service to our government as we set out to determine if Avastin's toxicities so outweighed its potential benefits that it should be pulled from the market as a breast cancer therapy?

Safety, safety, safety.

Concerns about the safety of food and drugs, and the impact on public health, were at the core of the formation of the FDA. But none of the legislation creating this regulatory body in 1930 actually focused directly on a drug's safety. Accurate labeling, yes. Prescribing limits and precise documentation of narcotics, sure. But drugs could still be sold that not only didn't work, but also simply weren't safe, because they hadn't been tested for safety prior to being marketed.

And that absence of a requirement to demonstrate a drug's safety would prove to be deadly.

Before the modern era of medicine, during the first few decades of the twentieth century, three of the top 10 causes of death in the United States were pneumonia, tuberculosis, and diarrhea/enteritis— all infections. Identifying drugs that could fight these infections— antibiotics—was thus a public health priority, worldwide.

Again, how remarkable that, one hundred years later, another infection—the severe acute respiratory syndrome coronavirus 2 (SARS-CoV-2), a coronavirus known as COVID-19—created a pandemic of epic proportions and vaulted ahead of cancer, heart disease, and the sum total of deaths from the two world wars, to be the leading cause of death in the United States during portions of 2020 and 2021.[28] A similar priority was placed on developing a vaccine for this infectious scourge.

In 1932, a German pathologist and bacteriologist, Gerhard Domagk, discovered that a chemical called protonsil protected against bacterial infections in mice. Protonsil was converted to an active ingredient called sulfanilamide, which could fight streptococcal infections in humans (one cause of pneumonia deaths, which were actually the no. 2 cause of mortality in the early twentieth century).[29] Over the next few years, pharmaceutical companies including Merck, Squibb, and Eli Lilly started to manufacture sulfanilamide mostly as pills and tablets.

The S. E. Massengill Company of Bristol, Tennessee, had a different idea—to create a liquid form of sulfanilamide that would be easier to ingest for patients, particularly children. But sulfanilamide didn't taste very good, so the company's chief chemist, Harold Cole Watkins, added other substances to the solution, including raspberry extract, saccharin, caramel—and the sweet-tasting solvent diethylene glycol.

More commonly known as antifreeze.

The company's internal control lab approved the appearance, flavor, and fragrance of the concoction. But testing for toxicity wasn't required under the Pure Food and Drugs law, or by its amendments. In September of 1937, 240 gallons of the liquid, called Elixir Sulfanilamide (figure 1.5), were distributed across the country in 633 shipments.[30]

And doctors started prescribing it.

By October, six patients from Tulsa, Oklahoma, who were prescribed the antibiotic had died of kidney failure. The doctor who gave these patients sulfanilamide, A. S. Calhoun, MD, was horrified at his unsuspecting role in the tragedy. He wrote in a letter to a colleague:

> Nobody but Almighty God and I can know what I have been through these past few days. I have been familiar with death in the years since I received my M.D. from Tulane University School of Medicine with the rest of my class of 1911. Covington County has been my home. I have practiced here for years. Any doctor who has practiced more than a quarter of a century has seen his share of death.

**Figure 1.5**
Elixir Sulfanilamide, an antibiotic that was easier to ingest, 1937. *Source*: http://www
.fda.gov/centennial/this_week/46_nov_12_nov_18.html.

But to realize that six human beings, all of them my patients,
one of them my best friend, are dead because they took medicine
that I prescribed for them innocently, and to realize that that
medicine which I had used for years in such cases suddenly had
become a deadly poison in its newest and most modern form, as
recommended by a great and reputable pharmaceutical firm in
Tennessee: well, that realization has given me such days and nights
of mental and spiritual agony as I did not believe a human being
could undergo and survive. I have known hours when death for me
would be a welcome relief.[31]

The American Medical Association and the FDA were notified.
They asked for samples of the drug and demanded to know the
composition of the compound from the Massengill Company. Before
long, the antifreeze was identified as the cause of death.

Responsibility for action fell to the commissioner of the new FDA, Walter Campbell, who was first appointed by Wiley as his chief inspector after passage of the 1906 Act, soon after Campbell had graduated from law school. He ordered the majority of his 239 inspectors and chemists both within and outside the FDA to investigate, at Massengill headquarters and at branch offices across the country. Included among them was a young graduate student, Frances Oldham Kelsey, who would go on to become quite famous for her work with the FDA. The company had already sent telegrams to more than a 1,000 salesmen, druggists, and doctors politely requesting return of the drug, but without indicating it was deadly. The FDA demanded a more pointed, second wave of messages, and a radio and newspaper campaign was initiated to warn the public about Elixir Sulfanilamide.

The next step was to try to retrieve the 240 gallons of the deadly solution that had been shipped around the country. A team of FDA inspectors scrutinized shipping records, distribution lists, and thousands of order slips; they tracked down the company's 200 salesmen to identify the drugstores and doctor's offices that had stocked the elixir. The team reviewed prescriptions to locate the purchasers of the drug—a particularly challenging task when some locations, like one in East St. Louis, Illinois, had filled prescriptions on which the only identification of the patient was "Mrs. Jackson" or, for a child, "Betty Jane," with no address provided.

Store by store, druggist by druggist, and prescription by prescription, the FDA team worked to find every patient who still had a bottle of the elixir, and to confiscate the remaining medicine. Inspectors went to extraordinary lengths in some instances to find discarded bottles: one inspector, hearing about a bottle tossed out of a patient's window, was able to track down the remaining ounce or two among the detritus of an alley.

Another learned of a patient who had died from the tainted antibiotic and heard that the custom in one small South Carolina community was to leave leftover medicines in the dirt over a person's grave. The inspector went over to the cemetery where this patient was buried, found his grave, and spied the sulfanilamide bottle, rising from the soil like an unholy crocus in early spring. Through their dogged efforts, the FDA's inspectors managed to recover 234 gallons and 1 pint of the original 240 gallons that had been shipped. The remainder had been consumed.[32]

All told, 71 adults and 34 children died as a result of taking the liquid antibiotic that was tainted with poison, as far east as Virginia, and as far west as California.[33] Many had the same symptoms that had affected the first six victims from Oklahoma, including kidney failure, severe abdominal pain, nausea and vomiting, and convulsions that are now recognized consequences of ingesting antifreeze.

In a heart-wrenching letter to President Franklin Roosevelt, one mother of a girl who died wrote:

> The first time I ever had occasion to call in a doctor for [Joan] and she was given Elixir of Sulfanilamide. All that is left to us is the caring for her little grave. Even the memory of her is mixed with sorrow for we can see her little body tossing to and fro and hear that little voice screaming with pain and it seems as though it would drive me insane. . . . It is my plea that you will take steps to prevent such sales of drugs that will take little lives and leave such suffering behind and such a bleak outlook on the future as I have tonight.[34]

The owner of the manufacturing company. Samuel Evans Massengill, was far less emotional, declaring sanctimoniously:

> My chemists and I deeply regret the fatal results, but there was no error in the manufacture of the product. We have been supplying a legitimate professional demand and not once could have foreseen the unlooked-for results. I do not feel that there was any responsibility on our part.[35]

His chief chemist did not agree. Horrified at the deaths his recipe had caused, on January 17, 1939, Harold Watkins committed suicide, using a gun to shoot himself in the heart.[36]

A 16-page report to Congress from Secretary of Agriculture Henry Agard Wallace (a future vice president under Franklin Roosevelt) was full of condemnation for the S. E. Massengill Company. Wallace lambasted an inadequate federal law that could not be invoked to head off more deaths. In fact, the only way the FDA could hold the company accountable for the disaster was by challenging the label's use of the word "elixir," which implied that the solution contained alcohol, which it didn't.[37]

Had the manufacturer called its medicine "Sulfanilamide Solution," the FDA could not have held it responsible for the deaths at all and would have had no legal authority to recover the medicine.

The report further stated that, "before the elixir was put on the market, it was tested for flavor but not for its effect on human life."[38] A few simple experiments would have averted the tragedy. Wallace cited other drugs that had injured patients, including dinitrophenol, used for weight loss, which had caused blindness and death in a few,[39] and cinchophen, a drug used for rheumatism, which had caused liver damage. Wallace implored Congress to regulate the distribution of highly potent drugs through an adequate Federal Food and Drug law.

Public outrage in response to the tragedy reached a crescendo, and Congress finally acted. Royal S. Copeland, MD, a physician and three-term senator from New York, became the principal author of what would become the Food, Drug, and Cosmetics Act. It passed both the House and the Senate, and President Franklin Roosevelt signed it into law on June 25, 1938.

The core of this law was the requirement that drug manufacturers file a New Drug Application (NDA) with the FDA, in which they submitted scientific data concerning the new drug product's composition, manufacturing process, quality control, and *safety*, and allow the FDA to have 60 days for its review. After 60 days, if the FDA did not respond to the manufacturer, the drug was by default approved for marketing. It also extended the FDA's authority to control the labeling of all drugs, including pamphlets concerning medicinal uses that accompanied the actual, physical medicine's container. Today this extends to brochures, press releases, advertisements, commercials, annual reports, and even scientific articles that a manufacturer associates with its drug product.

And it is still open to wide interpretation.

For five years, I edited a hematology magazine. Drug manufacturers often submitted just such an advertisement that looked for all the world like one of the independent, unbiased hematology articles we printed—same structure, same font, similar style, and sometimes even supposedly penned by a hematologist the drug manufacturer hired to endorse the drug (though in truth, the company usually hired a freelancer to ghostwrite the copy attributed to the hematologist). At the top of the page the word "advertisement" appeared in very small print, and thus was easy to miss. These ads, of course, supported use of the drug, and met the letter of the law in that they were truthful, if highly biased. We demanded that the ads be completely reformatted, to be distinctive from the content on which we reported with "ADVERTISEMENT" in large font, or we rejected the ads outright, so our readers wouldn't mistake the ads for the balanced reporting by one of our staff writers.

The FDA, which oversees ads for prescription drugs (the Federal Trade Commission oversees nonprescription, or over-the-counter drug ads), is clear that product-claim ads cannot be false or misleading. Ads must include the name of the drug, at least one FDA-approved use, and the most significant risks of the drug; they also must be balanced in presenting risks and benefits. The FDA doesn't get into nitty-gritty specifications of font type or size but leaves that up to the conscience and the bottom line for manufacturers paying different amounts for different types of print ads that appear in a journal or periodical.[40]

Broadcast product-claim ads, which are often limited to a 30-second commercial, must include the drug's most important risks in the audio, usually delivered in a soothing voice while the viewer watches heartwarming images of a family dining outdoors or a grandparent being adored by her grandchildren, so the risks don't *feel* as bad. Advertisers also have to disclose all the risks listed in a drug's prescribing information (by providing sources for viewers to find a drug's prescribing information, such as a toll-free number, or by including a reminder to "consult your doctor to see if sulfanilamide is right for you").[41]

Does direct-to-consumer advertising really work? One study from the early 2000s found that every $1,000 spent advertising cholesterol-lowering drugs was associated with 32 additional people being diagnosed with high cholesterol levels and 41 additional cholesterol-lowering drugs being prescribed—for life.[42] Another advertising campaign increasing "awareness" of onchomycosis (a fungal infection of the toe nails) increased new prescriptions for (you guessed it) an antifungal drug to treat the infections from 6.5 prescriptions to 15.2 prescriptions per 1,000 person-years.[43]

Cholesterol lowering and antifungal drugs are one thing. Cancer drugs, though, are really big business. The July 20, 2020, issue of the *New Yorker*—a publication not usually present on a list of high-impact medical journals—included an ad that implored readers who had lung cancer (or treated patients with lung cancer) to use a combination of drugs that harness the immune system to attack the cancer. The cost of the ad: $120,000. The cost for one patient to receive one year of those drugs: $200,000.[44]

Many of the 1938 law's specifics contained aspects of medication use that we take for granted today, and in any case would seem obvious: that the drug's safety reflects conditions of use prescribed in the drug's labeling; that labels contain a warning of drugs that could be habit-forming, such as narcotics; that active ingredients other than the main drug also be listed, and safe tolerances be set for unavoidable poisonous substances; that labels contain directions for use and warnings of use by children when it may be dangerous to their health; and that traffic in drugs that were prepared in unsanitary conditions be prohibited (and, by implication, that manufacturing facilities could be inspected). It also eliminated the Sherley Amendment loophole that necessitated proof of intent to mislabel drugs.[45]

To enforce the law, the FDA could invoke court injunctions, seizures, and prosecutions.

In an article written for the *Journal of the American Medical Association* in 1939, Theodore Klumpp, MD, who at the time was chief of the Drug Division at the FDA, predicted that the new law would lead to a lower incidence of poisoning, to more intelligent purchasing and use of drugs by the public, and, for the first time, to a doctor's implicit trust in the strength, quality, purity, and safety of the medications that would be prescribed to patients.[46]

All the things we take for granted nowadays when recommending and taking drugs.

The strength, quality, and purity of Avastin were not in question. But safety was.

The five voting members of ODAC and I, plus the one non-voting member present at the Avastin hearing, arranged ourselves at our table and took our seats. These were all people I had gotten to know over years of serving on the committee. We came from different backgrounds and a variety of specialties within cancer, and thus would each focus on slightly different aspects of the testimonies we were about to hear.

Frank Balis, MD, a tall, distinguished pediatric oncologist from Children's Hospital of Philadelphia, had taken the train down to join us.

Natalie Compagni-Portis, PsyD, was our patient representative from Oakland. I had served on previous ODAC panels with her. I appreciated her ability to ask probing questions about the scientific conduct of trials and to state simply and clearly the issues important to patients. She had been treated for breast cancer herself years earlier.

Ralph Freedman, MD, PhD, our elder statesman, was a gynecologic oncologist from the MD Anderson Cancer Center in Houston. He was old-school in his focus on questioning companies about their findings from pre-clinical studies—the basic tests in test tubes and animals that are conducted prior to drugs being tested in humans.

Brent Logan, PhD, was a statistician who specialized in bone marrow transplant clinical trials and hailed from the Medical College of Wisconsin in Milwaukee. He would help us understand some of the complicated analyses that could make study results seem better, or worse, than they actually were.

And Wyndham Wilson, MD, PhD, a lifer at the National Cancer Institute and a lymphoma specialist, was our ODAC chairperson, a role I would take over for him the following year. He had a couple of decades of experience in developing drugs and designing clinical trials at the NCI.

Our committee of six would make recommendations to the FDA on the fate of this breast cancer drug called Avastin in front of a mob: some there because it was their job; some for the spectacle; some hoping we would vote to remove Avastin from the market, and in so doing help secure the safety of the public; and some hoping we would recommend the drug remain available for those women with metastatic breast cancer who had few other options.

An additional non-voting member, Gregory Curt, MD, joined us on ODAC. He worked for the pharmaceutical company AstraZeneca. He often asked penetrating questions of the FDA about the interactions it had with other pharmaceutical companies or about the consistency of the bar it set for drug approval.

Seven of us in total. The number of ODAC members can vary meeting to meeting, depending on how many can attend, and how many are recused for potential conflicts of interest. Given the importance of this particular gathering, and the international media attention, the FDA was particularly cautious in selecting us as members, even dismissing one person just a couple of days before he was scheduled to join us.

The presiding officer for the FDA, Karen Midthun, MD, the director of the Center for Biologics Evaluation and Research, started the proceedings at 8:01 a.m.

> Good morning and welcome to this hearing. . . . I am acting in the capacity as presiding officer in this hearing. I am doing so at the request of Commissioner Margaret Hamburg. Based on the record created, Dr. Hamburg will make the final decision on the issues presented at this hearing. She will take into account what transpires at this hearing and the submissions to the public docket. Dr. Hamburg asked me to convey how seriously she takes this hearing and the need for the science to be presented and examined in an open, systematic and thoughtful manner.[47]

The cameras started clicking, and the television cameramen took panning shots of the audience, of Dr. Midthun, the FDA representative, and the Genentech employees, and then of us, sitting at our table, bracing for what would unfold in the next day and a half.

# 2

# And Finally, Efficacy

They were particularly disappointed because Christmas is apparently the season for sedatives and hypnotics. They kept calling me, and then just came right out and said, "We want to get this drug on the market before Christmas, because that is when our best sales are."

—Frances Oldham Kelsey, PhD, MD, 1960

As the Avastin hearings got underway on that hot and humid day in June 2011, a day when the temperature hit 90 degrees, the FDA's presiding officer, Dr. Midthun, outlined the four issues we would be considering over the course of June 28 and 29:[1]

1. Did two recent trials fail to verify the initial benefit that was seen with Avastin in women with metastatic breast cancer—the benefit that led to its initial approval?

2. Did the total available evidence for Avastin demonstrate that it was not, in fact, *effective* for the indication (metastatic breast cancer) for which it was approved?

3. Did the total available evidence for Avastin demonstrate that it was not, in fact, *safe* for the indication, and that the clinical benefit did not justify these risks?

4. If we decided that the drug should be withdrawn from the market, should the FDA allow continued approval of the drug for breast cancer while Genentech designed and conducted additional studies to try to demonstrate Avastin's benefit?

Each of these questions, in and of itself, had enormous implications. We were to decide if clinical trials enrolling thousands of women with breast cancer—which Genentech and a number of world-renowned breast cancer specialists had touted as undeniable successes in supporting the benefits of taking Avastin—were in fact abject failures. Then we were to vote on whether Avastin was effective at all in treating women with metastatic breast cancer. Question #3 was probably the most important from a public health perspective, asking if the drug fulfilled the criterion for safety required by the 1938 Food, Drug, and Cosmetic Act. And finally, if our conclusions fell somewhere in a gray zone of safety and benefit, was Avastin safe *enough* and did it demonstrate at least a *modicum* of benefit to justify keeping it on the market while a better clinical trial was designed?

I quickly wrote down the questions on a paper that I kept by my own microphone, as a reminder of what I would have to vote on the following day.

Dr. Midthun then introduced the first portion of the hearings:

> For the next two hours, we will be receiving comments from persons other than the parties [FDA and Genentech]. FDA places great importance on public participation in this process. The insights and comments provided can help the agency and this committee in the consideration of the issues before them.[2]

The open-mic session. This is where anybody—literally anybody—can register with the FDA ahead of time to offer a personal perspective on the drug being considered at the proceeding. Each person would have about four minutes; a light near the microphone would turn yellow when a minute was remaining, and red when time was up.

What an incredible demonstration of democracy in action.

What an emotional portion of these proceedings to witness.

We would be hearing directly from some of the women treated on these Avastin trials about whether they felt the drug was safe, and if it worked for them.

Safety, safety, safety.

With the passage of the Food, Drug, and Cosmetics Act in 1938, doctors, nurses, pharmacists, and patients could rest assured for the very first time that the nation's drug supply wouldn't harm them—or at least, they would be informed of what that harm could be, based on a drug's toxicity profile. But there was still no mention of efficacy—manufacturers were not required to prove, as part of a new drug application to the FDA, that drugs would actually work in treating disease, and in making people better.

Within two months of the 1938 act's passage, the FDA began identifying drugs such as the sulfa antibiotics that led to the tragedy ushering in the new law, drugs that could not be labeled for safe use by a patient. This in turn led to years of debates among the FDA, manufacturers, doctors, and pharmacists to decide what constituted over-the-counter medications (that could be used directly by a patient), and what medications necessitated doctor supervision (and thus could not be dispensed without a prescription).

Concurrently, from the 1940s to the 1960s, illegal sales of amphetamines and barbiturates increased, accompanied by aggressive marketing campaigns urging doctors to prescribe amphetamines for depression. Simultaneously, the US military distributed the stimulant Benzedrine—as a general medical supply, in emergency kits, and for routine use during aviation. During this period, the steadily growing, widespread use of these drugs caused more regulatory concern at the FDA than all other drug problems combined.[3]

To resolve the lack of clarity on the issue of which drugs could be safely purchased directly by consumers, and address (in part) the amphetamine and barbiturate problem, the next major legislation affecting the FDA came in the form of the Durham-Humphrey Amendment, co-sponsored by Carl Durham, a pharmacist representing North Carolina in the House of Representatives, and Senator Hubert Humphrey from Minnesota (later the 38th US vice president), who started his own working life in 1951 as a pharmacist in South Dakota. This bill made a distinction between over-the-counter (nonprescription) medications and legend drugs (those considered unsafe for self-medication, and thus necessitating not only a doctor's supervision, but also a bona fide prescription). In addition, it required that habit-forming drugs include the warning statement on the label, "Caution: Federal law prohibits dispensing without a prescription."[4]

The Humphrey-Durham Act also ushered in an era when many paid homage to the power of the pill.

Pharmacotherapy—in the form of both pills and injections—started to come of age in the 1950s as more and more people relied on medicines to eliminate conditions that had previously proven deadly (or at least somewhat annoying). And the pharmaceutical industry came to play a dominant role in manipulating what the public understood about medicine and the economics of treating disease.

The antibiotic terramycin was developed in 1950, and in 1951 the drug Antabuse was marketed as a cure for alcoholism. A massive trial of the polio vaccine developed by Jonas Salk was initiated in 1954, and an oral version developed by Albert Sabin was announced in 1956. A new penicillin—Penicillin V—came into being in 1957, a vaccine for measles in 1958, and a next-generation penicillin (methicillin) in 1959. Thorazine was available for mania, Ritalin for depression, Serpatilin for manic-depression. Bufferin could relieve pain. One advertisement showed a woman standing in her kitchen by the sink, near a stack of dirty plates, struggling to keep her eyes open from exhaustion. Dexedrine could fix that! Another promoted Compazine for "better management of mentally defective children." Tylenol could make their fevers go away. Doriden could help you get to sleep.[5] An advertisement for Distaval, a sedative and hypnotic marketed to pregnant women, shows a child opening a pill bottle when nobody is around to supervise her. Thank goodness it isn't a barbiturate that child is about to ingest and poison herself with because, as the ad extolled, Distaval was "outstandingly safe."[6]

Of course it was. After all, Distaval (figure 2.1) was otherwise known by its generic name, thalidomide.

Immediately following World War II, in 1946, Hermann Wirtz founded the company Chemie Grünenthal in Stolberg, West Germany. By 1947, it was the first to register and distribute penicillin in Germany. Almost 10 years later, it developed thalidomide and

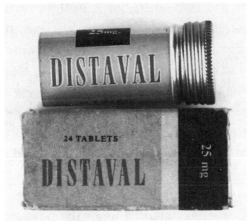

**Figure 2.1**
Distaval, also known as thalidomide, a sedative and hypnotic marketed to pregnant women from 1956 to 1962. *Source*: Museums Victoria, Copyright Museums Victoria/ CC BY (licensed as Attribution 4.0 International), https://collections.museumsvictoria .com.au/items/259289.

marketed it in Europe as the first safe sleeping pill, and one that was considered highly effective at treating pregnant women with morning sickness.[7] The company was so successful, in fact, that in some countries, the drug was almost as popular as aspirin.

But then on Christmas Day 1956, the daughter of a Grünenthal employee was born with no ears. It was such a random event, no one thought to link it to the new medicine the employee's wife had taken to help combat morning sickness during her pregnancy.[8]

In September 1960 the young pharmacologist Frances Oldham Kelsey, who had assisted with the sulfanilamide investigation and had just officially joined the FDA one month earlier, was given her first assignment: to review a new drug application for thalidomide that had been submitted to the FDA in June.[9] Kelsey had earned her PhD and later her MD at the University of Chicago. Her acceptance into its graduate program—at the time, an unusual accomplishment for a woman—came in a letter addressed to "Mr. Oldham," which made Kelsey wonder for years if the reviewer of her application had misread her first name as "Francis," and assumed she was a man.[10]

Thalidomide was to be distributed in the United States by the Richardson-Merrell chemical company of Cincinnati, Ohio, and Selma, North Carolina, under the brand name Kevadon. The company was chomping at the bit to get the drug approved and take advantage of the US market of pregnant women, given the success the pills had enjoyed in Europe. But Kelsey had concerns about the drug's application from the get-go.[11]

The information in it seemed both too good, and too inadequate, to be true.

Data on how thalidomide was absorbed from the stomach and intestines, and then excreted through the bowel or kidneys, was insufficient. The long-term toxicity studies, which weren't quite long enough, unbelievably seemed to indicate that large doses of the drug could be administered without deleterious consequences, even in the setting of other illnesses or with other drugs.

Kelsey described her concerns in a letter to Richardson-Merrell in November 1960, responding within the timeframe of the law that allowed the FDA 60 days to review a new drug application before a new drug would be approved by default. The company quickly replied back. But instead of providing well-designed studies supporting the safety of thalidomide, they sent Kelsey what amounted to individual testimonials.[12]

Kelsey's concerns were only heightened. Where were the safety data for this drug?

She requested more information from Richardson-Merrell, and the 60-day clock started again. The company's representative, Dr. Joseph Murray, escalated the pressure on Kelsey to approve his company's drug. He called and visited her repeatedly. He complained to her bosses that she was nit-picking and unreasonable (a description, I suspect, he would not have used if a man had been assigned to the review). The company had a warehouse full of the drug ready for distribution, anticipating a quick approval by the FDA. He wanted thalidomide on the market in the United States.[13]

Kelsey didn't give in to Murray's bullying. As she described it:

> They were particularly disappointed because Christmas is apparently the season for sedatives and hypnotics (sleeping pills). They kept calling me, and then just came right out and said, "We want to get this drug on the market before Christmas, because that is when our best sales are."[14]

The FDA did not cooperate with Richardson-Merrell's timeline.

Then, on December 31, 1960, a physician from Aberdeenshire, in the United Kingdom, A. Leslie Florence, MD, sent a letter to the *British Medical Journal* describing four patients: all of them had been receiving thalidomide (brand name Distaval), and all of them experienced numbness and tingling of their feet and hands, coldness of their extremities, imbalance, and muscle cramps. When the patients stopped taking the drug, their symptoms improved. In the understated style of medical journals at the time, Florence wrote:

It would appear that these symptoms could possibly be a toxic effect of thalidomide. I have seen no record of similar effects with this drug, and I feel it would be of interest to learn whether any of your readers have observed these effects.[15]

Kelsey read Florence's letter and requested additional drug toxicity information from Richardson-Merrell. She also reflected on her postgraduate work at the University of Chicago, in which her research revealed that the antimalarial drug quinine could cross the placenta in pregnant rabbits and affect the fetus. Given how the drug was being prescribed, as a sedative for pregnant women, she wondered whether thalidomide could do the same.[16]

In early 1961, Widukind Lenz was a senior physician at the Hamburg University Children's Clinic, in Germany. He was consulted about a few babies who had been born in a short period of time with malformed limbs. Imagine a hospital nursery with multiple newborn babies whose arms didn't extend much below their shoulders and ended in partially formed hands with two or three fingers; or whose legs, which didn't quite reach the knees, sprouted feet that appeared as if pasted on in no particular orientation. While this could occur as a result of genetic mutations, these types of mutations are rare, and wouldn't explain the epidemic of unusual babies he was seeing.[17]

Around the same time a young lawyer, Carl-Hermann Schulte-Hillen, and his wife consulted Lenz about their six-week-old son Jan, who also had been born with two short arms—a condition called phocomelia (from the Greek *phoke*, meaning "seal," and *melos*, meaning "limb"). A few weeks earlier, in fact, Carl-Hermann's sister had given birth to a girl with similarly shortened limbs. So had other people they knew.[18]

These were more than just random genetic mutations. Lenz and Schulte-Hillen agreed to work together to see if they could find a common cause. They drove around northern Germany in Schulte-Hillen's old Volkswagen trying to find other children with similar deformed limbs, and to question their mothers about the medications they took during pregnancy.

This wasn't an easy task. In that different era, children with deformities were hidden away, an embarrassment. So Schulte-Hillen carried with him a photo of Jan, to earn people's trust. When they did meet a family with a child who had phocomelia, Lenz would ask to search their bathroom medicine cabinet. Invariably, he discovered a bottle containing thalidomide—marketed as the brand name Contergan in Germany.[19]

Lenz initially found 14, and eventually a total of 46, children born with limb deformities he felt were associated with the use of thalidomide by their mothers during pregnancy (see an example of four children affected, figure 2.2). He compared facts about those mothers to details about 300 women whose children had no birth defects. He found that 41 of the 46 women with deformed babies had taken thalidomide, compared to none of the 300 women with unaffected children. On November 16, 1961, he called the medical

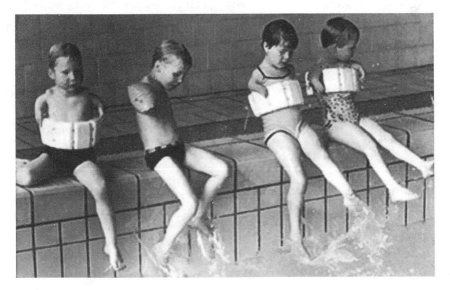

**Figure 2.2**
Four children affected by thalidomide.

director at Chemie Grünenthal and implored him to stop selling the drug.[20]

The medical director refused.

So Lenz went to the press and the German health authorities, which forced the pharmaceutical company to eventually capitulate to public pressure and pull thalidomide from the market on November 27, 1961. On December 16, 1961, an Australian obstetrician from Hurstville, South Wales, was the first to link thalidomide to birth defects in a medical journal, the *Lancet*. He wrote:

> Bony development seems to be affected in a very striking manner, resulting in polydactyly [extra fingers or toes], syndactyly [webbed fingers or toes], and failure of development of long bones (abnormally short femora and radii).[21]

Thalidomide continued to be sold for several months—in Belgium and Italy (under the brand names Softenon and Noctosediv), in Africa (as Valgis), in Canada (as Kevadon and Talimol), in Japan (as Isomin, Glutanon, and eight other proprietary names), and the list went on—despite the mounting evidence that the drug was profoundly teratogenic, meaning that it caused major birth defects.[22]

In March 1962, Richardson-Merrill withdrew its new drug application from the FDA. But by that point, approximately 10,000 children in 46 countries had been born with deformities thought to be caused by thalidomide.[23]

Chemie Grünenthal continued to deny the connection between their drug and birth defects for years thereafter.

The first person to approach the microphone at the Avastin hearings was Lisa Schlager, a vice president of Facing Our Risk of Cancer Empowered (FORCE), an advocacy group for people affected by hereditary breast, ovarian, and related cancers. Schlager was herself a carrier of the *BRCA1* (BReast CAncer gene) mutation—which is a type of tumor suppressor gene. Tumor suppressor genes help control the growth of a cell. A mutation in the gene disables it, which can allow cells to grow in an unfettered fashion—the basic definition of cancer. Approximately 3 to 5 percent of all women with breast cancer have a *BRCA* mutation. Women with breast cancer who have a family history of breast cancer are even more likely to carry a *BRCA* mutation. And a woman who is known to have a *BRCA* mutation, but has not yet developed cancer, has a lifetime risk of developing breast or ovarian cancer that may be more than 70 percent.[24] To minimize that risk, some women with the mutation choose to undergo prophylactic mastectomies or removal of their ovaries (as did the actress Angelina Jolie). Schlager had a personal stake in this decision, and didn't mince her words:

> We are strongly opposed to the FDA removal of the metastatic breast cancer label from the indication for Avastin. This change will halt access for newly diagnosed women with metastatic cancer who may benefit from the therapy. Likewise, insurance companies may use the FDA decision to restrict reimbursement for those currently benefitting and responding to the drug.[25]

She even read a quote from one patient who was a member of FORCE and on a clinical trial that included Avastin. The woman said she regularly measured the tumor in her breast with a ruler, and watched it shrink before her eyes.[26]

When Schlager finished, the audience erupted in applause.

Next up was Steve Walker, the cofounder of the Abigail Alliance for Better Access to Developmental Drugs, another patient advocacy organization. The Alliance was named for Abigail Burroughs, the daughter of the Alliance's other cofounder, Frank Burroughs. She was only 21 years old when she died from a horribly aggressive squamous cell carcinoma of the head and neck while trying to get access to an experimental drug, later called Erbitux, which (similar to Avastin) stops tumor blood vessel growth (angiogenesis). I could only imagine her father's frustration at watching his college-age daughter die when there was a drug available, in clinical trials, that might have helped her, but that she wasn't able to receive.

The Abigail Alliance decided to sue the FDA. They contended that FDA regulations kept Abigail from obtaining a potentially lifesaving treatment that her doctor recommended, violating her constitutional right to defend her life. They filed their suit in July 2003— two years after Abigail had died. The case worked its way through the courts until August 2007, when the US Court of Appeals for the District of Columbia voted against the alliance, finding that there was not a constitutional right to unapproved drugs by terminally ill patients. The Supreme Court declined to hear the case, and the path to get access to experimental treatments outside of clinical trials for people with limited options seemed to have ended.[27]

But 11 years later, what has since been called the Right to Try Act was passed by Congress and signed into law by President Trump on May 30, 2018. Frank Burroughs attended the signing ceremony.

At the microphone during the Avastin hearing, Walker didn't mince words, either:

> The Abigail Alliance strongly opposes the FDA's decision to rescind the accelerated approval of Avastin for the first-line treatment of metastatic breast cancer.[28]

He went on to say:

> I'd also like to note that this hearing is taking place within a procedurally corrupt administrative process. Dr. Pazdur [who was the director of the Office of Oncology Drug Products within the FDA] selects all appointed ODAC members from the nomination submitted for those posts. . . . None of the voting physicians on the panel appear to be engaged in treating breast cancer as a significant part of their clinical research or medical practice. . . . Dr. Pazdur's complete control of ODAC allows him to preordain the advice and opinions he receives from his committee, neutralizing the FDA's decision to observe separation of functions in this case and rendering this hearing essentially a sham.[29]

Again, the audience applauded. Those of us sitting at the small ODAC table shifted uncomfortably in our seats. It was the first time during these proceedings we were called out publicly, with someone questioning our authority to make a recommendation about withdrawing Avastin from the market. But it wouldn't be the last. I started to understand why I had been told days earlier that I should unlist my phone number and warn my secretary at work about the threatening calls I would receive after the hearing.

As an ODAC committee member, I had hoped the audience—and the public at large—would find it reassuring that we were people who understood, on a deep level, the scientific, medical, statistical, and operational issues underlying drug development and the construct of clinical trials: that we represented the interests of the public, patients, and even the pharmaceutical industry.

But Steve Walker had pointed out what anyone watching the proceedings saw as an obvious omission: Where were the breast cancer specialists?

Their absence can be explained by examining the FDA's extremely careful process for vetting members of its committees and avoiding even the semblance of impropriety as a result of a conflict of interest.

What would be considered a conflict of interest? There are some obvious examples: The FDA wouldn't want to invite someone employed by Genentech (or whose spouse or partner was employed by the company), or who owned stock in the company, to be an ODAC member for this hearing. That person would have a vested interest in the outcome of the deliberations. The FDA would similarly bar a doctor who had received speaking fees or honoraria for sitting on advisory boards for the company, or who was an investigator on a clinical trial sponsored by Genentech. Either situation might consciously or subconsciously influence a member's decision to favor the company's product.

Less obvious conflicts might also come into play. The FDA would also prohibit people from serving on ODAC if they had these same relationships with a company that manufactured a drug that *competed* with Genentech's Avastin for the treatment of breast cancer, as that person might have an interest in voting *against* Genentech's product.

Think about that for a second: any doctor who is a breast cancer specialist with particular expertise in the conduct of clinical trials in breast cancer patients would by definition likely be excluded from membership on an ODAC panel considering a breast cancer drug.

A panel just like ours.

Is that fair to breast cancer patients, or to the company bringing a breast cancer drug before the FDA? Can specialists in leukemia, lymphoma, gynecologic oncology, and pediatric oncology really deliberate about the safety and efficacy of a drug used in a patient population we don't care for ourselves?

Or can we reasonably translate the experiences of our own cancer patients to the those of women suffering from breast cancer?

Maybe it's actually better that none of us was a breast cancer specialist, because we shouldn't be considering our own, personal stories, and those of our patients, at all.

When I was training to be an oncologist, I once tried to use the experience of one of my patients to justify the treatment I wanted to give to another. Afterward, one of my advisors cautioned me: "The plural of anecdote is not data."

He meant that we may trick ourselves into thinking we are rigorously applying scientifically acquired data to inform future decisions, when we are really being driven by emotions surrounding a recent clinical success—or failure.

I see this all the time on our own leukemia unit in the hospital. A patient will suffer a pulmonary embolus—a blood clot that travels to the lungs, which is a relatively rare event in leukemia, despite how commonly it occurs in other types of cancers—and soon every patient who complains of shortness of breath over the subsequent week is sent for testing to rule out a pulmonary embolus!

We can be similarly tricked when serving on a high-level FDA panel.

Imagine I had recently been treating a breast cancer patient with Avastin and she had a fabulous outcome, with shrinkage of her tumor and no side effects.

Do you think this anecdote, fresh in my mind, would influence my vote on whether or not the balance of safety and efficacy of the drug warranted keeping it on the market?

Now, what if instead I had recently treated a patient with Avastin and she suffered liver failure and developed sepsis with a bacterial infection because the drug caused her immune system to tank?

How would I vote now?

If I were a breast cancer specialist, I might also vote in favor of a new breast cancer drug so I have another tool in my toolbox to offer my patients, even if it doesn't work that well.

Why? Well, imagine the following conversation:

I walk into my outpatient clinic room where my 35-year-old patient is sitting in a chair, waiting for results of her most recent scans. She has been receiving chemotherapy for metastatic breast cancer for four months, and now sports a scarf on her head and a white sweatshirt with pink lettering that reads "Fight Like a Girl!" She has children ages 8 and 10 at home, and in-between rounds of chemotherapy has made sure that their lives in school and their sports activities have continued uninterrupted.

I know what she's waiting to hear. I sit down and break the news to her as gently as possible. "So, the CT scans just returned, and they unfortunately show that the cancer, the mass, has gotten larger, despite the chemotherapy you just received. I'm really sorry."

My patient sighs. "I was worried that it was still growing. The pain in my belly, near my liver, was getting worse." Most of my patients know when their cancer has grown, or when it has returned. "What would you recommend I try next?" she asks.

I grimace a bit. "There isn't really another treatment option approved by the FDA, and the clinical trials we discussed exclude women with liver abnormalities, which unfortunately you have because of the cancer." She looks down at her hands, folded in her lap. She won't make eye contact with me. She knows what's coming next.

"I think it's time to talk about minimizing your symptoms, getting you to feel as good as you can, and spending quality time with your family."

She shakes her head. Not acceptable. "Isn't there anything you can come up with? I'm not ready to die yet." She looks up and meets my eyes. "I have two young children, and I want to live to see them graduate high school. You have kids. Wouldn't you want the same?"

If you substitute *leukemia* for *breast cancer*, I've had the same conversation with patients a few, awful times in my career.

Now, how does this conversation change if I have another drug I can offer?

My patient sighs. "What would you recommend I try next?"

"There's one more drug, recently approved by the FDA for women with breast cancer that won't go away after a couple of courses of chemotherapy. It works a small percentage of the time, but it has side effects that include liver failure and worsening of your immune system, making you more prone to infections."

"Are there any other options?" she asks.

I grimace and shake my head. "Not really. And the clinical trials we discussed excluded women with liver abnormalities, which unfortunately you have because of the cancer. The trials that led to this drug's approval also excluded women with liver abnormalities. So I can't say for sure that the drug would work as well for you, or that the side effects wouldn't be worse."

She sighs again and shrugs her shoulders. "Well, if that's all there is, I'll try it, no matter what the chances are. I have two young children, and I want to live to see them graduate high school."

We review the potential risks and benefits of receiving the next round of chemotherapy, and my patient agrees to proceed, allowing me to delay—if we're lucky—having the conversation about palliative care and hospice by another few months.

How can I be so sure that my patient will make the decision I imagine in the second scenario? I can't. Everyone responds differently to similar conversations, and not everyone may be willing to endure another round of chemotherapy.

A classic study asked 104 women with breast cancer, most of whom had undergone a mastectomy already, to estimate what survival benefit chemotherapy would have to provide to justify six months of treatment. More than 70 percent of these women said they would be willing to endure the risks of nausea, hair loss, fatigue, and infections, along with the time and emotional investment of being treated with three chemotherapy drugs, to achieve just a 5 percent greater chance of living five or more years.

On some conscious or subconscious level, those of us who practice oncology know this, and we will almost always advocate for having one additional drug to offer to our patients, for right or for wrong.

So is it better to have specialists on an ODAC panel support approval of that one additional drug because they have reflected on their experiences with countless patients who have walked that journey? Or because they imagine countless patients who will one day be able to use that drug? Or is it better to have some distance from those anecdotes, those biases, those conflicts, and those memories of the awful conversations when there were no options left, and thus possibly avoid an option that offers baseless hope? Who would be more likely to approve a drug to make it available to patients with terrible medical diagnoses who are in need, and who would be more likely to safeguard the health of the public?

Because once the FDA approves a drug and makes it available to patients, it's hard for the agency to pull it back unless the drug's safety concerns are particularly damning and dramatic—such as an increased risk of death in patients receiving the drug, or babies born with malformed arms and legs.

Only 17 so-called thalidomide babies were actually born in the United States.

But how could this have occurred when the drug had not yet been approved for sale? Richardson-Merrill had distributed more than 2.5 million thalidomide pills to more than 1,000 doctors in the United States on an "investigational basis"—essentially seeding the market, anticipating the drug's FDA approval. Almost 20,000 patients, in turn, received the drug, some of whom were pregnant women. As with the sulfanilamide disaster, the FDA field staff were mobilized to notify doctors, confiscate remaining pills, and warn patients.[30]

And as might be expected, the worldwide epidemic of limb and ear malformations in babies mirrored sales figures of thalidomide, and it ended abruptly in July 1962.

Frances Oldham Kelsey (figure 2.3) was celebrated. On July 15, 1962, Morton Mintz of the *Washington Post* wrote a front-page article about Kelsey titled "Heroine of FDA Keeps Bad Drug off Market." He described how "the skepticism and stubbornness of a government physician prevented what could have been an appalling American tragedy."[31] Other articles in the mainstream press followed, culminating in Kelsey receiving the "President's Award for Distinguished Federal Civilian Service" later that year. At the White House ceremony, President John F. Kennedy lauded Kelsey, saying that "Her exceptional judgment in evaluating a new drug for safety for human use has prevented a major tragedy of birth deformities in the United States." In 1962, a Gallup poll found that she was one of the 10 most admired women in the world.[32]

The American public seemed to recognize just how narrowly they had averted a nationwide tragedy. The time was ripe to resurrect a bill that had been introduced in 1960 by Senator Estes Kefauver of Tennessee.

A bill that would finally give the FDA more chops to regulate drugs.

But the bill had yet to gain traction because pharmaceutical companies opposed it, and thus was considered essentially dead.

**Figure 2.3**
Frances Oldham Kelsey, PhD, MD, "Heroine of FDA." *Source*: Image posted of Dr. Frances Kathleen Oldham Kelsey in the History of Medicine Collection, National Library of Medicine, photographer unknown, public domain, https://commons.wikimedia.org/w/index.php?curid=747686.

The pharmaceutical industry opposed Kefauver's efforts to strengthen the authority of the FDA because they felt that new pretesting requirements examining a drug's safety would actually *harm* patients by delaying those drugs from making it to market. They also (paternalistically) claimed that it would be a bad idea to publicize the side effects of drugs because it was the physicians' job to know these side effects and warn patients. During this Cold War era, the companies warned that increased regulation would give the government more control over the lives of US citizens.[33]

Some of these arguments were the same as those used in 1906 and 1938. They would be used again in the future, any time increased regulatory authority over drug manufacturing, distribution, and marketing was proposed.

The original 1960 legislation introduced by Kefauver, who sat on the Senate Antitrust and Monopoly Subcommittee, had frightened the pharmaceutical companies because of how it would hit their bottom lines. He felt the government should help control drug pricing and competition, and he had initiated hearings to expose unfair marketing practices that misled patients with their extravagant claims, resulted in excessive drug costs, and lacked scientific support of drug effectiveness. During the hearings, pharmaceutical representatives were openly berated for profiteering, and doctors were depicted as dupes to the marketing schemes of those companies.[34]

The original bill actually called for compulsory patent sharing, in which a company would be required to share its drug patents with competitors after only three years of market exclusivity, while collecting an annual royalty fee of 8 percent. It required a new drug be granted a patent only if its therapeutic effect was "significantly greater than that of the drug before modification"—meaning better than its predecessors. The bill also introduced a requirement that drugs be both safe *and* effective.

Kefauver had become famous a decade earlier when he headed the Senate Special Committee to Investigate Crime in Interstate Commerce (also known as organized crime). The committee hearings were televised live at a time when many Americans were buying their first television sets and were thus exposed to details about the mafia and how it operated. It cinched his reputation as being the public's champion in the Senate against crooked businessmen.

Now he would use that reputation to take on what he saw as the crooked pharmaceutical industry.

Kefauver introduced a revamped bill, co-sponsored by Representative Oren Harris of Arkansas, to Congress on July 19, 1962, to give new authorities to the FDA.[35] Major changes to the FDA's authority included:

- A requirement that manufacturers prove the *effectiveness* of drug products before they go on the market, and afterward report any serious side effects. (*Previously, only safety had to be demonstrated.*)
- A requirement that evidence of effectiveness be based on adequate and well-controlled clinical studies conducted by qualified experts. (*Testimonials from doctors and patients would not be enough.*)
- Study subjects on clinical trials would be required to give their informed consent. (*This stipulation rejected medical paternalism, in which doctors told patients what to do, and handed decision-making over to patients.*)
- It gave the FDA 180 days (*instead of the previous 60 days*) to approve a new drug application and required FDA approval before the drug could be marketed in the United States.
- It mandated that the FDA conduct a retrospective evaluation of the effectiveness of drugs approved for safety—but not for efficacy—between 1938 and 1962. (*This was known as the Drug Efficacy Study Implementation program.*)
- It allowed the FDA to set good manufacturing practices for industry and mandated regular inspections of production facilities. (*Previously, the FDA had no authority over the manufacturing process.*)
- It transferred to the FDA control of prescription drug advertising, which would have to include accurate information about efficacy and side effects. (*Gone would be claims, for example, of better managing "mentally defective children."*)
- It controlled the marketing of generic drugs to keep them from being sold as expensive medications under new trade names. (*This was one of Kefauver's biggest bugaboos. People shouldn't pay more for the same medicine just because it has a different name and is marketed to be more effective.*)

The Kefauver-Harris Amendment passed the Senate and the House quickly, on August 23, 1962, and was signed into law by President Kennedy on October 10, 1962. Estes Kefauver—who would die the following year on August 10, 1963, of a ruptured aortic aneurysm—considered the bill his finest achievement in 25 years of public service.

Safety, safety, safety.

And finally, efficacy.

The amendment greatly expanded the FDA's authority to include the consistency, standards, and sanctity of the drug manufacturing process, and the accuracy of safety and efficacy claims made to health care providers and the public; it gave the FDA adequate time to review new drug applications before they would reflexively be approved. It didn't ignore the many drugs already in existence with suspect claims on efficacy, and it evaluated more than 3,400 drugs approved only for safety between 1938 and 1962. By the early 1970s, the FDA had categorized approximately 600 of these drugs as ineffective and forced their removal from the market.[36] A few remain open (as of March 2022) without a final decision on effectiveness, such as extended-release oral nitroglycerin, and amphetamines.

With the atrocities of World War II still fresh in people's minds, including Josef Mengele's horrific experiments on Auschwitz concentration camp prisoners, the Kefauver-Harris Amendment recognized patient autonomy and patient rights, requiring a potential participant's voluntary agreement before enrolling in a clinical trial of experimental drugs. It eliminated confusing marketing practices that claimed one drug was superior to another, when the two were identical save for their name.

And 56 years after the Pure Food and Drug Act of 1906, it demanded that drugs be effective, ushering in the modern era of well-designed and controlled clinical trials as being the standard for demonstrating that drugs are safe, and that they actually work.

In August 1962, the FDA circulated a Notice of Proposed Rulemaking, which detailed requirements for the Investigational New Drug (IND) process. This was the mechanism by which companies could legally ship experimental drugs in interstate commerce for research purposes—the research that would be required to demonstrate a drug's safety and efficacy prior to a formal new drug application. It included a description of what would become the standard process for designing clinical trials of drugs, dividing them into three phases:

- Phase 1, to be conducted on a small number of patients to determine short-term toxicity, how a drug is distributed throughout the body after ingestion or administration, and how it is excreted.

- Phase 2, to be conducted on a limited number of patients with, or at risk for, the target condition to determine proof of concept of efficacy.

- Phase 3, to be conducted on a larger number of patients divided into two groups: those receiving the experimental drug, and those receiving standard of care or placebo.[37]

Meticulous record-keeping, along with monitoring of each trial for safety and efficacy, were mandated. That patients follow a consistent trial protocol was also a requirement. The FDA's power came from its ability to revoke an IND if investigators violated any of these requirements.

The events leading up to this point, of threats to the public health, public outcry, and legislation—and more threats to the public health, more public outcry, and more legislation repeated over and over— would form the basis for how the FDA gained regulatory authority, and deliberated over drug approval, for decades to come. Its focus would always be first and foremost safety, safety, safety—followed then by efficacy. The many steps a drug manufacturer had to take prior to even submitting a new drug application helped ensure that the medicines they might eventually hawk were safe or had manageable toxicities. And that they improved health.

But the years spent conducting those requisite laboratory and animal studies prior to giving the first granule of a drug to a human, and the time and enormous resources it would take to conduct the clinical trials themselves, would also delay getting necessary and potentially lifesaving medicines to the people who needed them most.

Margaret Hamburg, MD, the twenty-first commissioner of the FDA, who served from 2009 to 2015, would make the statement:

> With the passage of the [Kefauver-Harris] amendments, FDA was no longer a helpless bystander while unproven medicines were streaming into pharmacies and onto patients' bedside tables.[38]

Hamburg was the commissioner for the FDA when Avastin was granted approval for marketing to treat women with metastatic breast cancer.

# 3
# The Moxie to Do Battle

I don't think it is reasonable for you to set a number of people that need to be alive as a result of this drug in order to allow it to be sold. . . . My life should be enough, and it's not just my life but the lives of my family, friends, coworkers and everyone I meet.

—Heraleen Broome, 2011

People who enroll in clinical trials, like the people testifying in front of the FDA at the Avastin hearings, do so for a variety of reasons.

The first patient scheduled in my afternoon clinic a few years ago was a man named James Petrarcha, who drove about six hours— from a rural town in eastern Pennsylvania to the cancer center where I practiced in Cleveland—to consult with me. He had a leukemia that refused to be knocked out by a couple of rounds of chemotherapy and was interested in enrolling in a clinical trial of a new therapy.

It was late November, which in northeast Ohio looks a lot like the thick of winter in other parts of the country. Snow was threatening, as it would be through Easter, and the skies had taken on a hue of lackluster gray that usually didn't encourage visitors that time of year.

But Cleveland offered Mr. Petrarcha another advantage: his cousin, Theresa, who lived only a half hour from our cancer center, could provide him with a place to stay and would act as his caregiver for any treatment he might receive during the trial.

This was the type of trial first described by the FDA a good fifty-five years earlier, in its 1962 Notice of Proposed Rulemaking, detailing the requirements for its Investigational New Drug process.[1]

When I walked into the examination room to meet Mr. Petrarcha, he was sitting next to his cousin in a gray chair that matched the Cleveland skies; he wore a black sweatshirt with the word *Italia* written in white, block letters over an image of the Italian flag. His cousin was still wearing her winter coat, with a Cleveland Browns scarf loosened around her neck. I introduced myself and sat down by the tiny desk in the room to review what I had learned about him from his electronic medical record, the same one used by his doctor in Pennsylvania. Fortuitously, we subscribed to the same medical record software, so I could read the written notes and interpret the laboratory results from blood draws taken hundreds of miles away.

Mr. Petrarcha was 70 years old. He had held a variety of jobs over the course of his life, working for most of it as a plumber. But he defined himself by his very first one.

"I was a boxer, doc, light heavyweight," he told me, lifting his arms from the sides of his chair in my examination room and giving the air a couple of jabs.

At this point in his life, though, he had crossed the 175-pound weight limit for light heavyweight, the 200-pound limit for cruiserweight, and had landed squarely in heavyweight territory. He looked like an aged version of the movie fighter Rocky, though his voice was gravelly, more like the Burgess Meredith character, Mickey Goldmill, Rocky's trainer.

"I fought in Madison Square Garden—twice!" Jimmy told me.

"Wow! What was that like?" I asked.

"Incredible. The crowds were amazing back then!" he said, his arms still raised for combat, his eyes refocusing on a distant past. The trips to New York City, the hotel rooms, his prep time in the locker room before the fight, the noise from the crowd as he walked to the ring, the feel of bending over to squeeze in-between the ropes surrounding the ring . . . the bell, the surge of adrenaline as the fight started . . . it was all too much to explain beyond "incredible." I never asked him if he won the bouts. Just having the moxie to do battle there had been the point.

His cousin came with him to the appointment, to help him ask questions about his condition and recall what I said, but also to keep him focused.

"Jimmy, we gotta talk to the doctor about your leukemia," Theresa gently reminded him, in a way that told me she was used to his reminiscing about his glory days—and she loved him for it, or in spite of it.

"Yeah, what do I have to do to get rid of my leukemia? I'll try anything," he said to me earnestly. "I heard you had a study going on here. I want in!"

Jimmy was first diagnosed with acute myeloid leukemia, or AML, nine months earlier. AML is a cancer of the cells in the bone marrow that initially comes on fast, like a raging bull. People often go to the doctor or to the emergency room thinking they have the flu and then get the shock of a lifetime (as does the nurse or doctor taking care of them) when the labs return horribly wrong: with a sky-high white blood cell count (the cells of the immune system that fight infections); a half-normal hemoglobin (the measure of red blood cells), which indicates profound anemia; and a platelet count (the platelets help stop bleeding) one-tenth where it should be. Sometimes, people with platelet counts this low come to the doctor's office or the emergency room with recurrent nose bleeds, hemorrhages in the eye, or worse—a stroke.

AML is considered a "liquid" tumor: this is different than breast cancer, where the rogue cells whose capacity to divide and proliferate outpaces other cells around them and form a lump; and different than lung cancer, where the corrupted cells grow in an uncontrolled fashion and create a mass in the chest. Leukemia cells spread like a wildfire, expanding rapidly to fill the narrow confines of the bone and torching the remaining, normal, bone marrow cells. Those normal bone marrow cells are the ones that make the red blood cells and the platelets. The factory making those red blood cells and platelets is destroyed, causing the low blood counts.[2]

The leukemia cells, called *blasts*, are an immature version of white blood cells. When he was diagnosed with leukemia, Jimmy had 80 percent of his bone marrow consumed by blasts. Stuck in their puerile state, the blasts don't have the capacity to combat infectious invaders. So, while a leukemia patient's white blood cell count may be elevated—sometimes 40 or 50 times normal—those cells are ineffectual at fighting infections caused by bacteria or fungi.

The only way to restore the bone marrow's function, and those critical white blood cells, red blood cells, and platelets, is to annihilate the blasts and allow the normal bone marrow cells to grow back.

And the only way to annihilate those blasts is to use chemotherapy.

This is not straightforward in people considered to be "older adults" with AML, commonly defined as over 60 years of age. One approach is to use aggressive, intensive chemotherapy, which consists of two drugs (daunorubicin and cytarabine) administered over seven days in the hospital. Patients receiving these drugs have to remain in the hospital for four to six weeks as they endure the side effects of the chemotherapy, which can lead to death in as many as 15 to 20 percent of those who receive the treatment. This type of chemotherapy, though, can also lead to a remission in up to 60 percent of older adults, and even a cure in a lucky few.

High risk, high reward.

Another option is to use less intensive chemotherapy (usually the drugs azacitidine or decitabine) that can be given in an outpatient clinic, like the one in which I was seeing Jimmy. The chance that one of these drugs could cause significant side effects or even death is much less (typically under 5 percent), but so is the chance of achieving a remission (approximately 20 percent).[3]

Lower risk, lower reward.

Jimmy, fighter that he was, chose the more aggressive approach when he was diagnosed. He endured a lengthy hospitalization lasting six weeks in Pennsylvania, and he managed to achieve a remission.

But remission is not the same as cure. Remission means that, following chemotherapy, the blasts have receded to account for less than 5 percent of the bone marrow as the red and white blood cells and platelets have returned to their normal, pre-leukemia levels. It is a snapshot in time.

The wildfire of blasts, though, can smolder, and they can be rekindled. Four months later, that's exactly what happened in Jimmy's bone marrow.

His leukemia came roaring back, and his blasts rose from 3 percent to 30 percent of his bone marrow. His oncologist in Pennsylvania tried treating him with the less intensive azacitidine, but after two courses of therapy, the blasts rose to 40 percent.

Jimmy's doctor then tried adding another drug—venetoclax—to the azacitidine. A recent study had shown that the combination of this new drug with either azacitidine or decitabine in 145 older adults with AML could lead to a remission in 67 percent of patients—more than three times what was expected from either the azacitidine or decitabine alone.[4]

But that didn't work either.

Running out of options, Jimmy's doctor suggested he come see me. And, like the many women participating in the Avastin studies, Jimmy felt that his best prospect was to enroll in a clinical trial.

On that day in June 2011, Heraleen Broome, a 74-year-old woman from Oakland, California, was the first patient to approach the microphone to talk about her experience with Avastin. She wore glasses that arched up at each side and had a face that was warm and expressive. I liked her instantly. She greeted everyone with a "Good morning" and started to eloquently describe her own, reluctant, intimate association with breast cancer. She was diagnosed with Stage 1 disease in October 2000, for which she was treated with a lumpectomy, chemotherapy, and radiation therapy. But two-and-a-half years later, the breast cancer returned with a vengeance, not only to the breast where it started, but also planting multiple tumors in her lungs. In July 2003, she started taking Avastin on a clinical trial.

> Within a few days, all of my tumors were shrinking and many had disappeared. That was almost eight years ago. . . . There is life after chemo fails you, this life made possible by Avastin in my case.[5]

Then, as if that wasn't personal enough, Ms. Broome talked about her family, and said plainly what many in the audience were thinking:

> I simply don't understand how the FDA can [say] that Avastin does not provide meaningful results of meaningfully prolonging life. I owe the last seven-and-a-half years to Avastin. Those years have seen my grandchildren grow up and they have taken me on wonderful trips to Europe and Asia, places I would never have gone without Avastin. . . . I don't think it is reasonable for you to set a number of people that need to be alive as a result of this drug in order to allow it to be sold. It seems to me that my life should be ˙enough, and it's not just my life but the lives of my family, friends, coworkers and everyone I meet.[6]

What she had said was so moving. The applause that followed her statement was thunderous, as people in the audience nodded their heads in agreement.

She wasn't the only woman with metastatic breast cancer treated with Avastin on a clinical trial who came to the microphone to tell her story.

Patricia Howard, a teacher for 21 years from Smithtown, New York, described herself as a "wife, mother, sister, aunt, and grammy" who enjoyed the births of three grandchildren while on the drug. After talking about her own breast cancer story, and the improvement she experienced with Avastin, she reminded us, "I'm not just a piece of anecdotal evidence. . . . I'm not just a statistic."[7] The women treated with Avastin who appeared at the FDA in 2011 had led full lives, with loving families, and had stories that stretched back years or even decades preceding their identity as a "subject" on a clinical trial.

As Jimmy reviewed his own full life, he told me he had smoked cigarettes from the end of his boxing career, in his mid-20s, until the age of 40. I also read in his medical record that, while Jimmy's AML was first diagnosed nine months previously, the flame for it may have been sparked a decade earlier, when he was treated for prostate cancer.

"Oh yeah, I almost forgot about that," Jimmy said, when I mentioned it. "They put those radiation seeds in my prostrate"—he pronounced the organ as if describing someone kneeling before a god, an endearing malapropism that elicited a smile from his cousin. "It hurt like a bugger, but then the cancer was gone. My PSA, they can't even measure it, it's so low!"

It's a common misconception that cancers arise because of a single, isolated, tragic genetic event that leads to the uncontrolled growth of a cell. That can occur with a couple of cancers (chronic myeloid leukemia is an example in which one genetic mutation—an exchange of genetic material between chromosome 9 and chromosome 22—leads to such a cell).[8] But more commonly it takes a series of genetic mutations (mutations that are acquired—in other words, not passed down to other family members) before the monster cells that grow out of control are created.[9]

What causes those mutations to occur? Mostly just dumb luck. If a cell is 99.9 percent accurate at making a perfect copy of itself to create its progeny, then 1 time out of 1,000 it will copy its own genetic material (the blueprints for that cell) the wrong way. Most of the time the result is genetic garbage, a nonfunctional cell, and that cell dies or is eliminated by the immune system.

But what if another 1 time out of 1,000 the cell that is created actually survives? And the immune system doesn't scavenge and eliminate it, like it's supposed to? That cell will then pass down this new genetic code to its progeny, and somewhere along the line, either because the cell has already demonstrated it has a proclivity toward error, or because of some outside insult, additional genetic errors occur. Eventually, those errors can drive the cell (and they are, in fact, called "driver" mutations) to reproduce faster than other cells around it, or to ignore the body's normal signals that tell it to stop growing.

That's when cancer occurs.

Thinking about it statistically, it can take years or even decades for enough of those "1 in 1,000" genetic mutations to arise—and for the immune system to miss them—before they lead to cancer.

That's why cancer occurs most frequently in people older than 60. And with multiple steps that lead to the cancer, that's why it's so hard to develop a drug that can target just one of those steps (and why it's appealing to develop a drug like Avastin that instead targets the blood supply to the cancer).

The exception occurs when people are born with a genetic mutation that gives them a proclivity to develop cancer—as might occur with a woman carrying a BRCA1 mutation. Lisa Schlager, the vice president of the advocacy group for people affected by hereditary breast, ovarian, and related cancers, is an example of a woman who is not only more likely to develop breast cancer, but also to develop it at a younger age, as the genetic cascade of events that normally takes decades to occur got a jumpstart in her at birth.

What are the "outside insults" that can push the process along? Excess intake of alcohol over long stretches of time can do it. So can smoking. In fact, we conducted a study in people with a bone marrow cancer called myelodysplastic syndrome (which can worsen to become AML) in which we examined in detail the smoking histories of our patients to determine whether there was an association between cigarette smoking and specific genetic abnormalities in the cancer.[10]

What we found was fascinating.

Smoking is not a simple binary risk factor—meaning, "Do you smoke, yes or no?" If you've ever seen family members or friends who smoke, you realize that not everybody smokes the same amount. Some smoke a few cigarettes per week, when they are around their friends; others smoke three packs of cigarettes a day, and they have the yellowed fingers and teeth to prove it! Some people smoked a bit in college and then gave up the habit, while others smoked for a couple of decades in their 20s and 30s but stopped because of the first report of Surgeon General Luther Terry, MD, on smoking and health in 1964, which linked smoking to lung and laryngeal cancer and chronic bronchitis.[11] Or they stopped because a spouse told them to give up the habit when a child was born, or because the "damn things just got so damn expensive" (to quote one patient). I've had patients who smoked very little (perhaps a few cigarettes each week) for decades, some who smoked a lot for decades, and some who smoked a lot for just a few years.

We determined that, indeed, smoking played a role in the stepwise progression of genetic mutations that led to the cancer. Smoking led to specific genetic mutations that occurred more frequently in patients who smoked than in those who didn't. But even more incredibly, we found that people who smoked more intensively (the three-pack-per-day crowd, compared to the half-a-packers) developed unique genetic mutations, and that these were distinct from the mutations that occurred in people who smoked very little, but for long periods of time.

We also found that, sometimes, the genetic mutation that occurred with smoking was the very first that led down that grim-rose path toward cancer; other times, that genetic error was the second, or third, or even fourth mutation.

Smoking is also a risk factor for developing breast cancer.

Complicated, isn't it? But it helps explain why not everyone who smokes gets cancer, and why not everyone who gets cancer has smoked in the past. These genetic events can occur just through mathematical probabilities and random, uncontrollable events, and not all smoking is the same. The period in people's lives when they smoke may add to the genetic chaos at just the right time, or just the wrong time. Sometimes, also, the immune system blinks, missing its chance to remove bad cells.

Cancer is complicated, which is why one, or two, or even three rounds of chemotherapy may not be enough.

It's also why the stories told by the women participating in the Avastin studies were so important, as the factors leading to each woman's breast cancer diagnosis, and her experience receiving Avastin, could be quite different.

A moment of realization shined in Jimmy's eyes when I asked him about the treatment for his prostate cancer.

"Wait, doc, you think those radiation seeds I got for the prostrate could have caused the leukemia? That's what my doctor back home said coulda happened."

"It's possible," I told him. "Always hard to know in retrospect."

He shrugged his shoulders. "What's done is done. I need to get that other cancer treated regardless."

Jimmy's question was more complicated than he may have intended. Just like with heavy or extended smoking or alcohol ingestion, treatment for other cancers—either with chemotherapy or radiation therapy—can cripple a cell's DNA, leading to genetic damage (figure 3.1). That is actually the reason these treatments are often used—when the DNA (and thus the genes) of a cell are disrupted, the cell dies. Since cancer cells grow faster than other cells in

# Multiple Steps Leading to DNA Damage, and Then to Cancer

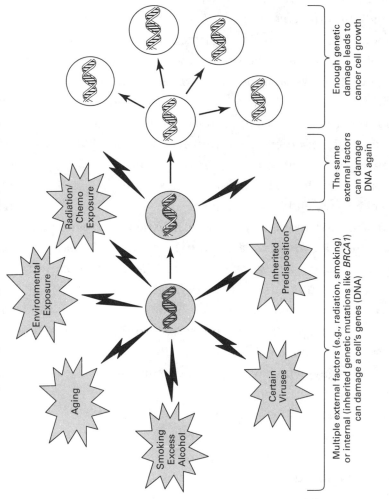

**Figure 3.1**

Damage to a cell's genes can cause damage to result in cancer cell growth.

the body, they are the ones most susceptible to the DNA crippling effects of chemotherapy and radiation therapy.

But other, normal cells can also sustain genetic damage. If this happens, they can die too. As an example, when the cells in hair follicles, which are growing all the time, are affected by chemotherapy or radiation therapy, they die. As a consequence, people may lose their hair when undergoing treatment for breast cancer.

But what happens when cells exposed to chemotherapy or radiation don't die? What if the DNA damage leads to genetic mutations that are then passed on to a cell's progeny? And what if those mutations predispose the cell to acquiring additional genetic mutations?

Leukemia, or other second cancers, can result. But is this true for radiation therapy used to treat prostate cancer?

On the one hand, it makes total sense: the prostate is nestled in the pelvis, which happens to be a bone rich in those bone marrow stem cells that make the red blood cells, the whites, and the platelets and which, if corrupted, can lead to leukemia. If the radiation treating the prostate misses its target and instead hits those juicy stem cells, theoretically they could be damaged.

On the other hand, with almost 200,000 men in the United States diagnosed with prostate cancer each year, and approximately 60,000 treated with radiation therapy, why don't I have a leukemia clinic filled with guys who have to excuse themselves to use the restroom frequently?[12]

In another study, we examined approximately 10,900 men treated for prostate cancer. About 5,100 of those men received some type of radiation treatment (either radiation seeds, called brachytherapy, which are placed into the prostate itself to release their radiation into the cancer cells; or external beam radiation therapy, meaning a machine outside the body aims radiation beams through a person's skin at the prostate[13]). The other 5,800 men had their prostates removed surgically. They served as our "control" group—men with prostate cancer, but who weren't treated with radiation therapy.[14]

When we looked at the raw numbers, it appeared that men treated with radiation were more likely to get myelodysplastic syndrome— the bone marrow cancer that could evolve into leukemia: 25 men, versus only 6 in the prostate surgery group.

But it wasn't a fair comparison. Men who choose radiation therapy for prostate cancer are older than men who choose surgery (an average of 68 years old versus 60 years old in our study). And older age can also lead to developing myelodysplastic syndrome or any other cancer. Why? Because the cumulative effects of those mathematical probabilities of developing genetic mutations result in cancer occurring more commonly in older adults. This is known as a "confounding variable" in a study—a factor that is associated with a risk factor (getting treated with radiation therapy) as well as with an outcome of interest (developing myelodysplastic syndrome).

You can see why it is so important to have statisticians like Brett Logan participate in ODAC meetings at the FDA. They help us identify the traps (like confounding variables) that could cause study findings to be misinterpreted; sometimes accidentally, but sometimes deliberately to favor one result over another.

When we adjusted our analyses for the age difference, the difference in developing the second cancer between those who received the radiation therapy and those who had their prostates removed surgically disappeared. And rates of developing myelodysplastic syndromes were similar to rates in other, older men in the population who never had prostate cancer.[15]

But does that mean that getting treated with radiation for prostate cancer is risk-free?

Our conclusion from the study was that there didn't appear to be a higher risk of myelodysplastic syndrome developing in this population of men receiving radiation therapy for prostate cancer *during their lifetime.*

That's an important caveat. It can take years or decades to accumulate enough of those genetic mutations to cause myelodysplastic syndromes or leukemia. If a man is treated with radiation therapy for prostate cancer at age 80, he will probably not live long enough for enough mutations to occur and lead to the second cancer. But a man treated with radiation at the age of 60, like Jimmy, might.

Hodgkin lymphoma, which is one of the first cancers to be successfully treated with radiation therapy, is also one of the few cancers that tend to affect people who are younger. As Hodgkin's often involves a tumor in the chest, radiation to shrink that tumor may have to pass through overlying breast tissue. One study found that people surviving Hodgkin's are at risk of secondary cancers— particularly breast cancer—even 40 years after their Hodgkin's diagnosis.[16]

Cancer is complicated. Identifying risk factors for cancer is even more complicated. Assessing the efficacy of a drug to treat cancer, when even a single diagnosis like "breast cancer" includes many different types of breast cancer with many different causes, can be even more complicated still.

"It's possible," I had told Jimmy when he asked whether the radiation therapy could have caused his leukemia. But I felt that I hadn't given him a straight answer to his questions yet! Second cancers like acute leukemia are much harder to treat, and much harder to cure, than cancers like leukemia that arise out of nowhere—called *de novo* cancers.

His leukemia sure was acting like a second cancer.

I shifted gears and took a deep breath before launching into a discussion with Jimmy about clinical trials. This was a similar discussion, I imagined, that the thousands of women who participated in the Avastin studies had engaged in with their doctors.

"Before we start talking about trials, I want to make sure you know that it's okay to say enough is enough, and not to pursue another treatment for your leukemia," I told Jimmy. I looked him in the eyes so he would know I was being sincere, that this was a viable approach. With the possibility that he had a second cancer, and the recalcitrance it had already shown to three different treatments, the chance that any other therapy would now work was vanishingly small.

Theresa nodded her head vigorously, as if she and Jimmy had engaged in this same conversation more than once, and so that he would see that she supported it.

But Jimmy shook his head. "Nah doc, I'm not ready to throw in the towel yet. I'm still tough as nails!" He lifted his arms again and gave the air a couple of jabs.

His cousin just shook her head and rolled her eyes a bit, smiling. Jimmy being Jimmy.

I had to smile also. I wondered if he had ever let a trainer stop a fight early, or if he always went the distance during his boxing days. "We do have a clinical trial open, and I wonder if this is the one your doctor in Pennsylvania was thinking about. It involves a type of treatment that isn't chemotherapy. Instead, it tries to bring your own immune system into the ring to fight the leukemia. It's called *immunotherapy*."

Jimmy nodded. I couldn't tell if he had heard the term before or not. "I like the sound of that!" he said.

The theory behind immunotherapy is fascinating, and it makes total sense considering how cancer develops: part of the process involves the multiple genetic mutations that occur over a lifetime; but part of it also involves what happens when the immune system's surveillance mechanism fails to remove the abnormal cells that become cancer. If we can somehow teach the immune system to go back, identify, and scavenge the cancerous cells, then maybe it can replace chemotherapy entirely in ridding the body of cancer. These sorts of immunotherapy approaches are also regulated by the FDA.

I described a clinical trial with just such an approach to Jimmy and Theresa.

"The goal of the treatment, of course, is to get rid of the leukemia that we can find—to get you in a remission. The chance we can do that is low, less than 20 percent, maybe even less than 10 percent," I told him.

Jimmy grimaced. I always feel terrible giving my patients these withering odds. But I would feel worse if I gave people false expectations about their chances, and they spent their last days on this earth stuck in a hospital when they would have chosen otherwise if they had just heard the truth to start with.

"But it could be rough," I continued. "Four weeks in the hospital, where you'll be cared for by nurses, nurse practitioners and physician assistants, residents and fellows, pharmacists, and me. The treatment will drop your blood counts down to those low levels you had when you were first hospitalized for your leukemia."

"Yeah, I remember," Jimmy said. "They had to give me blood and platelets every other day."

"Right," I agreed. "And the risk of infections from your low immune system will be even worse than it is with the leukemia alone. But in addition, this immunotherapy comes with a side effect called 'cytokine release syndrome' that could give you bad joint and muscle aches, shortness of breath, fevers, even drop your blood pressure so much you could end up in the intensive care unit." CRS is an inflammatory response by the immune system that affects the whole body. This is the same syndrome that makes people infected with COVID-19 so sick, and lands many of them in intensive care units.

His eyes almost glistened. "Bring it on doc, I'm ready for it." He raised his arms once more and jabbed the still air in front of him.

"I don't want to sound harsh, but you could even die going through this," I told him. I looked him in the eyes again as he let his arms drift down to the sides of his chair. Theresa was quiet, glancing at him first, and then at the floor.

"Yeah, I know that doc. I know that." He spoke softly. "But if I don't do something, I die anyway."

I nodded, acknowledging the cruel circumstances, the odds he was up against no matter his decision.

I had reviewed with him the risks, benefits, alternative treatment options, and personnel involved: the core elements of informed consent for a treatment trial, as mandated by the Kefauver-Harris Amendment of 1962.

"One more question," Theresa piped up. "This immunotherapy, has it been used in other people with leukemia before? Or is Jimmy here gonna be like a guinea pig? No offense, Jimmy."

He laughed. "I've been called worse."

More and more women stepped up to the microphone to testify about how Avastin had benefited them. None would have called herself a guinea pig for participating in a breast cancer clinical trial.

Nancy Haunty was a 41-year-old woman from Seattle who had 14 breast cancer tumors in her liver and more than 30 in her lungs. She started Avastin on a clinical trial and was doing well 21 months after her diagnosis. She even spent four days climbing to the summit of Mount Adams, the second highest peak in Washington State, at 12,000 feet. "I can't think of a better way to describe progression-free survival," she commented, referencing the study's endpoint, a measure of the time period during which the cancer didn't get any worse from when she started Avastin.[17]

Crystal Hanna had short, brown hair and wore a pink top, the neckline of which framed a silver cross hanging from a chain around her neck. She was a 35-year-old woman from Parkersburg, West Virginia, and had been diagnosed with breast cancer almost three years earlier. At the time her son was a year old and her daughter was 4. While taking Avastin as part of a clinical trial, she saw her daughter get baptized, took a vacation to Disney World, and attended her brother's wedding. She pleaded with the FDA, and with us:

If the FDA removes the breast cancer indication from [Avastin's] label, my insurance likely won't pay, and I can't afford the drug otherwise. If you were me or I was your loved one, wouldn't you want a specialist recommending treatment and the freedom to choose the best options?[18]

Others followed: representatives from breastcancer.org, the Marti Nelson Cancer Foundation, the Colon Cancer Alliance, the Kidney Cancer Association, the Cancer Support Community, and more women who themselves were treated in clinical trials with Avastin. These were the most moving testimonies, and the hardest to ignore. Survival curves and percentages of trial subjects experiencing toxicities were one thing; real, breathing people talking about their lives were another thing entirely.

Applause, applause, applause followed each and every one of these brave women who walked up to the microphone and spoke candidly about her cancer journey. All told, 13 women with breast cancer treated with Avastin and other chemotherapy drugs shared their stories with us, and we heard from their husbands, friends, and doctors, and from other advocates for women with breast cancer.

Thirty-four people in total. It was awe-inspiring.

They were living their lives. They had children and grandchildren. They were not aggregates of data. They were women with breast cancer who were healthy enough to participate in a clinical trial with an investigational new drug and to then get in a car or on a plane and travel to the White Oaks facility in Rockville, Maryland, to remind everyone at this hearing what was at stake. And they credited Avastin with still being alive.

Way back in 1962, the government had developed detailed requirements whereby manufacturers could distribute drugs across state lines for investigational purposes—the FDA called it the Investigational New Drug process—one such purpose being to conduct clinical trials in people to determine whether the drugs were indeed safe and effective.[19]

But before a drug can be administered to people, it has to be either designed or discovered. More recently, drugs have been designed to target abnormalities unique to the cancer—perhaps a specific genetic mutation that drove that cancer down its dastardly path of destruction and dominance over the body: the genetic mutations *FLT3* in acute myeloid leukemia, for instance, or *HER2/neu* in breast cancer, or it might be a mutation in the dystrophin gene in Duchenne muscular dystrophy.

How long does it take to design such a drug? The *Her2/neu* gene was first described as playing a role in cancer development in 1979.[20] Five years later, the protein produced by this gene, which contributed to the uncontrolled growth of cancer cells, was identified, and then it took another three years before the gene and protein were linked to the recurrence and spread of breast cancer.[21] This work was performed by Robert Weinberg, PhD, at the Massachusetts Institute of Technology; Dennis Slamon, MD, at the University of California, Los Angeles; Stuart Aaronson, PhD, at the National Cancer Institute; and Michael Shepard, PhD, and Axel Ullrich, PhD, both scientists at the pharmaceutical company Genentech, among other researchers.[22]

Then Slamon and Ullrich approached leaders at Genentech—the same company that would later develop Avastin—about developing a drug to target the protein produced by the *HER2/neu* mutation. But at the time the company had disbanded its oncology branch and wasn't interested.

Until two years later, in 1989—when the mother of a senior vice president at Genentech developed breast cancer. Partially as a result, and after years of planned innovation, resources to support drug development for breast cancer materialized. Trastuzumab, also known as Herceptin, was created.[23]

As the last three letters of the name implies, trastuzumab is a Monoclonal AntiBody, meaning it has an antibody portion that binds to a specific protein on the outside of the cancer cell linked to *HER2/neu*. In the same way, antibodies our own body manufactures can bind to proteins on specific infections to get rid of them—like the antibodies measured after the COVID-19 vaccines, which can protect us against severe viral infections. The first woman enrolled in a 16-patient clinical trial of trastuzumab was recruited in June 1992. Thanks to the advocacy efforts of a number of breast cancer groups and physician scientists, the drug gained FDA approval for the treatment of women with metastatic breast cancer in September 1998.[24]

Almost 20 years after the gene that it targets was first described.

Thousands of drugs have been in existence for decades, through many attempts over time to rein in disease. Most of those attempts have unfortunately been fruitless—few drugs ever make it to a clinical trial, never mind getting approved by the FDA. It is estimated that only 14 percent of all drugs in clinical trials win approval from the FDA, and only 3 to 4 percent of investigational cancer treatments ever get approved.[25]

What happens to all of these frustrated medicines? Are they tossed down an industrial sink? Relegated to an island of misfit pharmaceuticals?

As it turns out, they are catalogued and assembled into a chemical library. Scientists can screen that library for a disease indication or a specific target on a diseased cell (like *HER2/neu*) that might not have been recognized when the drug was first designed, years or even decades earlier. A technique called high-throughput screening, which uses robots, detectors, and software, can allow 100,000 compounds to be screened in a single day!

These drugs are first added to artificial cells (in test tubes or to shallow wells on a plastic plate) that resemble the cells one might actually find in the diseased body, like breast cancer cells or leukemia cells. Let's imagine putting these drugs in the ring with Jimmy's leukemia cells.

Drug A, a poorly trained welterweight, might put on its gloves, but Jimmy's cells just shrug it off, and keep growing.

Drug B might then enter the ring. Maybe it lands a couple of good punches in the second round and slows the growth of Jimmy's cells for a while, but then they rev up and keep dividing as if the drug was never there.

Drug C is then pitted against Jimmy's cells, and whoa! They don't know what hit 'em. Knocked to the mat, they sit there, stunned, but they don't die. Maybe they get up to fight again, maybe not.

Drug D, however, annihilates Jimmy's cells: 100 percent kill rate, no survivors. It's as if, channeling Muhammad Ali, Drug D knocked out Jimmy's cells in the first round. Folks, we have a winner!

Drug D, now back in the lab in test tubes or wells, may then be modified by a chemist to enhance its activity against the cells even further, reduce its effects on other cells, and improve its absorption into the cells and the body. The drug, now referred to as a "lead compound," may be added to the cells at different doses, and even for different amounts of time, to see what the lowest dose that kills the cells might be.

Some drugs continue testing on cells that mimic major organs in the body, to assess whether toxicities exist. Others may need to then be given to animals for these assessments.

Let's say an investigator takes Drug D and administers it to a special type of mouse—one that has the disease she's trying to eliminate. If the drug is being developed to treat breast cancer, the mouse might have a breast cancer tumor that has been stimulated to grow in its hindquarters, where the effects of the drug on the tumor can be observed more easily. The investigator tries one dose of Drug D and thinks the tumor might have shrunk a bit, but the mouse dies. She tries a lower dose. Same outcome. Then a lower dose. And so on until the mouse survives. But there's a problem: the dose is so low that the tumor doesn't shrink.

So much for Drug D. It's safe, but not effective in a mouse. Time to go back to the drug screening studies, or further refine this lead compound.

The investigator goes through the same process. Finally she identifies a compound that kills cells in a test tube and kills the tumor in the mouse. She continues to administer her lead compound—in her mind, she has named it Tumorminimab—but in the process she has to look for other side effects in her animal. One drug kills the tumor and doesn't kill the animal, but it severely damages the animal's kidneys and liver.

Effective, but not safe. Scrap that one.

Another compound kills the tumor and doesn't kill the animal, but studies in pregnant animals show that it causes severe birth defects or even fetal death.

Do we want another thalidomide on our hands?

This can take a lot of time, a lot of false starts, a lot of dashed hopes, and a lot of going back to the drawing boards. It can also take a lot of money. Millions of dollars exploring the safety and efficacy of dozens of candidate drugs before they ever make it into a human being.

Drug discovery and drug development isn't easy.

It is only after a drug has cleared these hurdles and gotten the nod from the FDA that it can then be used experimentally in people (figure 3.2). And only then can it move to the types of clinical trials in which thousands of women had participated to test Avastin, and in which Jimmy was now considering for his resistant leukemia.

How do lead compounds—and eventually approved drugs—get their names? A good friend and colleague, David Steensma, MD, once explained it to me.[26]

Remember that our investigator gave the name Tumorminimab to the drug she used in her clinical trial with the mouse. (As with the real drug trastuzumab, the last three letters indicate a monoclonal antibody that minimizes the size of tumors.) Drugs are first given identifiers made by combining letters and numbers. The letters may

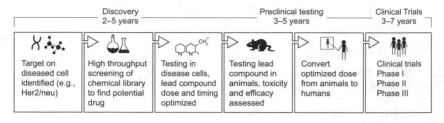

**Figure 3.2**
Getting a drug to market can take more than a decade, from the time of discovery, to testing, and through clinical trials.

reflect the company that developed the molecule (PF-1234 could be a Pfizer drug, whereas LY-5678 could come from Eli Lily) or how the drug works (STI-571—later known as Imatinib or Gleevec and used to treat chronic myeloid leukemia, is a Signal Transduction Inhibitor).

A drug's generic name can come from how it works, its development history, or its actual chemical structure. A pharmaceutical company gets first crack at the name, and then negotiates it with regulatory agencies, which make sure the name doesn't promise more than the drug can deliver (thus, no drug can be named Cholesterolbegone!) or that it will be confused with other drug names (a testosterone drug couldn't be named Himatinib).

A portion of a drug's name can include how it works, as with monoclonal antibodies and their "mab" suffixes. Tyrosine kinase inhibitors tend to end in "mib" (as with imatinib), protesome inhibitors with "zomib" (as with bortezomib), cholesterol lowering drugs with "statin" (not "begone!"), and so on.

The next step? A national or international nomenclature committee, the members of which focus on name clarity, including how to pronounce a drug's name. For example, α-(N-Phthalimido) glutaramide became the now infamous thalidomide, and not phthalidomide, which is harder to say.

For brand names, the marketing arms of pharmaceutical companies tend to step in, though these, too, need to be approved by regulatory agencies. Focus groups have shown that doctors tend to remember names with hard to pronounce consonants such as J, Q, X, and Z, and to associate these letters with high-tech, innovative science, and thus are more likely to prescribe them.

What about the drug being considered on that fateful June day in 2011? Bevacizumab, the generic name for Avastin, thus includes "ci" (for cardiovascular, perhaps as it works on vascular endothelial growth factor); "zu" (shorthand for humanized), and "mab," as it is a monoclonal antibody.

# 4

# Trials and Tribulations

What I suffered physically was worth what I've accomplished
in life. A man who is not courageous enough to take risks will
never accomplish anything in life.

—Muhammad Ali, 1984

The clinical trial process, by which a drug makes the long journey
toward the study that might lead to its FDA approval, includes four
phases, each designed with specific objectives in mind, as shown in
table 4.1.

Phase 1, or more dramatically, "first in human" clinical trials,
look at drug safety. Take "Tumorminimab," the fictitious tumor-
shrinking drug named in chapter 3, as an example. By the time a
Phase 1 trial is started, prior testing has already determined the best
way to administer the drug: as a pill, by vein, or under the skin. We
may already have found, for example, that Tumorminimab is one
of those drugs that are disabled or destroyed by the stomach's acid
and won't be very effective if given in pill form—that it has to be
administered under the skin or by vein, or by pill only if it is combined with another chemical that prevents its acid demise.

**Table 4.1**

| Trial Phase | No. of People (Subjects) Included (Approximate) | Objectives and Design |
|---|---|---|
| 1 | 3–75 | *Safety*: Determine drug dose, frequency, tolerability, side effects (toxicity)<br><br>Usually single study arm (non-comparative)<br><br>Can include patients with multiple disease types |
| 2 | 30–300 | *Safety and Efficacy*: Assess drug side effects and whether it works<br><br>Usually single study arm, can be two study arms (comparative)<br><br>Usually includes patients with single disease type |
| 3 | 100s–1,000s | *Safety and Efficacy*: Assess drug side effects and whether it works<br><br>Always two or more study arms (compare to standard of care)<br><br>Includes patients with single disease type |
| 4 | 100s–1,000s | *Safety and Efficacy*: Also known as post-marketing or surveillance study<br><br>Assess rare side effects, efficacy in subgroups<br><br>Can include patients with multiple disease types |

But what about the dose? And how frequently should the drug be administered?

Some of these questions would have already been answered in the cell or animal studies, where the peak and trough levels of a drug's concentration in the animals' bloodstream are assessed. The dose and frequency of administration are adjusted until the right balance is attained, blending into the equation the need to ensure that the dose and frequency work to kill the tumor and aren't too toxic to the animal or its organs. Scientists can then use a formula to determine the appropriate dose in humans.[1]

For example, if a drug is given at a dose of 0.2 mg daily in a mouse, that might translate to 50 mg daily in a human. So 50 mg should be the starting dose for a Phase 1 study, right?

Wrong. The starting dose might be 10 mg, which almost certainly won't work to shrink the tumor. But it's also not likely to cause severe toxicities in people, which could shut the drug development program down.

Phase 1 studies are often designed using a method called "3+3."[2] Three patients are enrolled at a drug's starting dose, say 10 mg. If none of those three patients experience a major toxicity, the next three patients are enrolled on the study at the next higher dose level, say 30 mg. If those three don't suffer major side effects, the dose then might be escalated to 50 mg for another three patients—the dose predicted to be effective in humans based on the 0.2 mg dose in mice. The process continues, exposing patients to progressively higher drug dose levels.

But what happens if one of the first three patients has kidney failure while on the drug, and there's a reasonable likelihood that the drug caused that kidney failure? Another three patients are enrolled to the study at the same dose level because, after all, it may have been just bad luck that this patient developed kidney failure: maybe she became severely dehydrated over the weekend because she was outside in the blistering Miami sun playing with her grandchildren and forgot to keep up with her fluids, which could have damaged her kidneys and would have occurred whether or not the experimental drug had been given.

If those additional three patients (the "+ 3" of the "3+3" design) are able to take the drug without a major incident, then the next group of three can be enrolled onto the 30 mg dosing group.

But if one of those additional three also experiences a major drug toxicity like liver failure or a dangerous heart arrhythmia—these are called *serious adverse events* or *SAEs*—then the drug is pretty much dead in the water. The same is true if two of the first three patients suffered a serious adverse event.

So all of the time, effort, and resources that went into drug discovery and animal testing for this particular drug is for naught. Time to start over.

That's why, in Phase 1 trials, the starting doses of a drug are unlikely to be effective: they are set purposely low to make sure they won't cause serious toxic reactions or death in humans— and thereby also kill a drug's prospects for approval before it gets a chance to work.

So it stands to reason that if you're a patient looking for a drug that is effective at treating your disease, be it breast cancer or rheumatoid arthritis, you may not want to be in one of the first couple of dosing groups in a Phase 1 study.

In reality, though, it's unlikely that these types of toxicities would occur at such a low dose of 10 mg, when the projected dose in humans should be 50 mg. Let's say instead that nothing bad happened at the 10 mg and 30 mg dosing groups, but the kidney failure and cardiac arrhythmia occurred at the 50 mg dose in two separate patients. Then, the investigators involved in the Phase 1 study would conclude that the 30 mg dose was the *maximum tolerated dose*—the MTD. That would be the dose moving forward in larger studies.

Phase 1 studies also look at other factors important in giving medicines to humans, such as the distribution of the drug throughout the body, whether the dosing schedule is truly the correct one, and how the drug is eliminated—in urine or feces. (It has to get out of the body somehow!)

But there's no mention of efficacy, is there? (Look again at the Phase 1 row in table 4.1: you won't find the word "efficacy" in the Objectives and Design column.) Here's where we enter the ethical badlands of Phase 1 clinical trials.

Why do people participate in Phase 1 clinical trials, if ostensibly the purpose of such a trial has nothing to do with whether or not a drug works? In one study, surveys asking this very question were mailed to 287 adult cancer trial participants and 65 parents of pediatric cancer trial participants. When the adult patients were asked the primary motivation for participating in a clinical trial, 45 percent of those who were enrolled in a Phase 1 trial said they were motivated by the possibility that they would *receive medical benefits* from the treatment.[3]

But the primary purpose of Phase 1 trials is to find the right drug dose and to assess safety of that drug. In these trials, the chance that a drug will be at all effective and a patient's cancer will shrink is historically only 5 to 10 percent.

The next highest motivations for adults participating in Phase 1 trials was *trusting the study doctor* (17 percent), *to maintain hope* (15 percent), and *to help future patients* (4 percent). This last category is considered medical *altruism*, as is wanting to help advance medical science. These tend to be more common in patients with better prognoses.[4]

Why, then, did so many of these patients agree to participate in a Phase 1 trial if they were hoping for an effective drug?

Imagine you're Jimmy, with a leukemia that has continued to burn despite multiple rounds of chemotherapy. Your doctor tells you that there aren't any more treatment options available, so you'd better go to the university hospital nearby, or to one of the big academic hospitals where they might be running a clinical trial of a new drug.

To a guy like Jimmy, who really feels pretty good most of the time except for when he needs a blood or platelet transfusion—and who tells you, "I'm not ready to throw in the towel yet. I'm still tough as nails!"—why does a clinical trial become the next treatment step, sometimes regardless of what that trial entails or any promises that the drug might work?

Likely because his doctor told him one exists. The same might be true for a woman whose breast cancer spreads after her initial treatment of lumpectomy, chemotherapy, and radiation therapy— like for Heraleen Broome—and then she hears from her doctor about an Avastin clinical trial.

But more commonly, those of us involved in clinical research may not be effectively communicating the true goals of such an early phase trial. And ineffective communication can lead to *therapeutic misconception*—the belief that the purpose of the research is to directly benefit the individual patient enrolling on the trial. In reality, a study that focuses on a drug's safety, its distribution in the body, and its correct dosage is most likely to help only future patients, not current ones, who take the drug.

Another study examined how doctors involved in these types of studies and families of pediatric cancer patients communicated about the risks and benefits of participation in a Phase 1 trial during the informed consent process. These conversations were audio recorded for 85 families, and doctors had an average of 14 years of experience caring for children with cancer—these were experienced healthcare providers.[5]

The findings from the study are revealing.

Risks were discussed 95 percent of the time, with 81 of 85 families. It is a bit surprising that this didn't occur 100 percent of the time, as these Phase 1 trials involved chemotherapy.

Therapeutic benefits were discussed almost as frequently—88 percent of the time, for 75 of 85 families. The quality-of-life impact on the child were discussed just as often. To be fair, a range of therapeutic benefits and quality of life were described: from no benefit and a decreased quality of life to major benefit and improved quality of life. In 13 percent of conversations, though, the clinical trial was actually described as a bridge to another therapy or to extend life. One doctor told a child and her family:

If she is benefiting from this drug, she would take it for a year according to the study. . . . I don't anticipate she would be on it for a year. . . . I think at some point we would want to get her to immunotherapy.[6]

These were all discussions involving Phase 1 trials, in which efficacy is never a primary objective. Altruism was also a part of these conversations 41 percent of the time.

So, why *do* patients agree to participate in Phase 1 trials? It's possible that they misunderstand the intent, either because it isn't communicated clearly by an investigator, or because they may be hoping for an effective drug despite the expressed goals of the trial. People at the end of life are also altruistic; and on a few occasions patients have told me that their main motivation for participating in research is to help others, as part of their legacy.

And sometimes patients are walking the treatment treadmill. They just see the trial as the next step—or are told as much.

Jimmy wanted to know if he would be a guinea pig if he participated in a clinical trial.

"This drug has already been given to a series of patients with your type of leukemia and other cancers of the blood and bone marrow to find the right dose, and to see what side effects occur," I told him and Theresa. "This is the next phase of trials, where it's given to a larger group of patients with just your type of leukemia. It's called a Phase 2 trial."

"Round 2!" Jimmy interrupted. "I usually did pretty good in the second round!"

Theresa shook her head. "Jimmy, listen to the doctor, he's trying to explain this!"

I laughed. What a pair these two were. "Now we have to check to see if you're eligible for the trial."

"Why wouldn't they take me?" he asked. Good question.

In a Phase 2 study, all of the patients included will be given the dose that in the Phase 1 study was determined to be the maximum tolerated dose. Phase 2 trials might enroll anywhere from 30 patients to 200 or even more, all with the same disease. (See the appendix for an example of the criteria considered for those who wish to enroll in a Phase 2 trial to treat myelodysplastic syndromes, a type of bone marrow cancer.) Every patient treated during the study receives the experimental drug, and side effects to the drug continue to be monitored extremely closely—just as they were on the Phase 1 study—but especially so in this larger group of patients, where there may have been as few as three patients treated at the maximum tolerated dose from the Phase 1. But this time, the primary objective of the study is to assess whether or not the drug is effective.

Should be straightforward, right? If a drug is effective, the disease should go away.

But efficacy is not always so cut and dried. Let's return to Tumorminimab. It performed well in a Phase 1 trial, in which the maximum tolerated dose was 30 mg. In that Phase 1 trial, which enrolled patients with a variety of cancers, the investigators noticed that two patients with lung cancer who happened to receive the 30 mg dose had some shrinkage of their tumors—one patient had a 30 percent shrinkage, and another a 20 percent shrinkage. Based on this—on the experience of just two patients—the drug's manufacturer decides to design a Phase 2 trial just for lung cancer patients, and at the 30 mg dose.

Sound absurd? This is actually how decisions are made about target patient populations for drug development. This and, of course, economic motivators: It's probably appealing to investors in a pharmaceutical company, or to a company's board, to develop a drug for a disease like lung cancer, which affects 220,000 people yearly in the United States.[7] It's a harder sell to develop a drug and bring it to clinical trials for a "boutique" indication like Gaucher disease, in which the body deposits abnormal proteins in organs, where they accumulate and cause those organs to enlarge, along with bone abnormalities, and even brainstem dysfunction. It is equally serious to lung cancer, leading to death at a very young age, but it only affects 1 in 60,000 people yearly (whereas 1 in 16 people is affected by lung cancer in the course of a lifetime).[8]

A Phase 2 trial is designed to try to meet a target rate of efficacy, based on past experience with the experimental drug or with other drugs used for the same disease indication. For Tumorminimab, let's assume the Phase 2 trial is focused on patients with lung cancer that has returned despite two prior attempts at treating it. In this setting, other drugs might shrink the tumor perhaps 15 percent of the time. The investigators on the trial may aim for an improvement with the new drug that doubles that rate—to 30 percent.

Notice how precisely the target population is defined—those for whom lung cancer has returned despite two prior attempts at treating it. Part of the reason for this precision is that a company developing a drug already has an eye toward getting the drug approved by the FDA, and for that to occur the drug's indication—the disease, disease stage, and at what point in treating the disease the drug should be used—has to be defined clearly for the drug's label.

Notice also how the target population for Tumorminimab are those patients who have an end-stage cancer—one that has grown despite previous treatment. Most cancer drugs evaluated in clinical trials are administered to this group. Why them, as opposed to patients who have just received a new lung cancer diagnosis?

First, because patients with end-stage cancer don't have many treatment options remaining, and a new drug for them could make the greatest impact. Second, from an ethical standpoint, giving a new drug that hasn't yet been proven to be safe or effective makes more sense when there aren't other great options, as opposed to in the frontline setting when other drugs have been shown to have the appropriate balance of safety and efficacy.

This ethical calculus changes when the new drug is combined with a standard drug for use initially, or, when the new drug has been proven to work extremely well in cancer that has returned or has not gone away following initial therapy (what we call cancer that has relapsed following treatment or is refractory to treatment); it then makes good sense to compare this highly effective drug to the standard, up-front treatment.

A lung cancer patient with a new diagnosis has treatment options that include surgery, radiation therapy, chemotherapy drugs such as carboplatin and taxol, and immunotherapy drugs like nivolumab or ipilimumab. Other lung cancer drugs can target specific genetic mutations within the cancer itself: crizotinib (Xalkori) or ceritinib (Zykadia), for instance, target the anaplastic lymphoma kinase (ALK) genetic mutation; ramucirumab (Cyramaza) and bevacizumab (Avastin), the latter being the same Avastin used in breast cancer, target a protein that helps the blood vessels that feed the tumor form.[9]

For lung cancer that returns after this initial round of chemotherapy, the same options may still be available, except for the treatment that was already used. The available options—especially those approved by the FDA—diminish substantially when lung cancer returns, or doesn't go away, following this second round of therapy. Thus the opportunity to develop a new drug.

I remember the day my Mom was diagnosed with lung cancer and we faced some of these decisions.[10]

"I want you to talk to me like I'm one of your patients, not like I'm your mother."

Her voice came over the car's speakers via the Bluetooth connection to my phone as I drove home. She had left a voicemail an hour earlier asking me to call her back, which was never a good sign. My mother, still working as an administrator in Rhode Island at age 74, was not the type to mince words, nor ask for a return call to discuss trivialities. I asked her what was going on.

"I had a cold that wasn't getting any better, so I went to an urgent care clinic to get some antibiotics."

I avoided the temptation to remind her that most colds were viral, and that antibiotics don't alter their duration. Naturally, she knew that I would tell her that, and thus the reason she didn't mention she was going to urgent care in the first place. So it goes for mothers and sons. She continued.

"They took a chest X-ray, and my primary care doctor called me the next day to tell me that they found a 'shadow' in my lung, and that I needed to get a CT scan of my chest to see it more clearly."

By this point I was holding my breath and bracing myself for what would come next: the beginning of every cancer story, when the seemingly innocent cough, lump, or common cold takes a sinister turn, and the unexpected replaces what was expected.

"She called me this afternoon and told me I have lung cancer, and I have to schedule a biopsy."

I only vaguely processed the other cars on the road and the clouds breezing past the stagnant sky, the rest of the world moving on as mine suddenly stood still.

"Okay," I said, buying time to find some of the words I had heard family members of my own patients use for reassurance. "There are still a lot of things a mass in the lungs could be, like an infection, or scar tissue. It's not cancer yet, until a biopsy shows that it's cancer." So the saying in oncology went, "Tumor is a rumor, tissue is the issue." I continued. "You haven't gotten a biopsy yet, right?"

"Well, no. But my doctor seemed pretty sure this was cancer," she answered.

"It's not cancer yet," I said, trying to convince myself as much as her.

Over the next few days, I played an unfamiliar role, similar to the husbands and sons of all of those women treated with Avastin who approached the microphone to tell their stories.

Rather than doctor providing information, I became the family member trying to obtain it, and also attempting to help schedule a procedure in an unfamiliar hospital many states away. My mother's doctor quickly faxed me the report from the CT scan, which described a lobulated mass more than 3 centimeters long, typical of cancer. Scheduling the biopsy proved more challenging, though, and after several phone calls the best the interventional radiology department could provide was a tentative date, 10 days in the future. We entered the purgatory of waiting for a cancer diagnosis.

Each March, my mother accompanied my family and me as we fled the stubborn Cleveland winter for the warm, sandy beaches of Sanibel Island in Florida. Our yearly migration fell during those 10 days, and she insisted we keep to our tradition, as the trip might distract her from the ominous, impending diagnosis.

But as I lay next to her on lounge chairs by the pool, I could see her attention drift from the Dick Francis novel in her lap to some indeterminate space in the distance, as she formulated her next "if this is cancer" question:

> If this is cancer . . . what are the next tests I will need?
> . . . will I have surgery?
> . . . will I get chemotherapy?
> . . . should I consider a clinical trial?
> . . . can I keep working?
> . . . when will we know?

One evening, we went for dinner on nearby Captiva, and afterward walked to the beach. A crowd had gathered, and as a bagpiper played, the sun set over the Gulf of Mexico, flaming orange and gold as it was swallowed by the water. When it finally disappeared, the crowd erupted in applause. My 12-year-old daughter came over to me, laughing.

"Can you believe everyone clapped?" she asked. "Like there was ever a doubt the sun would make it!"

I glanced over at my mother, whose expression was complex, as if seeing the sun set on yet another day was no longer so guaranteed.

We all returned north and my mother underwent the biopsy, which confirmed that she had cancer. It was rotten news, but in a twisted way almost a relief that we knew what we were dealing with, could make plans, and had emerged from the wretched period of waiting.

She came to my hospital and met with a good friend of mine, Nate Pennell, MD, PhD, who also happened to head up our lung cancer program. How strange, to be sitting in the patient chair next to my Mom, like the Avastin husbands or sons, dutifully taking notes about her treatment options, as this man who helped coach my son's baseball team gave her advice on the therapeutic path that had the best chance of prolonging her life. This man who, in the cruelest of ironies, had lost his own mother to lung cancer—he knew how we were still reeling from the news of the diagnosis, and how best to guide us.

She underwent surgery. One lobe of her right lung was removed, and then she underwent routine CT scans, every three months, to make sure the cancer wasn't returning—just as the women on the Avastin trials underwent regular CT scans to assess their tumors. The first few were all clear, but about a year after her surgery, a small mass appeared, measuring less than 1 centimeter in diameter. Nate and others in the lung cancer group agreed that it was concerning for lung cancer, and recommended that, this time, she undergo radiation therapy. After one week of treatment, the mass was gone, and she again entered a remission.

Ironically, for the purposes of this book, and typical of many interventions in medicine, the radiation treatment she received has not been supported through randomized trials and approved specifically for the indication of "relapsed lung cancer" by the FDA—yet it is commonly used.

What happens if the cancer returns for a third, unwelcome appearance?

She could take one of the other treatments—chemotherapy, immunotherapy, or targeted therapy—that she hasn't tried yet. She could also consider entering a clinical trial of a new drug.

If she, like Jimmy, were determined to be eligible.

There's a common saying among clinical researchers, usually muttered through gritted teeth, that you almost have to be an Olympic athlete to make it on to a clinical trial, given the rigid restrictions of eligibility criteria.

Some of those criteria make good sense. For example, a clinical trial of a drug to treat lung cancer should require that a person actually have lung cancer to be eligible for the study. It is also sensible that a study enrolls patients reasonably healthy enough to benefit from the drug. A person who is moribund and at death's door, who wouldn't receive the drug if it were approved, thus shouldn't be enrolled.

But many eligibility criteria require near perfect liver, kidney, and heart function; no other medical conditions, such as heart failure, HIV, or neurologic conditions; no recent cancer diagnoses (other than the cancer for which the trial is intended). And they exclude children and pregnant women.

Why deliberately exclude so many patients who may be desperate for a drug to treat a life-threatening diagnosis like cancer, or debilitating neurologic conditions like multiple sclerosis?

The people designing such trials (many of whom work for pharmaceutical companies) argue that extremely healthy patients are necessary to preserve the sanctity of the trial, so that an underlying medical condition isn't confused with a side effect to a drug.

For example, a patient who has lung cancer and also severe heart disease (this is a common scenario, as smoking can lead to both the cancer and the heart disease), receives Tumorminimab on a clinical trial for the lung cancer, and four days later suffers a heart attack. Should his myocardial infarction be blamed on the drug, or on his known heart disease? In other words, would he have suffered the heart attack on the same date regardless of receiving Tumorminimab?

If his heart attack occurs when taking Tumorminimab as part of a Phase 1 trial, and an investigator decides that there is a possible association between the drug and his attack, then the number of milligrams of the experimental drug he took could be declared toxic, and future patients may receive a dose that is too low to effectively treat their cancers.

On the other hand, if no patients with heart disease are enrolled in the trials of Tumorminimab, and the drug is eventually approved by the FDA, should I, in my practice, give the drug to patients with heart disease, when I don't know if it's safe for them?

Let's consider some implicit biases and conflicts of interest that provide incentives for restricting enrollment to patients who are relatively healthy.

Healthy patients live longer, and they tend to have improved health when given an experimental drug. Patients on a trial who achieve better health and live longer make a drug seem more effective than it might be for patients who didn't start out as healthy, which increases its chances of gaining regulatory approval. If the person who designed the trial works for a pharmaceutical company, that person will probably hold stock options whose value will increase if the drug gets approved. If the person designing the trial is an academic investigator, he or she has a better chance of writing a scientific manuscript describing the results of the trial that will get accepted to a high-profile medical journal if the drug is shown to improve patient outcomes. This will lead to greater fame, and possible academic promotion.

Think that I'm suggesting conspiracy in the ranks? Multiple studies have shown that a strong bias exists favoring the publication in scientific journals of clinical trials that have "positive results" showing that an experimental drug is effective, compared to trials that have "negative results" indicating that an experimental drug works no better (or worse) than existing therapies.[11]

One such analysis examined over 1,100 studies included in the Cochrane Database of Systematic Reviews in which some form of treatment for a medical condition was compared to placebo or no treatment at all. The Cochrane Database is known for its scientific rigor in vetting well-conducted clinical trials to make treatment recommendations. This analysis found that trials in which a treatment was favored had a 27 percent higher probability of being included in the Cochrane studies. Additionally, results showing no evidence of toxicities to an experimental drug were 78 percent more likely to be included than trials showing that adverse events existed.[12]

And sometimes, the efficacy of a drug in a clinical trial is exaggerated, while the toxicities are downplayed or dismissed as being "expected in this patient population," to help a study get accepted to a medical journal.

Unfortunately, "spin factor" is just as common in science as it is in politics.

Not all of the speakers who approached the microphone at the 2011 FDA hearing supported Avastin. Some saw the "positive results" from the clinical trials as spin, worried that the toxicities had been minimized in publications, and called them out.

And not all of the women who participated in the Avastin trials could be in Rockville that day to speak on their own behalf. Even among the so-called Olympic athletes who cleared the trial eligibility hurdles, some got sick and died from Avastin.

Helen Schiff was affiliated with SHARE, a breast and ovarian cancer support organization, with a special focus on medically underserved communities, that has been around since 1978. She had been diagnosed with breast cancer in 1989 and joined the organization soon after. Schiff and a majority of SHARE leaders felt Avastin should not remain on the market:

> Like everyone else, we wanted Avastin to succeed in metastatic breast cancer, but we are honest enough to admit that it did not. . . . For every woman here testifying, there are other women we know—a member of our group who bled out every orifice of her body and another woman . . . in Florida who had a brain hemorrhage . . . who don't come to testify. I just want you to remember that they exist, too.[13]

There was no applause from the audience.

Christine Brunswick was 58 years old and vice president of the National Breast Cancer Coalition. She had been diagnosed with breast cancer 20 years earlier, when she first joined the NBCC, and told the audience that she was living with metastatic disease. She was well known in the breast cancer advocacy world and was even celebrated by former secretary of state Hillary Clinton for being an "extraordinary advocate for women" and for her work with the NBCC "on Capitol Hill, with the White House, and the scientific community and her passion for helping women around the world."[14] I anticipated this well-respected leader of a well-respected advocacy group to be another champion for Avastin. But what she said took me by surprise.

> Avastin has been shown to be unsafe and ineffective for breast cancer patients. The FDA's decision on Avastin must be based on scientific evidence from well-done trials and cannot be based on any one individual story, no matter how compelling. This decision cannot be driven by anecdotes. It must be driven by science.[15]

She went on to say plainly and unequivocally:

> We now know that women died because of this drug. . . . It does not significantly keep the disease at bay, it surely is not a cure, and it does not extend life. The drug does raise false expectations.[16]

In less than two years, on February 25, 2013, Christine Brunswick would die of complications from her breast cancer. A public service fellowship through the American Bar Association would be named in her honor.

But on that day after she spoke at the FDA, there was no applause for her. Then, 34-year-old Kimberly Jewett followed her to the microphone.

> I am completely disgusted to have to follow somebody like that. She apparently has not listened to the many women who are standing here today and have benefited from Avastin.[17]

Applause, applause, applause.

Of the 34 people who spoke that day, many were funded by Genentech, Avastin's manufacturer, to make the trip to the FDA. Many were concerned about the precedent a decision to withdraw Avastin's approval for metastatic breast cancer would set for therapies of other cancers. All of the women who spoke who had been treated with Avastin had been eligible to participate in these important trials—we never heard from those who wouldn't have been eligible for the trials, but were treated with Avastin anyway, after its accelerated approval. Many credited Avastin with living to see that day.

But only four clearly supported the FDA's pulling the drug from the breast cancer market.

The women who spoke on behalf of Avastin at the FDA hearing had been considered "Olympic athlete" material when they were deemed eligible for one of the Avastin trials. They hadn't been excluded despite the biases and conflicts of interest that play a role in overly restrictive eligibility criteria.

But can a less sinister explanation exist for the restrictive criteria? What about simple laziness?

A few years ago, I was approached by a woman named Abby Statler, who worked in our research compliance group, about clinical trial eligibility criteria. A research compliance group reviews the conduct of clinical trials within a medical center to ensure that patients are treated according to the rules of the clinical trial protocol and then sees to it that any deviations to the stipulations of those protocols (most of which are quite minor) are corrected.

A minor deviation might result, for example, when a patient who was supposed to have his urine checked for an infection every two weeks while on the clinical trial only had it checked once during one of those two-week periods. People who work in compliance groups tend to be rule followers. The word *anal* might even be used to describe them: in clinical research we take it as a compliment; you want someone who's anal overseeing the safe conduct of research that affects patients. Super-talented compliance workers also think about the implications of restrictive trial guidelines on the ability of patients to get the care they need.

Abby was just this sort of person, and she had a question for me.

"Why does it seem like every clinical trial has the same eligibility criteria?"

I asked her what she meant.

"Well, I was reviewing a trial in lymphoma patients, and it excludes patients with kidney and liver abnormalities that are pretty mild. Same with cardiac function and neurologic abnormalities. Then I looked over a lung cancer trial—same exact exclusion criteria. Same with a trial in patients with colon cancer. And for acute leukemia."

"Too identical to be an accident, huh?" I asked.

"Yes!" she exclaimed. "It's like they were cut and pasted from one protocol to another."

"That's because they were cut and pasted from one protocol to another," I said, smiling at her insight.

She looked at me hesitantly. "Really?"

Unfortunately, yes. Imagine you're a clinical researcher, or you work for a pharmaceutical company, and you're tasked with writing a brand new, from scratch, clinical trial of a new drug to fight kidney cancer. You will need to put together a protocol that logically presents the scientific and medical justification for why a clinical trial of this new drug is necessary, and that clearly provides instructions for how to conduct it—clearly enough that every doctor, nurse, pharmacist, and research coordinator who participates in the study, at any cancer center around the country or internationally, will treat every patient exactly the same—like an instruction manual for how to give the drugs and monitor the patients.

You need to include some background information about kidney cancer, its seriousness, and why it's so important to develop a new drug to get rid of it. You'll also discuss the drugs you want to study in the trial, and how they work; you'll want to review studies that were conducted in test tubes and in animals before the drugs were given to people, and initial studies in people, including how the drug is distributed around the body, how it is excreted from the body, and known toxicities. A lot of these sections might be copied from previous trials conducted in people with the same cancer or in which the same drug was used, because the disease being treated is just as serious, regardless of the trial, and the same initial pre-clinical drug studies will be referenced whenever the drug is used in a trial.

Based on those studies, you'll describe how you arrived at the doses you're going to use in the trial, and your primary objectives in conducting the trial: for Phase 1, safety and to find the right dose; for Phase 2, efficacy and safety; and for Phase 3, that the drug is more effective than the standard treatment, and that it is safe.

Next, you're going to describe the schedule of the drugs you're intending to give—the design of the study, both in the protocol text and in a table or figure. Some people even include a flow diagram picturing the length of a treatment cycle—often 21 or 28 days—and on which of those days the drug is administered.

Then comes the eligibility section, which lists the patients who should be *included* in the trial, like those with a diagnosis of kidney cancer, and which patients should be *excluded* from the trial. As Abby had pointed out, the *excluded* section often lists people with mild kidney, liver, cardiac, and neurologic abnormalities.

A reasonable person might think that those exclusion criteria would be based on what toxicities were seen in animals or the first few people treated with those drugs. But this is where standard templates for writing a clinical trial hurt patients. Many people who write the trials just use the already formatted eligibility criteria that others have used for other clinical trials, and that favor the healthiest of patients to enter clinical trials.[18]

"That's terrible," Abby said, when I explained this to her. "But what if it's a pharmaceutical company testing the drug for a bunch of different diseases. Does the company use the same template?"

"Sure it does. And so do we, at our cancer center. We use standard clinical trial templates that are supposed to be adapted to studies for any cancer subtype. So do other cancer centers, to make it easier for investigators who are writing their own protocols."

"Is there a way we could show scientifically that this is happening?" she asked, her eyes defiant about the injustice.

Abby spent the next year doing just that. She decided to focus on studies in which patients with hematologic malignancies were randomized to receive either standard chemotherapy, or a new drug (either the new drug only, or the new drug combined with the standard chemotherapy). She examined 1,353 trials published over a five-year period to identify 97 trials with eligibility criteria that were available for her to review. These trials enrolled almost 44,000 patients. She wanted to answer two questions: (1) Did the eligibility criteria actually reflect the drug toxicities that were known prior to the start of the randomized trial, or did they have nothing to do with those toxicities? (2) Did patients enrolled on the trial actually experience any of the dreaded side effects to the drug that were the basis for the eligibility criteria?[19]

The answer to the first question was a resounding NO. Almost 90 percent of the trials had eligibility criteria that excluded patients with abnormal kidney, liver, or heart function. Although previous observations suggested that 21 percent of the drugs used in these trials had the potential to cause kidney damage, a whopping 74 percent of the trials excluded patients with abnormal kidney function! The same held true for liver damage, and heart abnormalities. Not surprisingly, the answer to the second question was similar: exclusion criteria had little to do with the toxicities to drugs that patients actually experienced on the trial.

Abby got her MPH, and then decided to pursue a PhD in Public Health. For her thesis, she took these findings to their logical next step.

She examined 13 leukemia studies conducted through the National Cancer Institute's Southwest Oncology Group between 2005 and 2015. Of the 2,351 patients enrolled and treated on those studies, she discovered that 10 percent were found to be ineligible for the trials after the fact. They were treated on study essentially by accident, as they should been excluded based on the restrictive eligibility criteria. But when compared to the patients who actually met the eligibility criteria, ineligible patients were just as likely to go into remission from their leukemia, to live as long as eligible patients, and to experience the same rates of side effects to the drugs being used in the trials.[20]

The eligibility criteria for these leukemia clinical trials that were funded through taxpayer dollars were overly restrictive, needlessly excluding patients from participating.

What if the notion of liberalizing cancer trial eligibility criteria were taken to its extreme? In what sounds like a choice for contestants on the television show Let's Make a Deal, investigators at the MD Anderson Cancer Center in Houston, Texas, offered 109 patients who would otherwise be considered ineligible for standard clinical trials for a type of leukemia one more option: a trial whose eligibility criteria were actually the ineligibility criteria of the other trials![21]

And what were the results of this trial, which included only imperfect candidates, with abnormal function of their kidneys, hearts, livers, lungs, neurologic systems, or with other cancers? Their leukemia improved at the same rates, and they experienced comparable toxicities, to patients with normal organ function enrolled in other similar trials.

The FDA and the National Cancer Institute are giving more credibility to clinical trials that enroll the types of patients (called *real world* patients) who are actually most likely to receive the drug once it is approved, as opposed to the Olympic athlete types. But most clinical trials still enroll only the healthiest of patients despite this: the fear that people with other illnesses might have side effects erroneously attributed to a study drug, and that this would hurt the chances for that drug to be approved by the FDA, still prevails.

Jimmy decided to enroll in the clinical trial. I gave him the study's informed consent: the 12-page document reviewed the risks, benefits, alternatives, and personnel who would be involved in his care in much more detail than I did. Unlike most commercial "terms and agreements," it is a standard requirement by institutional review boards that this document spell things out at a sixth-grade reading level—to be accessible and understood by most adults. I encouraged him to take it home and read through it, or at least to take an hour and read it while he was still in clinic. Jimmy just shook his head.

"Nah doc, I trust you," he said, flipping through it quickly before arriving at the final page, where he signed his name. So much effort goes into trying to ensure that patients are truly informed about the treatment they're about to receive. Some of my patients do take the document home and read it over. A handful return with notes and ask additional questions. But most do what Jimmy did, just sign on the final page without reading it closely.

Informed consent is tricky. How can I, as someone who doesn't have leukemia, and hasn't been through other cancer treatments, and can't truly distance myself from the two decades of experience I've had in treating leukemia patients, provide a true picture of what the experience of receiving chemotherapy or immunotherapy will be like to someone like Jimmy, or to a patient with a new leukemia diagnosis? I try to meet my patients where they are. Sometimes I draw pictures or charts to illustrate risks and benefits. I've even asked patients to repeat back to me what they've heard.

But does that mean they're truly informed?

Jimmy came back to clinic the following day so we could draw some blood for a series of laboratory tests that would determine Jimmy's eligibility for the trial. We also checked his EKG, sent him for a chest X-ray, and had to perform another bone marrow biopsy: even though we knew Jimmy's leukemia had returned, and we could measure the leukemia cells in his bloodstream, the trial required that leukemia be shown in a bone marrow biopsy within two weeks of starting the trial. In fact, this was one of the major reasons why patients who were analyzed in Abby's study were supposedly ineligible for the Southwest Oncology Group leukemia trials—they had undergone a bone marrow biopsy earlier than this two-week window. I apologized to Jimmy for his having to undergo another biopsy.

"It's no problem, they don't bug me too much," he said, magnanimously. Then again, his pain tolerance was a heck of a lot higher than mine.

No surprise, Jimmy's bone marrow still had leukemia in it. Luckily, his kidney and liver blood tests, and his EKG, were pretty normal.

"Congratulations, you made it into the study!" I told Jimmy, a few days later in the same clinic room.

He stood up with his arms in the air. "The winner, and still champion, Jimmy Petrarcha!" he exclaimed. Theresa and I laughed. He was irrepressible.

A week had passed since our first visit. Add to that another couple of weeks from when Jimmy had been told his leukemia wasn't getting any better with that third course of chemotherapy. Add to that the fact that he was still willing (and able) to travel hundreds of miles from home. Patients enrolling in clinical trials must be healthy enough to qualify, and their disease must remain quiescent enough to not make them sick before they start the treatment.

They're not just Olympic athletes. They're Olympic gods.

We admitted Jimmy to the hospital the following day and got started on the experimental treatment. He did well at first, even teasing me and the medical team that we were being overly dramatic about the possible side effects from the drug. The leukemia cells vanished from his blood stream, and he made himself at home in his hospital room, wearing his own bathrobe for our visits. Of course, he charmed the nurses, and even demanded that Theresa bring in an old photo from when he was in his late 20s, in which he was dressed in a boxing outfit and looked for all the world like Chuck Norris. He hung it on the hospital wall, facing his bed. This is how he saw himself, battling leukemia.

Then one morning we learned he'd had a rough night. Jimmy's nurse mentioned his severe joint pain, and that his blood pressure was low. Both were evidence that the cytokine release syndrome (CRS)—a side effect of the immunotherapy, which I'd explained to him early on—was kicking in.

When we walked into the room, he greeted us loudly from his bed, but it was forced, and through clenched teeth. Theresa sat in a chair nearby. When I extended my hand to shake his, he looked at me sheepishly, and couldn't reciprocate.

"Shoulder hurt you so much you can't lift your arm?" I asked.

"It's not that bad, doc," he said. His cousin rolled her eyes. I again reflected on the fact that as a former boxer, his pain tolerance must have been incredible, and I remembered reading something Muhammed Ali had said back in the 1980s, reflecting on his career: "What I suffered physically was worth what I've accomplished in life. A man who is not courageous enough to take risks will never accomplish anything in life." [22]

I told Jimmy that we would start a drug to combat the CRS and relieve the pain.

"But you know, if the side effects from the treatment get to be too much, we can always stop," I said. Theresa nodded, reinforcing what I said.

But Jimmy shook his head, saying, "Don't you dare stop that chemo. Keep it comin'!" Like Rocky speaking to Mickey while Apollo Creed was clobbering him.

So we did. His pain improved with the CRS drug, and he weathered infections and bleeding from his gastrointestinal tract over the month-long hospitalization.

Part of conducting a clinical trial is documenting the adverse events that occur and trying to determine if they are related to the drug, or to the underlying disease, or to neither. Drug toxicities would certainly be front and center in the Avastin hearing.

With everything that had occurred to Jimmy, this list ran pages long.

Cytokine release syndrome. Definitely related to the drug.

Joint pains. Definitely related to the drug. They were caused by the CRS.

Infection. Possibly related to the drug's effect on his immune system. But possibly related to his underlying leukemia, too, which almost by definition is a cancer of the immune system. People with leukemia get infections.

Low platelet count. Possibly related to the drug's effect on his bone marrow. But possibly related to his leukemia, too.

Gastrointestinal bleeding. Probably not related to the drug. His platelets were low, though, which predisposed him to bleed, and which may have been due to the drug. But the low platelets may have been due to the leukemia, too.

This process, called attribution of adverse events, is obviously not straightforward, and explains why medication labels aren't necessarily reflective of side effects that can be linked to a drug. For every adverse event to which I thought there was a *possibility* the drug played a role, a drug manufacturer has to report that adverse event to the FDA, which may then add that toxicity to a drug label if the drug gets approved.

A month-long hospitalization. And at the end of that month, his leukemia returned despite the treatment, like the raging bull that it was at its genesis. We stopped the treatment and discharged him to his cousin's house.

I felt terrible that he had traveled all that way for a clinical trial, and then had to endure such severe side effects and an eternity on our inpatient leukemia unit—the trials and tribulations—all to be back where we started.

When I walked into his room in my outpatient clinic, he again greeted me with a broad smile, easing himself from the chair he occupied next to Theresa to a standing position so we could shake hands. He was moving slower than he had been a month earlier, but he remained undaunted.

"I'm so sorry this drug didn't work to get rid of your leukemia and that you had to spend all that time in the hospital," I said to him.

He waved me off. "Doc, it was worth a shot, right? And I figure, maybe you guys learned something by studying me, and I help someone else in the future." Altruism.

I nodded. "I'm sure you did Jimmy. I'm sure you did." I started to talk with him about transitioning his care toward palliating his symptoms, rather than treating the leukemia. But he waved me off again.

"What's next?" he asked.

"Jimmy, there doesn't have to be a *next*," Theresa said. "Maybe you should take a break, recover a little."

Jimmy shook his head. "I'm recovered enough. I'm ready for another drug." He lifted his arms from his side and jabbed the air, weaker than before.

I again reviewed with him all the treatments he had been through, the side effects from those treatments, and the time he had spent in the hospital. I was probably hoping on some level that he would recognize the futility of everything that had been tried before, and thus the likely futility of anything that would be tried in the future.

He wasn't buying it, though.

"What's next?" he repeated.

I quickly glanced over to Theresa, who just shrugged her shoulders. "We tried," she was saying, without actually saying it.

I talked with Jimmy about another study we had available of an experimental drug for people with different types of blood cancers, a Phase 1 trial.

"The goal of the study is to find the right dose of the drug and to see what side effects happen when people receive the drug," I explained.

"What's the chance the drug will work?" Jimmy asked.

"I don't know, Jimmy. This is the first time it's being used in people who have leukemia."

He was relentless. "What's your best guess?"

I sighed and gave him my best estimate, based on how well patients with persistent leukemia, despite multiple courses of treatment, respond to yet another round of chemotherapy.

"Probably only 5 to 10 percent," I said.

"Good enough for me," Jimmy said.

We tried the other experimental drug for a couple of months but this, too, proved ineffective. His leukemia kept growing, and he was becoming increasingly dependent on blood and platelet transfusions. We both agreed it was time to stop that drug, too. He decided to head back to Philadelphia.

"I just wanna go home for a couple of weeks and recover my strength. Then I'll be back," he promised me. He looked smaller this time in my exam room, as if he was sitting in the chair at the corner of the boxing ring at the end of the eleventh round of a brutal bout. I told him I thought that was a super idea. We hugged each other goodbye.

It was the last time I would see him. A few days later, his cousin called to let us know that he had died, and how appreciative he was of our care.

I felt terrible that he had spent his last few months in a foreign city, withstanding the blows of aggressive chemotherapy. I don't know that I would have done the same.

But maybe to him, just having the moxie to do battle had been the point all along.

The Avastin hearings were going to be a war.

That was abundantly clear when Terry Kalley, the man who organized the protest outside the FDA's White Oak campus, and whose wife Arlene would die from her breast cancer in August 2015, approached the microphone in the Great Room, still wearing the pink T-shirt he had sported earlier in the day.

> The FDA has treated these women as expendable, innocent statistics in the face of a regulatory machine on autopilot, a bureaucracy unencumbered by any ethical controls. Your callous indifference is terrifying patients. Their anxiety is excruciating, your prolonged silence deafening.[23]

Again, members of the audience nodded their agreement as FDA representatives looked at him without reacting or didn't regard him at all. Kalley continued, this time staring directly at those of us occupying the ODAC table:

> Make no mistake. This hearing is a death trial, not of Avastin, but of the women who rely on Avastin to stay alive. You are personally responsible for the consequences of your own vote. A vote against Avastin by each of you is a vote against thousands of women.[24]

# 5
# Starve a Tumor, Feed an Industry

You can't win in this job. If you approve a drug, they accuse you of lowering standards. And if you don't approve it, you're the worst thing since the Nazi death camps and should be killed.

—Richard Pazdur, MD, 2009

After the open-mic session on Day 1 of the 2011 Avastin hearings concluded, I was emotionally spent. As I'm sure many others in the audience were, too.

The tales these women told were awe inspiring—the glimpses into their lives ranged from the terrible moment of learning that they had breast cancer; to the periods of remission and the awful news of relapse or progression; to the return to health and the simple victories of leading normal lives with their families, even while being treated with chemotherapy. The passions of the many speakers for or against Avastin, and their reminders of what they felt was at stake with a vote to withdraw Avastin's FDA approval for metastatic breast cancer or to keep it on the market, resonated with me, as I bet it did with the six other members of ODAC. I felt as if hours had

**Figure 5.1**
Richard Pazdur, MD, now director of the FDA's Oncology Center of Excellence, formerly director of the Office of Oncology Drug Products within the Center for Drug Evaluation and Research. *Source*: https://www.fda.gov/about-fda/fda-organization /richard-pazdur.

passed since the presiding officer made her opening statement, but when I checked my watch, it was only 10 a.m.

After a short break, the FDA's Center for Drug Evaluation and Research (CDER, the arm of the FDA that regulates over-the-counter and prescription drugs) gave a two-hour presentation kicked off by Richard Pazdur, MD (figure 5.1).

Rick, at age 59, described as "greyhound thin" as a result of his dedication to cycling and a vegetarian diet, was the director of the Office of Oncology Drug Products (ODP) within CDER. He had been with the FDA for 11 years, having spent the previous 11 years at the MD Anderson Cancer Center in Houston, Texas, where he oversaw their drug trials. When he first came to the FDA, he referred to the agency as a "secretive world" similar to the Catholic Church, as the decisions it made about whether or not to approve drugs went on behind closed doors. He has since worked tirelessly for transparency within the FDA operations and procedures.[1]

Pazdur was the person who ultimately had selected me to be a member of ODAC. I found him to be measured in his decisions, insightful into the science of cancer and chemotherapy drug development, and an inspiring leader to the many who worked for him in ODP. He had a piercing intellect. The office worked as a close-knit team of about 150 oncologists, pharmacists, toxicologists, and other specialists, supportive of each other and dedicated to making decisions based on the underlying truth of a drug's safety and efficacy. They viewed their jobs as a public health mission, always keeping an eye on how a new drug might help a population of patients, or how it might hurt them.

Rick could also be funny; he was once said to "laugh like Charles Nelson Reilly."[2] A few times during ODAC meetings in which I took part, a member of the committee would grill a pharmaceutical company representative about some questionable aspect of a clinical trial. Out of the corner of my eye I would see Pazdur, sitting in his usual end chair on the left arm of the horseshoe table, closest to the audience, smiling and rolling his eyes, exaggeratingly shrugging his shoulders and raising his arms, as if pantomiming "This is what we've been telling them all along!"

At one meeting in 2010, ODAC members deliberated over the efficacy of an anti-hormone drug, dutasteride, at decreasing a man's risk of developing prostate cancer. A couple of urologists from Johns Hopkins and Memorial Sloan Kettering Cancer Center stood to testify. They became so impassioned about their respective points of view that they started shouting at each other, completely ignoring the ODAC chair's instructions to settle down.

Pazdur would have none of this. Laughing, he stopped the usually reserved proceedings, asked a member of his team to bring a couple of chairs over to these learned professors of urology, and told them to sit in their chairs, like school children, and speak only when spoken to, or he would kick them out of the Great Room for good!

He was also exquisitely skilled politically, having remained in his position through a number of administrations led by different parties. He carefully weighed his obligations about meeting the treatment needs of different patient populations against guarding the safety of the public, and he seemed also to consider the political ramifications of giving either of these duties short shrift.

Pazdur constantly reminded members of ODAC, the pharmaceutical sponsors, and the audience that the FDA's responsibility was to dispassionately weigh the study results in making its decisions. That day in 2011, he spoke to this point again:

> While we acknowledge the pain and suffering caused by cancer, our job in making decisions about drug approval is to focus on the available scientific evidence. Our regulatory decisions are based on data from adequate and well-controlled clinical trials. They are not based on consideration of the drug's cost or decisions by third-party payers regarding reimbursement.[3]

But he was not naive to the economic impact of regulatory decisions made by the ODP. I'm sure Pazdur knew that a decision to withdraw Avastin's breast cancer approval would cost the company $1 billion in annual revenue. When I interviewed for ODAC membership, after giving a talk to dozens of his team's members and meeting with a smaller contingent to answer questions, Rick took me to the FDA's cafeteria for lunch. As we approached the cashier, he made sure to remind me that, as a government employee, he was not allowed to pay for my meal, but that I would be reimbursed the nominal amount by the FDA in due time.

I decided to save all US taxpayers the expense by springing for the sandwich myself.

We discussed the nuts and bolts of ODAC and my duties as a member. At one point during our conversation, I asked him if he ever felt bad about a negative decision for a drug, when that decision could mean, particularly for a small pharmaceutical company with only one or two drugs in the pipeline, that the company would go out of business.

He smiled and shook his head a bit. "Investors aren't stupid," he told me. "If a drug works really well for a particular cancer, the company making the drug will have adequate funding, and it's also more likely the drug will get approved. It's only when a drug isn't that great that funding becomes an issue."

Lessons learned. Focus on the science, on the data coming from the trials. The people making investment decisions often know the data as well as we do. The money will follow. Emotions—feeling bad for a company—aren't part of it.

But what about emotions for the patients affected by these decisions?

Barry Kramer, MD, MPH, the director of the National Cancer Institute's Division of Cancer Prevention and a lifer within the National Institutes of Health, once commented to me that, within academic medicine, you often spend your career trying to get credit for your work. But within the government, you spent it trying to avoid attribution.

While I liked and respected Pazdur a lot, and admired his political acumen, he could not avoid attribution.

In fact, he was often a lightning rod for the frustrations expressed by patients and pharmaceutical companies about the lack of progress in cancer therapies. Patient advocates called him a murderer, and others referred to him as an obstructionist bureaucrat, to which he responded:

> You can't win in this job. If you approve a drug, they accuse you of lowering standards. And if you don't approve it, you're the worst thing since the Nazi death camps and should be killed.[4]

Playing on the death-camp metaphor, the consequences of negative decisions by Pazdur and his team—not only for patients who have been deprived a drug but also for investors—were described by one reactionary healthcare worker as a "Holocaust.[5]"

Avastin had been approved by the FDA, in combination with chemotherapy—a drug called paclitaxel—for the treatment of women with metastatic breast cancer. What happened during its development that led to these proceedings on whether or not that approval should now be withdrawn?

Starting with the basics, Avastin is a type of drug known as an angiogenesis inhibitor—it blocks the growth of the blood vessels that feed a tumor, and which are necessary for that tumor to receive nutrition and survive.[6]

The field of angiogenesis research was founded in part by Judah Folkman, MD, born in Cleveland, Ohio, in 1933. As a child he was influenced by the teachings of his father, a rabbi, and his mother's love of science. After graduating from Ohio State University, he attended Harvard for medical school and remained there for his entire career. He completed a surgical residency at Massachusetts General Hospital.[7] Even four decades later, during my own training at Mass General, where I completed my residency in internal medicine, people were still telling Judah Folkman stories. During his time there, surgical interns were on call (spending the night taking care of patients) every other night. Rumor had it that Folkman decided it wasn't worth spending money on an apartment that he would occupy only half the time, so he also spent his non-call nights in one of the on-call rooms, and literally lived at the hospital for the year! See Folkman in his lab, figure 5.2.

In 1971, Folkman published a seminal article in which he described the vigorous growth of blood vessels in the presence of a tumor, and that the tumor itself released chemicals that attracted blood vessels and encouraged their growth, thus ensuring its own nourishment.[8] These chemical *growth factors* were later identified and called *fibroblast growth factor* (FGF) and *vascular endothelial*

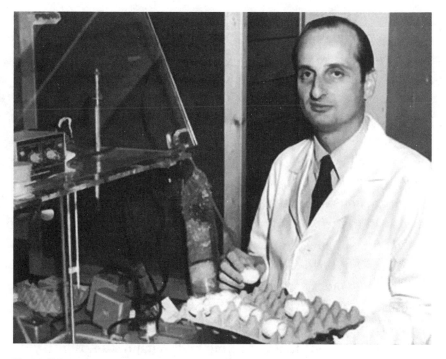

**Figure 5.2**
Angiogenesis researcher Judah Folkman, MD, conducting an experiment with chick eggs, 1974. *Source*: Photo from Folkman lab from Anca-Maria Cimpean, Domenico Ribatti, and Marius Raica, "A Brief History of Angiogenesis Assays," *International Journal of Developmental Biology* 55 (2011): 377–382.

*growth factor* (VEGF).[9] VEGF was eventually discovered by scientists at the pharmaceutical company Genentech, under the direction of Napoleone Ferrara, PhD, in 1989.[10] Folkman later found that even so-called *liquid* tumors, like the bone marrow cancer multiple myeloma, depended on blood vessel growth for their survival.[11]

Once these growth factors were defined, drugs that could block their effects could be developed, or discovered. Scientists in Folkman's lab, who were also ophthalmologists—Joan Miller, MD, Anthony Adamis, MD, and Robert D'Amato, MD—were studying diabetic retinopathy—vision loss in people with diabetes brought about by excessive blood vessel growth. In the mid-1990s, they conducted experiments in which they administered antibodies to VEGF to primates; the experiments showed that the primates who received the antibodies did not develop the blood vessel growth in their eyes associated with the retinopathy.[12]

At around the same time, the scientists recalled that another drug had been found, years earlier, to prevent the growth of blood vessels, and they wanted to see if it would work in rabbits. They first injected FGF into the corneas of the rabbits, to encourage the growth of blood vessels, and then gave the rabbits the drug. Sure enough, rabbits who received the drug had a reduction in blood vessel growth in their eyes by 40 percent!

That drug's name was thalidomide.[13]

The reason it had caused such severe birth defects became clear. Thalidomide blocked the growth of blood vessels in the limb buds of fetuses. Limb buds eventually grow to become arms and legs—unless their blood supply is cut off, as occurred with exposure to thalidomide, in which case the limb buds remain stumps.[14]

At around that time, a man in his 30s living in New York City was dying from multiple myeloma, despite multiple rounds of chemotherapy. His wife, Elizabeth Jacobsen, who was a lawyer, was diligently researching any possible next treatment steps her husband could pursue. She read about how multiple myeloma depended on enhanced blood vessel growth, and the work Folkman's lab was doing to identify treatments to block blood vessel growth. She gave the lab a call, and actually spoke to Folkman directly. He told her about the study they had conducted with thalidomide in rabbits, and suggested she contact a multiple myeloma specialist, Bart Barlogie, MD, at the University of Arkansas, to see if he would be willing to treat Jacobsen's husband with this storied drug.

She called Barlogie, and he agreed.

But unfortunately, thalidomide didn't work for her husband, and he died months later from his myeloma. It didn't work in three other patients, all treated under compassionate use protocols, meaning, not part of a formal clinical trial, but because these patients had no other options.

And then, it did work in a patient who had received multiple other rounds of chemotherapy. And it worked within three months of starting the drug.

This inspired Barlogie to design a Phase 2 trial in which 84 patients with similar, advanced multiple myeloma received thalidomide, from December 1997 through June 1998. And this drug, this maligned drug that had caused such horrors around the world almost 40 years earlier, and which had led to such massive change in the authority of the FDA, worked to shrink the cancer in about one-third of the patients treated on this study.[15]

Folkman's theories seemed to be playing out in real patients.

Meanwhile, Ferrara, the scientist at Genentech, continued to focus on the VEGF growth factor, and in 1993 he developed an antibody that blocked its function and inhibited the growth of sarcomas (a soft tissue cancer) and glioblastomas (a type of brain cancer) in mice.[16] Encouraged by these results, Ferrara then eventually convinced the management team at Genentech to create a version of the antibody that would work in humans.

It had taken over two decades since Folkman's famous paper had been published, along with his and Ferrara's and others' focus and dedication to the belief that stopping the blood vessel supply to tumors was critical to beating back cancer. They persisted against a dubious scientific community, similar to how the pioneering breast cancer surgeon Bernard Fisher worked to convince doctors that Halsted's disfiguring radical mastectomy could be modified. Finally, a monoclonal antibody—one of those *mab* drugs that could thwart blood vessel growth—was ready to try in people.

And that drug was bevacizumab, or Avastin. In 1997, two Phase 1 clinical trials were started.[17]

The first trial enrolled 25 patients with a variety of cancers. Each was treated with just Avastin. Side effects to Avastin included bleeding within the tumor in three patients, headaches, and nausea, and a maximum tolerated dose was established. There were no responses, though—nobody's tumors had significantly shrunk.[18]

The second Phase 1 trial recruited 12 patients with advanced cancers and treated them with Avastin, but this time combined with a second chemotherapy drug. In this trial, patients experienced diarrhea and suppression of their immune system, both of which were blamed on the second chemotherapy drug, and not on Avastin; 3 of the 12 patients had a response—their tumors shrank—and the dose was determined to be 5 mg or 10 mg of Avastin.[19]

Based on these results—that Avastin appeared to be well tolerated when administered alone, but with more side effects when given along with chemotherapy, and that it led to improvement in a total of 3 out of 37 patients treated (just 8 percent)—a series of Phase 2 trials were initiated the following year.

The Phase 2 studies included trials of Avastin combined with chemotherapy in patients with metastatic colorectal cancer, in patients with advanced lung cancer, and Avastin alone in patients with kidney cancer.

In the colorectal cancer trial, 105 patients were enrolled; 40 percent had a response to the combination of Avastin plus chemotherapy (tumors shrank), and for those who had a response, the response lasted for an average of about 9 months. The average survival for patients enrolled on the study was over 21 months.[20] Similar results were seen in the lung cancer trial: in 99 patients enrolled, 32 percent had a response that lasted an average of over 7 months, and patients lived an average of 18 months. Side effects included formation of blood clots, high blood pressure, infections, and some people had nose bleeds.[21]

In patients with kidney cancer, where Avastin was used alone, the first of 115 patients was enrolled in October 1998. The time it took for the tumors to worsen (called tumor *progression*) was about 5 months, and patients lived, on average, about 14 months. Similar to the other trials, patients experienced high blood pressure, bleeding, and blood clots.[22]

A decision was made to try to get Avastin approved by the FDA in patients with metastatic colon cancer, and a Phase 3 trial was started.

At the 2011 Avastin hearings, Pazdur continued his opening remarks on behalf of the FDA's Center for Drug Evaluation and Research:

> My colleagues and I will explain why CDER has proposed to withdraw approval of Avastin's indication for the treatment of patients with metastatic breast cancer. We will explain the scientific basis for our conclusion, that, number one, Genentech's required confirmatory trials failed to verify a clinical benefit of Avastin in treating patients with metastatic breast cancer, and two, the totality of the data submitted to the FDA show Avastin is neither safe nor effective to support the breast cancer indication.
>
> Finally, we will explain why the law, the science, and the public health policy all counsel against permitting Avastin's breast cancer indication to remain on the label while Genentech designs and conducts additional studies.[23]

There was no humor as he talked, none of the glint in his eyes I had seen at previous ODAC meetings. This was serious business, and Rick didn't want to be placed in this position of leading a public hearing any more than anyone else in the room; probably he felt that Genentech should have withdrawn their drug for breast cancer voluntarily to avoid these proceedings. He continued:

> While CDER and Genentech disagree about many issues to be discussed today, one issue about which there is no dispute is that Avastin has not been demonstrated to improve overall survival in patients with metastatic breast cancer in clinical trials. Five clinical trials in breast cancer have failed to demonstrate an overall survival benefit when Avastin is added to various chemotherapy regimens.

Further, the available data fail to demonstrate that Avastin improves quality of life outcomes in patients with metastatic breast cancer. If data submitted to the agency demonstrated any of these benefits, we would not be here today.[24]

"Trials failed . . . neither safe nor effective . . . has not been demonstrated to improve survival . . . trials failed . . .": Pazdur was making the case that the basics for full drug approval in the United States had not been fulfilled for Avastin, despite its early promise. All eyes in the audience were fixed on him; the expressions on the faces of the many people who had testified at the microphone were grim.

As I explained in chapter 4, the objective of Phase 1 trials is to assess drug toxicities and to establish the maximum tolerated dose. For Avastin, those side effects included bleeding, headaches, nausea, and (when given with chemotherapy) diarrhea and suppression of the immune system.

Phase 2 trials continue to examine drug safety, but at this stage investigators begin to determine whether a drug is effective in a specific disease. For colon cancer, the combination of Avastin and chemotherapy led to responses (significant tumor shrinkage) in about one-third of patients, and as more patients were treated, more side effects emerged—high blood pressure, bleeding, infections, and the development of blood clots.[25]

Phase 3 trials are considered the gold standard of clinical research; they are the studies the FDA prefers to consider before approving a drug. In these trials, patients are chosen randomly to participate in different treatment scenarios: to receive a study drug versus standard therapy; or a study drug combined with standard therapy versus the standard therapy alone. The goal is once again to assess efficacy—but this time, comparing efficacy directly to standard therapy—and, of course, to continue to explore safety.

Is it ethical to randomize patients to a study drug versus a placebo? In some cases, yes. For example, if a person has a disease that is not life threatening (let's say a simple wart), and there is no urgency to treat it, a "standard" approach might be to not treat the disease at all, and to randomly assign such a patient to receive the study drug Wartbegone versus a placebo. In this situation, a person wouldn't necessarily be harmed—though perhaps would be annoyed—if a wart is treated with a placebo.

Is that ever an ethical approach to treating a person with cancer? If a cancer is not life threatening, and the standard approach would be to not treat it until that cancer causes symptoms, the answer is yes.

Chronic lymphocytic leukemia is often diagnosed because a person who otherwise feels well has a slightly high white blood cell count that is detected on routine labs. A famous study randomized such patients to starting chemotherapy immediately (with a drug called chlorambucil) versus waiting until that person developed symptoms to start the chemotherapy—an initial "no treatment" study arm. A total of 1,534 patients were enrolled to this trial between 1980 and 1990. With over 12 years of follow-up, the study found that, although the chlorambucil was able to slow progression of the leukemia, it had no impact on overall survival: patients starting chemotherapy immediately lived just as long as those who waited to start chemotherapy when their cancer demanded it.[26]

But what if the cancer *is* life threatening? In rare circumstances, when there are absolutely no treatments available, then again it may be ethical to randomize patients to receive a placebo.

This was the case in early 2000s for patients with hepatocellular carcinoma—a primary liver cancer. The drug sorafenib, similar to Avastin, can prevent the formation of the blood vessels that feed a tumor, and it also works to stop cancer cells from growing directly. A Phase 3 trial was designed in which 602 patients with liver cancer were randomized to receive either the sorafenib or a placebo. Patients treated with sorafenib lived almost 3 months longer than those receiving placebo—an average of 10.7 versus 7.9 months. Based on this study, in 2005 sorafenib was the first drug ever approved for the treatment of hepatocellular carcinoma.[27]

After 2005, then, it would no longer have been ethical to randomize patients with newly diagnosed liver cancer to receive a placebo, because a new standard of care had been established. Future study drugs would need to be compared to sorafenib.

In the Phase 3 trial for patients with metastatic colon cancer, Avastin was combined with the chemotherapy drugs irinotecan, fluorouracil, and leucovorin (abbreviated IFL) and compared to IFL without Avastin. The first of the 813 patients (who came from the United States, Australia, and New Zealand) was enrolled in September 2000, and the final patient in May 2002. On average, patients entering the study were 60 years old and had a very good performance status, meaning that their cancer was causing minimal or no symptoms at all—typical of the Olympic athletes you might expect to be eligible for such a trial. Patients receiving Avastin had an average overall survival that was 20 months and one week, compared to 15 months and two weeks for patients who just received the IFL chemotherapy. And this difference was significant—meaning, statistically, with a confidence level of over 99 percent, it was not due to chance alone.[28]

Patients receiving Avastin and IFL also had a progression-free survival that was 10 months and two weeks, versus 6 months and one week for patients who received IFL alone, and this difference was also statistically significant.[29]

Progression-free survival means that patients receiving Avastin spent a longer period of time with their cancer not getting worse—either not enlarging much, or not spreading further. But it doesn't, in and of itself, mean that a patient survived for a greater period of time, or had an improved quality of life, because of the study treatment—what the FDA sometimes refers to as the efficacy standard of "lives longer or lives better." It just means that the cancer didn't worsen for a longer period of time.

Still, living an average of about five months longer, or a 44 percent reduction in dying, is a pretty big deal for someone with cancer that has already spread.

Toxicity from Avastin and IFL was worse than for IFL alone, with severe toxicity about 10 percent worse. As could have been predicted from the earlier trials, patients receiving Avastin had higher rates of high blood pressure, diarrhea, and a low immune system, but not of blood clots. Another side effect that emerged in six patients treated with Avastin was bowel perforation.

These side effects are serious and may not be acceptable for a drug like Wartbegone, where the medical condition itself (an annoying wart) is not life threatening. But metastatic colon cancer is serious, and patients receiving Avastin lived about five months longer because of the drug. The totality of the data—balancing the safety against the efficacy in light of a life-threatening diagnosis—looked pretty good.

The FDA thought so, too. And based on this study, on February 26, 2004, the FDA approved the angiogenesis inhibitor (combined with chemotherapy) for the treatment of metastatic colon cancer.[30]

Judah Folkman's grand theory—that if the blood supply to a tumor (and thus, the tumor's supply of sustaining nutrients) could be disrupted, that tumor would be eliminated and a person with cancer could live longer—had finally resulted in the approval of a drug by the FDA three decades later, and just four years before he would die of a heart attack on his way to a scientific meeting.

Two-and-a-half years later, on October 11, 2006, Avastin would gain its second approval, again in combination with chemotherapy (carboplatin and paclitaxel), but this time for the treatment of advanced lung cancer. This approval was also based on a Phase 3 trial in which 878 patients were enrolled in the study between July 2001 and April 2004. They were randomized to receive either Avastin with chemotherapy, or chemotherapy alone.[31]

Those receiving Avastin lived an average of 2 months longer than those who were treated with just chemotherapy—12.3 months versus 10.3 months, with a reduction in the chance of dying of 21 percent. Progression-free survival was also improved for the Avastin group by about seven weeks, at an average of 6.2 months versus 4.5 months for the chemotherapy-only group. Both differences were statistically significant. Rates of serious adverse events were also significantly higher in the Avastin treatment arm, and similar to what was seen in the colon cancer study: low immune system, bleeding events, high blood pressure, headache, and also kidney problems and rash.

As more patients were treated with Avastin, more side effects started to emerge.

The benefits for lung cancer patients of adding Avastin to chemotherapy—of living longer, and of having an extended period of time during which the cancer didn't worsen—were more modest, at an average of just a few weeks. For colon cancer patients, those survival benefits had been an average of 4 to 5 months.[32]

Did the totality of data, the balance of safety and efficacy, again in a patient population with a life-threatening illness who had few other options, justify the approval for patients with advanced lung cancer? While the FDA may not acknowledge it, the bar for approval is lower for a drug that has already been on the market for 30 months, and that involves expansion of a drug's label to include a new indication (lung cancer), as opposed to an entirely new label.

In part that's because, with additional use in thousands of patients, the presumption is that serious, heretofore unrecognized toxicities likely would have emerged. Additionally, doctors around the country have developed some comfort level with giving a new drug, recognizing side effects to that drug that emerge, and hopefully managing those side effects better. Thus, risk is perceived to be reduced because of what's already known about a drug, as opposed to the unknown, rarer toxicities of a drug that is approved based on data from a few hundred people (or a few dozen, in some cases). For example, when the COVID-19 vaccines were administered to millions of people, instead of the thousands on clinical trials, rare side effects such as low platelet counts, cardiomyopathy, and the neurological condition Guillain-Barré syndrome were recognized (and contributed to vaccine hesitancy for some).

People were increasingly concerned about the cost of newly approved therapies, though—particularly those with modest benefits, like Avastin, in people with lung cancer. An article that appeared in the *New York Times* six months prior to Avastin's lung cancer approval, anticipating what would come, decried the approximate $100,000 yearly cost of the drug, and predicted that Avastin, which had already taken in over $1 billion in the previous year, was predicted to grow in sales nearly seven-fold, to $7 billion by 2009.[33]

Interestingly, one year later, the drug would be approved for the treatment of breast cancer.

Genentech cited the inherent value of life-sustaining therapy to justify the exorbitant costs, steering away from the usual justification provided by pharmaceutical manufacturers, of recouping the millions of dollars in research and development costs. William H. Burns, the chief executive of Roche's pharmaceutical division (they were a majority owner of Genentech) and a member of Genentech's board, made the self-righteous comment:

> As we look at Avastin pricing, right now the health economics hold up, and therefore I don't see any reason to be touching them.[34]

Meanwhile patients, oncologists, and Genentech employees were eagerly awaiting results to report out from a randomized, Phase 3 trial of Avastin combined with the chemotherapy paclitaxel, versus paclitaxel alone, in women with metastatic breast cancer. This study—called E2100 (the "E" stood for Eastern Cooperative Oncology Group)—was conducted through the National Cancer Institute (NCI) cooperative group mechanism.[35]

The concept of cooperative group trials came about in 1955, when the NCI formed a Clinical Studies Panel. It concluded that cancer research would progress faster if cancer centers worked together to enroll patients—particularly those with rare cancers—onto the same studies. Congress appropriated $5 million to the NCI to create the Chemotherapy National Service Center, which organized a number of these cooperative groups around the country. The trials that emerged from these groups set the standards for care for a variety of cancers. They helped debunk the utility of particularly aggressive (and disfiguring) treatments such as radical mastectomy for breast cancer, for instance. They also targeted certain particularly aggressive chemotherapy regimens for lymphoma that led to higher rates of infertility and secondary cancers—meaning, the lymphoma treatment led to the development of other cancers years later—but worked no better than standard regimens.[36] The Eastern Cooperative Oncology Group was one; the Southwest Oncology Group (the leukemia trials from which my PhD student, Abby Statler, had conducted her study) was another.

The E2100 trial enrolled its first of 722 patients in December 2001, and its last patient in May 2004; 7 percent of these women did not meet eligibility criteria and were excluded from efficacy analyses. The reasons for their disqualification included having a CT scan slightly more than the four weeks prior to enrolling on the trial, a stipulation that Abby Statler, PhD, had determined to be not only silly but also unrelated to a drug's safety or efficacy.[37]

Women receiving Avastin along with the chemotherapy had a progression-free survival that was about 6 months longer than women receiving just chemotherapy—at an average of 11.8 months versus 5.9 months, and this was a statistically significant difference. The average overall survival between the groups did not differ, though: 26.7 months for those receiving Avastin, versus 25.2 months for those who didn't. Similar to what was seen in other Avastin trials, patients receiving the drug combined with chemotherapy were more likely to experience serious infections, high blood pressure, headache, and kidney problems.[38]

The investigators tried to assess if women being treated with Avastin, who went a longer period of time without their tumors worsening, had a better quality of life than those treated with chemotherapy alone, even if they didn't live longer. This is the "lives better" aspect of efficacy that the FDA considers.

These assessments are also referred to as "patient reported outcomes," that is, straight from the horse's mouth. The questionnaire that they used—the Functional Assessment in Cancer Therapy—Breast (FACT-B)—was developed by David Cella, PhD, a professor at Northwestern University, and it was widely accepted as being valid and reliable for assessing quality of life in women receiving treatment for breast cancer. It would pose a statement, such as "I have a lack of energy," and ask women if they agreed with that statement to answer: not at all; a little bit; somewhat; quite a bit; or very much.[39]

These FACT-B forms were divided into sections that contained a series of statements focused on physical well-being ("I feel ill"); social/family well-being ("My family has accepted my illness"); emotional well-being ("I worry about dying"); and functional well-being ("I am sleeping well"); and an additional section with statements specific to concerns expressed by women with breast cancer ("I am self-conscious about the way I dress" or "I have certain parts of my body where I experience pain").[40]

On the E2100 trial, women in both arms of the study, receiving chemotherapy with or without Avastin, had a similar drop in their quality-of-life scores on the FACT-B. Trial participants reported their outcomes to be worse, regardless of the therapy they received.

These were the data submitted by Genentech to the FDA in 2007 for the approval of Avastin, in combination with paclitaxel, for the treatment of women with metastatic breast cancer.

Why did it take so long, when the last woman had enrolled in the trial in December 2004? To report the results accurately, investigators and the pharmaceutical company had to allow women a sufficient amount of time to remain on their treatments and to follow them for tumor progression and survival. If women with metastatic breast cancer lived for an average of slightly more than two years, then the investigators and Genentech would wait at least that long for a sufficient number of "events" (breast cancer progression or death) to occur before reporting the results.

What would the FDA do now, though, with a drug that seemed to delay the time it took for tumors to grow, but did not appear to enable women with metastatic breast cancer to live longer or to live better?

For the first of three times, the FDA would ask the Oncologic Drugs Advisory Committee for its opinion about Avastin's role in treating breast cancer. ODAC met on a cold, sunny day on December 5, 2007—before my time on the committee—to hear the evidence.

The FDA first asked the committee of nine voting members to discuss whether progression-free survival alone without a demonstrated survival advantage should be considered a measure of direct clinical benefit in the initial treatment of metastatic breast cancer.[41]

Members of ODAC expressed concern over Avastin's toxicities (serious adverse events occurred at a rate that was 20 percent higher for women receiving Avastin than for those receiving chemotherapy alone) and if the drug would do more harm than good to patients.

But one committee member pointed out that many women had actually received other treatments before enrolling on the E2100 trial, making it difficult to directly compare survival for these women, whose breast cancer was diagnosed earlier, to the survival for those women who received E2100 therapy as their first treatment.[42]

Cancer is complicated: first, because the number of genetic mutations that occur, which lead to the cancer, can result in one person's breast cancer being entirely different from another's; and second, because cancer can be treated in a variety of ways when first diagnosed. As a result, clinical trials are never quite as "clean," despite all of the restrictive eligibility criteria, as we would like. Other committee members agreed.

ODAC members also expressed concerns about the quality of the data collected—meaning its accuracy and consistency from what was reported by individual sites around the country and by Genentech, compared to the FDA's own analysis of the data.[43]

The quality—and believability—of data submitted to the FDA by pharmaceutical companies in support of a drug is naturally critical for assessing the safety and efficacy of drugs, as Frances Oldham Kelsey, PhD, MD, well knew when she evaluated thalidomide.[44]

In the case of Avastin, CT scans may be used to first diagnose tumors like breast or lung cancer (which leads to a biopsy confirming that diagnosis). CT scans then allow doctors to follow those cancers over time, to assess whether they shrink when exposed to radiation therapy or chemotherapy, and whether they grow back after being surgically resected (as with my mom's lung cancer), or when a patient "loses a response" to radiation or chemotherapy—a progression.

It turns out that progression may be in the eyes of the beholder. Discrepancies between what a local site's radiologist or oncologist calls a progression, and what a centralized, independent reviewer might call a progression, can occur up to 30 percent of the time.[45]

Incredible, that almost one-third of the time, one doctor might say a woman's breast cancer has gotten worse, and another will say that the same woman's breast cancer hasn't changed. Or the opposite.

Overall survival, on the other hand, is usually quite accurate: most doctors agree on whether a patient is alive or dead.

Given concerns about data accuracy, and the lack of a patient-reported outcome or overall survival advantage for women treated with Avastin, the ODAC members then discussed the six-month improvement in progression-free survival. They felt that most patients would conclude that no progression is better than progression, even if "better" could not really be quantified.

The FDA then asked ODAC members to vote on the following question:

> Are the data provided sufficient to establish a favorable risk/benefit analysis for the use of Avastin plus paclitaxel for first-line treatment of patients with metastatic breast cancer?[46]

In a razor-thin margin, the members of ODAC, on that cold day in December 2007, voted 5 to 4—*against* recommending approval of Avastin for the treatment of metastatic breast cancer.[47] Immediately after the decision, shares in Genentech's stock fell 8.4 percent, before trading on the stock was halted.

But two months later, on February 22, 2008, the FDA reminded the country, and the world, that ODAC's vote and comments on a drug's clinical trial data is *advisory*, not compulsory, and the agency approved Avastin anyway for the treatment of metastatic breast cancer. It was one of the rare instances in which the FDA would decide to make a move counter to ODAC's recommendations. In 2021, the FDA would approve the controversial Alzheimer's drug manufactured by Biogen, aducanumab, despite an advisory committee similar to ODAC virtually unanimously voting against its approval. This led to almost uniform reprobation of the agency by scientific experts, and to the FDA's subsequent backtracking on the drug's label indication.[48]

In response to the news that, against ODAC's opinion, the FDA had approved Avastin on February 22, 2008, Genentech's shares immediately rose 8 percent in afterhours trading.[49]

To some, the decision appeared to water down the threshold for approval of cancer drugs. As Rick Pazdur explained:

> We wanted to have the regulatory flexibility to approve effective drugs where there isn't overall survival.[50]

Pazdur then indicated that the FDA had sympathy for the view that delaying tumor growth, even in the absence of an improved overall survival, "may be a direct clinical benefit in itself."[51]

Fran Visco, the president of the National Breast Cancer Coalition Fund (the patient advocacy group on behalf of which Christine Brunswick had spoken, against Avastin, at the 2011 hearings) was blunt in her assessment of the FDA's decision:

> We believe that they have lowered the bar. Our goal is to get the best treatments out to patients that really will be effective and safe. This particular circumstance will not advance that goal.[52]

Barbara Brenner, executive director of the advocacy group Breast Cancer Action, echoed Visco's sentiments:

> The bar has been lowered for the approval of cancer drugs and that is a loss for patients, period. We all want good drugs as long as they provide a real benefit. This drug does not.[53]

But it was not a complete victory for Genentech. The FDA mitigated its own risk with Avastin in breast cancer patients by granting the drug *accelerated* approval. This regulatory mechanism allowed drugs for life-threatening diseases to reach the market on the basis of data that is reasonably likely to translate to a clinically meaningful benefit, such as "lives longer" or "lives better." It requires the conduct of another trial, usually a randomized, Phase 3 trial that will demonstrate that benefit.

Neither Dr. Pazdur nor David Schenkein, a senior vice president of Genentech, would comment on whether an overall survival benefit would need to be demonstrated in such a trial to obtain full FDA approval.

And luckily for Genentech, they already had just such a trial in the works.

# 6

# A Viral Scourge

*. . . I'd go*
*around the house with a rag of ammonia*
*Wiping wiping crazed as a housewife on Let's*
*Make a Deal the deal being PLEASE DON'T MAKE*
*HIM SICK AGAIN faucets doorknobs the phone*
*every lethal thing a person grips*
—Paul Monette, "The Worrying," 1988

The coronavirus pandemic, a blight that started in late 2019 in Wuhan Province, China, has infected more than 500 million people worldwide and killed more than 6.2 million as this book goes to press.[1] Anyone might look at these numbers and marvel at the sheer human devastation they represent, just the way I and countless other people, before the coronavirus began to run rampant, reacted when reading statistics about the flu pandemic of 1918–1919: it is estimated that 500 million people were infected by that flu (at the time, one-third of the world's population), and over 50 million died worldwide.[2]

But the sense of desperation—of lives lost, of living in constant worry for the health of your family, friends, and heck, even yourself—remains at arm's length unless you've actually lived through an infectious pandemic:

Until you learn for the first time that—WHAT? The virus started in animals before infecting people—with some conspiracy theorists believing it came from a laboratory as a type of bioterrorism—and with media reporting it can be passed by someone who has no symptoms at all, may be aerosolized and transmitted in body fluids, lives on surfaces undetected for days, and is at least 10 times more deadly than the flu.

Until you've experienced the fear of getting infected with a virus that might be able to kill from an innocent sneeze.

Until you read in the news about efforts to quarantine people—or even to castigate or target them—because of certain ethnic characteristics or "unhealthy" behaviors.

Until you've been the one to hoard Lysol wipes and paper towels—and don't forget the toilet paper.

Until you've established a "hot zone" in your garage for the contaminated groceries you tempted fate by shopping for or having delivered, and you participate in the existential exercise of opening that Lysol container to wipe down the container itself, along with every other package you just purchased, before bringing it all into the "safe zone" of your home.

Until you've scrubbed all the flat surfaces you can identify, your car's steering wheel, your house keys, unsuspecting door knobs, even your children, and still wonder if it's safe to hug them.

Until you've been the one coming home from your job at the hospital where you cared for others with the virus and, as the Providence, Rhode Island, emergency room doctor Jay Baruch, MD, wrote:

> You remove your scrubs outside and pad downstairs to the washing machine in the basement. You're sure the neighbors see more of you than anyone should. You fear their young children will be

permanently scarred by this hairy man hopping around the other side of the fence.[3]

Until you've seen friends young and old—who shouldn't be dying—die, and doctors and nurses working in intensive care units and ERs use and reuse and reuse again what were supposed to be single-use, disposable masks and plastic shields because there isn't enough equipment to protect them adequately from the patients they're treating.

Until you've felt helpless witnessing death and despair wrought by a virus with no effective treatment and no vaccine.

Indeed, until you've actually lived through a viral plague, it's hard to understand the urgency people feel to motivate a recalcitrant and at times misguided and even misleading government to acknowledge the deadliness of an infection, enact legislation that makes it easier to diagnose, monitor, and prevent or eliminate the virus, and tear down a wall of bureaucracy to safeguard the health of a newly threatened public.

All of this was true in 2020 and 2021 amid the coronavirus pandemic. And it was true in the 1980s in the thick of the AIDS crisis.

Just as with the passage of the Wiley Act in 1906, the Food, Drug, and Cosmetics Act following the sulfanilamide tragedy in 1938, and the Kefauver-Harris Amendment in 1962 following the thalidomide scandal, in which health crises begat changes in how drugs were regulated; so, too, AIDS was the sort of deadly illness, deliberately ignored and with research and drug development underfunded by a callous government, that spurred patient groups to set a new standard for protest and advocacy, with the goal of getting drugs approved quickly to treat life-threatening illnesses.

On June 5, 1981, in the medical journal *Morbidity and Mortality Weekly Report*, the Centers for Disease Control and Prevention disclosed that five men from Los Angeles—ages 29 to 36, all previously healthy, and all gay—had contracted a rare type of lung infection: *pneumocystis carinii* pneumonia. PCP (later named *pneumocystis jiroveci* pneumonia when the infectious organism was reclassified as a fungus, from a protozoan) had previously only been seen in people who were profoundly immunosuppressed as a result of congenital immune conditions, or from cancer or chemotherapy to treat cancer. All of the men were also infected with a virus, called cytomegalovirus, or CMV. Within the time between the men's diagnosis and the report's submission, two of the men had died. In an editorial note accompanying the article, the author matter-of-factly commented:

> The occurrence of pneumocystosis in these 5 previously healthy individuals without a clinically apparent underlying immunodeficiency is unusual. The fact that these patients were all homosexuals suggests an association between some aspect of a homosexual lifestyle or disease acquired through sexual contact.[4]

The article was picked up by the *Los Angeles Times* and the *San Francisco Chronicle*, and within days the CDC was flooded with stories of similar cases of the same pneumonia and of a rare skin cancer—Kaposi's sarcoma (figure 6.1)—also found exclusively in gay men who were living in California and New York.[5] Named for Moritz Kaposi, a Viennese physician who in 1872 first described the condition in older men of Mediterranean or Jewish extraction, KS was seen previously only in the elderly, with a low, annual incidence rate in the United States of 0.02 per 100,000 citizens.[6] A follow-up report from the CDC dated July 3, 1981, described 26 gay men, ages 25 to 51, with the same skin cancer and pneumonia diagnosed within the preceding two-and-a-half years.[7] The CDC report led to the first mention of this new cancer epidemic, on the same day, by the *New York Times*, in which the reporter commented:

> The cause of the outbreak is unknown, and there is as yet no evidence of contagion.

He then presciently added:

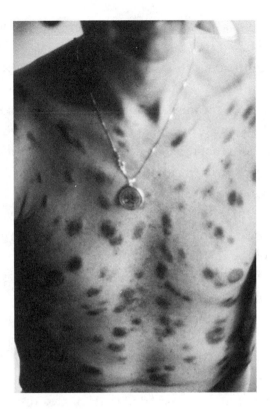

**Figure 6.1**
An HIV-positive man with Kaposi's sarcoma on his chest and abdomen. *Source*: Paul
A. Volderberg, MD, University of California San Francisco, https://www.hiv.va.gov
/provider/image-library/cancers.asp?post=1&slide=173.

Cancer is not believed to be contagious, but conditions that might
precipitate it, such as particular viruses or environmental factors,
might account for an outbreak among a single group.[8]

Ironically, the sobering article appeared on the same newspaper
page as an advertisement from a local bank extolling readers, the day
before Independence Day, to "Sing out on the 4th!"

The fireworks surrounding the spread of what would eventually
be called acquired immunodeficiency syndrome, or AIDS, were just
beginning.

The term "gay cancer" soon entered the public lexicon and was
later referred to by researchers as Gay-Related Immune Deficiency or

GRID. By the end of 1981, 270 gay men were diagnosed with GRID, 121 of whom had died.[9]

It wasn't until about six months later, in June 1982, that GRID was linked to an infectious agent, though whether that was a virus, bacteria, or "micro-organism" had not yet been established. By that point, over 350 people had been diagnosed with the immunodeficiency syndrome. That number now included not just gay men, but also heterosexual women and men, and intravenous drug users.[10]

The following month, health officials reported on 34 recent immigrants from Haiti who had severe immunodeficiency, 16 of whom had died. They had similar, unusual infections as the gay men with GRID. Four of the Haitians were women.[11]

Young, previously health people were dying in droves, and nobody knew the cause.

It was quickly becoming apparent that this could no longer be referred to as a gay man's disease, and on September 24, 1982, the CDC used the acronym AIDS for the first time to describe the epidemic.[12] That day, Representative Henry Waxman, a Democrat from California whose district included parts of Los Angeles, where the first unusual pneumonia cases were described, and Representative Phillip Burton, another California Democrat from San Francisco, introduced the first legislation to allocate $5 million to the CDC for AIDS surveillance, and $10 million to the National Institutes of Health for AIDS research.[13] By December, AIDS was also detected in infants. Anthony Fauci, MD, of the National Institutes of Health, the man who would become the nation's doctor during the coronavirus pandemic 37 years later, acknowledged the possibility of maternal-to-fetal transmission of the disease, meaning that AIDS was blood-borne and not tied simply to promiscuous behaviors.[14]

Supporting this discovery, AIDS was detected in those receiving blood and plasma transfusions—a particular risk in people suffering from hemophilia, who are born with a deficiency in a factor that helps the blood to clot, not only leaving them prone to bleeding episodes that necessitate the transfusions but also needing treatment with plasma-derived factor replacement.[15] This was the disease that plagued the Romanovs, the royal Russian family, and descendants of the British monarch Queen Victoria, during the nineteenth century.[16] From 1981 to 1984, 50 percent of people with hemophilia would become infected with the virus that was eventually determined to have caused AIDS.[17]

In 1982, 853 people died from AIDS in the United States. This number jumped to 2,304 deaths in 1983, 4,251 in 1984, and 5,636 in 1985.[18]

According to the CDC, more than 50,000 people were diagnosed with AIDS in the United States from 1981 to 1987, and 96 percent of those people died.[19]

From 1988 to 1992, more than 200,000 people in the United States were diagnosed with AIDS, 90 percent of whom died.[20]

There didn't appear to be any flattening of those curves over the 12-year period.

Not until May 1983—almost two years after the first report of the unusual pneumonia in five gay men—did Congress pass its first bill committing $12 million of funding for AIDS research and treatment.[21]

Compare that to the weeks it took Congress in 2020 to fund $1.25 billion in research on COVID-19, in which sexual orientation couldn't be implicated as an etiology.[22] Even accounting for inflation, this amount is still 42 times what was earmarked for AIDS.

Similar to public response during the coronavirus pandemic, people were terrified of catching AIDS (or, more accurately, the human immunodeficiency virus that was found to cause the syndrome), and still didn't have a clear understanding of how it was transmitted. In September 1983, another report from the CDC tried to both clarify this issue and call out the unfounded biases that were being associated with AIDS:

The classification of certain groups as being more closely associated with the disease has been misconstrued by some to mean these groups are likely to transmit the disease through non-intimate interactions. This view is not justified by available data. Nonetheless, it has been used unfairly as a basis for social and economic discrimination.

The occurrence of AIDS cases among homosexual men, IV drug abusers, persons with hemophilia, sexual partners of members of these groups, and recipients of blood transfusions is consistent with the hypothesis that AIDS is caused by an agent that is transmitted sexually or, less commonly, through contaminated needles or blood. About 91% percent of reported cases have occurred in these patient groups. Among the remaining cases, there has been no evidence that the disease was acquired through casual contact with AIDS patients or with persons in population groups with an increased incidence of AIDS. AIDS is not known to be transmitted through food, water, air, or environmental surfaces.[23]

This CDC clarification was eerily similar to its clarification in May 2020 about the unlikelihood of contracting COVID-19 from casual contact with surfaces.

Yet prior to May 2020, as was true with our understanding of AIDS prior to September 1983, those of us armed with a container of Lysol wipes could relate to the evocative lines from "Worrying" by the poet and activist Paul Monette, who wrote in response to caring for his AIDS-infected partner in the 1980s:

"I'd go / around the house with a rag of ammonia / Wiping wiping crazed as a housewife on Let's / Make a Deal the deal being PLEASE DON'T MAKE / HIM SICK AGAIN faucets doorknobs the phone / every lethal thing a person grips."[24]

In September 1983, the same month as the CDC's "clarification," Dr. Joseph Sonnabend was treating AIDS patients at his office on West 12th Street in New York City when he was issued an eviction notice by the building's board of directors, for fear that he or his patients would spread AIDS to other building occupants. Sonnabend, a South African–born physician who held an MB (a bachelor's degree in medicine; equivalent to MD in the US) and was an MRCP (Member of the Royal College of Physicians)—and one of the first to notice the immune deficiency that became known as HIV/AIDS among his gay male patients—had been building his medical practice and eventually conducting AIDS research in the building since 1977. In response, he engaged the state's attorney general and the Lambda Legal Defense and Education Fund, which jointly filed the very first AIDS discrimination lawsuit, against the cooperative apartment complex.[25]

Lambda Legal was established in 1973 with a mission to safeguard the civil rights of lesbians, gay men, bisexuals, transgender people, and eventually anyone living with HIV.[26] Other advocacy groups were created in response to the fear surrounding AIDS, and the paucity of information about its cause, spread, and treatment.

Probably the most famous was the Gay Men's Health Crisis, founded in January 1982 in New York City by six gay men: the playwright and screenwriter Larry Kramer (figure 6.2), along with Nathan Fain, Lawrence Mass, Paul Popham, Paul Rapoport, and Edmund White, at Kramer's Manhattan apartment. They initially raised money for research into Kaposi's sarcoma, but in May of that year opened a hotline to answer questions about the new gay plague.[27]

The first night it went live, they received 100 calls. People were desperate for help.

The group expanded by recruiting volunteers to help people suffering from AIDS with basic tasks, such as grocery shopping and laundry, and even with home nursing care, as healthcare providers themselves feared caring for AIDS patients and refused to enter their homes. Other programs soon followed, to help patients navigate the healthcare system and identify federal assistance programs. They provided funding for Lambda Legal's defense of Dr. Sonnabend and fought for increased government support of AIDS research.

**Figure 6.2**
Larry Kramer, a founder of the Gay Men's Health Alliance, of the activist group ACT UP, and author of "1,112 and Counting" with Molly, his Wheaten Terrier, New York City, 1989. *Source*: Photo by Robert Giard, © Estate of Robert Giard, https://makinggayhistory.com/podcast/larry-kramer/.

The Gay Men's Health Crisis held benefits to raise money for AIDS research and disseminated education materials. But a clear cause of AIDS and how to keep from contracting the disease—never mind how to treat it—still wasn't clear. They and others were highly critical of the FDA and other government agencies involved in drug development. Government scientists were accused of being more interested in maintaining the rigorous scientific standards of research and clinical trials than in providing real options for the thousands of patients who were dying as a result of AIDS.[28]

But those government workers received little support from the executive branch under President Reagan, who at the time refused to even utter the word publicly.[29]

Then in 1983 Larry Kramer published "1,112 and Counting," a blistering assessment on how AIDS had affected the gay community in the New York Native. In this essay he attacked a sluggish government, an uninformed medical community, and arcane policies in research that prevented the rapid dissemination of knowledge. As he put it:

> If you write a calm letter and fax it to nobody, it sinks like a brick in the Hudson.[30]

Also in 1983, San Francisco General Hospital opened the now famous Ward 5B, the first dedicated inpatient AIDS hospital unit.[31]

And in 1983 the televangelist Jerry Falwell famously declared on his "Old Time Gospel Hour" program that AIDS was "a judgment of God upon moral perversion in this society."[32]

Fear of the new, mysterious syndrome led to hate and blame, but at the time no treatment for the disease.

Up to this point, though, doctors, nurses, and even AIDS organizations could do little more than offer comfort care when the inevitable opportunistic infections or cancers arose, and then attempt to ease the transition to death.

A major breakthrough came in May 1983, a couple of years after the infectious consequences of AIDS had first been described. In a heated and very competitive months-long race to be the first laboratory to isolate the cause of the disease, French and American scientists (in particular Luc Montagnier of the Pasteur Institute, who was awarded the Nobel Prize in Physiology or Medicine for his work, and Robert Gallo of the National Cancer Institute) published research findings in the same month. They established that these patients were infected with what would be called the human immunodeficiency virus, HIV, and announced that they were able to produce large quantities of the virus.[33]

Identification and production of the virus were the necessary steps needed to finally initiate drug testing to combat the plague, which was still running more rampant than ever, still misunderstood, and still widely feared: even as late as October 1984, the *New York Times* reported that AIDS could be transmissible in saliva—an inflated claim that took two years to debunk.[34]

That same month, San Francisco closed its bathhouses in an attempt to thwart high-risk sexual activity that could spread the virus, a move not entirely dissimilar to the closing of restaurants and bars nationwide in 2020 during the coronavirus pandemic.

The year 1985 marked its own AIDS "milestones" when the actor Rock Hudson became the first major public figure to acknowledge having AIDS, and when President Reagan finally mentioned AIDS publicly, for the first time acknowledging its existence. In June 1985, Ryan White, a teenager who had hemophilia and was HIV positive from the tainted blood product and clotting factor supply, was officially denied readmittance to his middle school. At the end of this cruel year, a *Los Angeles Times* poll found that a majority of Americans favored quarantining people who had AIDS, and nearly half favored requiring government-issued identification cards for those who tested positive for the disease.[35]

Where were the drugs needed to treat AIDS? And given the national urgency to identify a treatment for the thousands of people dying from this malicious and unforgiving virus, and the infections and cancers it begat, why wasn't there a regulatory mechanism to bring hopeful drugs to market in an accelerated way, as quickly as possible?

On February 25, 2008, Avastin received just such an accelerated FDA approval for the treatment of metastatic breast cancer—another malicious and unforgiving disease.[36] It was based on results from the E2100 study, in which women treated with Avastin combined with the chemotherapy drug paclitaxel had an average progression-free survival of 11.8 months, compared to 5.9 months for women who received the chemotherapy alone—a 5.9-month improvement.[37]

But while it took longer for breast cancer to worsen in women treated with Avastin compared to women receiving chemotherapy alone, the average overall survival had been similar in both groups, at a little over two years.[38]

This type of accelerated approval required post-marketing studies to confirm (and hopefully improve upon) the initial benefits seen in the original E2100 study. These trials were underway around the time of Avastin's accelerated approval, in 2008.

In fact, Genentech actually had two opportunities to demonstrate that the progression-free survival advantage for women taking Avastin, seen in the initial E2100 study, was not a fluke, and could even translate to an overall survival advantage, with women taking Avastin actually living longer.

The first study, abbreviated AVADO for Avastin And Docetaxel, was structurally similar to the E2100 trial, and enrolled patients from March 2006 through October 2007. A total of 736 women with metastatic breast cancer were randomly selected to receive a chemotherapy cousin of paclitaxel called docetaxel, or to be treated with docetaxel combined with two different doses of Avastin. Women receiving the chemotherapy docetaxel alone had a progression-free survival average of 7.9 months—a bit more than women receiving paclitaxel alone on the E2100 study.[39]

Those receiving docetaxel combined with Avastin on the AVADO study had an improvement in progression-free survival that amounted to just a little over three-and-a-half weeks more than those getting docetaxel alone.

Weeks, not even months. In fact, a full five months *less* of an improvement for those receiving Avastin than what had been seen in the original E2100 study. Overall survival was no different between the groups.

Rates of bleeding, lowering of the immune system, fever, and in general serious side effects were all higher among women receiving Avastin.[40]

The second trial, called RIBBON-1 for Regimens In Bevacizumab for Breast Oncology (the uninspired acronym alone may have presaged where this trial was headed), enrolled 1,237 women with metastatic breast cancer to receive one of three different types of chemotherapy alone (some of which were similar to the paclitaxel or docetaxel chemotherapy used in other studies), or combined with Avastin. The first woman entered the trial in December 2005, and the final woman was enrolled in August 2007.[41]

The average progression-free survival for women treated with chemotherapy alone that was similar to the paclitaxel or docetaxel chemo used in the other studies was almost identical to that seen in the AVADO study, at eight months. Those who also received Avastin enjoyed an average improvement in progression free survival of an additional 5 weeks for those treated with a chemotherapy similar to previous studies, and 12 weeks for women treated with other types of chemotherapy combined with Avastin.

That is still far inferior to what was seen in the original E2100 study (the basis for Avastin's accelerated approval). Again, overall survival did not differ between the groups. And again, toxicities were higher for those treated with Avastin, including bleeding, a suppressed immune system, fever, and high blood pressure.[42]

Following accelerated approval of a drug by the FDA, post-marketing confirmatory trials have to "verify and describe the anticipated effect on irreversible morbidity or mortality," and be completed in a timely fashion.[43] These trials enrolled patients by the time of Avastin's initial approval and followed those patients appropriately for meaningful outcomes that included overall survival. So, yes, they were timely.

But had they verified Avastin's effect, first seen in the E2100 trial, on mortality—on progression-free survival or (better yet) on the "lives longer" FDA bar of overall survival?

In 1985, as I mentioned earlier, there were no FDA approved drugs to treat HIV/AIDS.

Desperate patients were being hawked nostrums and cure-alls to treat HIV/AIDS in the 1980s that a century earlier—before there was even a semblance of an FDA and in the absence of drugs with proven safety and efficacy—would have made Hamlin's Wizard Oil or Brandreth's Vegetable Universal Pill proud: these "remedies" included Vitamin C, hydrogen peroxide, and even imitation nonoxynol-9 spermicides such as Lubraseptic, which promised to "Reduce the risk. Increase the pleasure."[44] The promotion of hydroxychloroquine for the treatment of COVID-19 decades later smacked of the same exploitative opportunism. None of these drugs was effective at preventing or treating AIDS.

But a discarded cancer drug was.

Azidothymidine, also called AZT or zidovudine, was originally developed as a potential chemotherapy in the 1960s by Jerome P. Horwitz, PhD, of Wayne State University and the Michigan Cancer Foundation in Detroit.[45] At the time, it was thought that cancers could be caused by viruses, which was later proven to be correct in cancers affecting the cervix, rectum, head and neck, and some lymphomas, to name a few. Like many other cancer drugs, azidothymidine acts like a Trojan Horse with its resemblance to thymidine, the sugar used to build and copy DNA, the genetic blueprints for cells. When AZT was administered to quickly growing cells in a test tube—cells that grow like cancer—it inserted itself into the genetic machinery of the cell and blocked the cell's ability to copy its own DNA. A cell that can't copy its DNA can't continue to grow and divide. Unfortunately, at the next stage of drug development—testing the drug in mice—AZT didn't work, and it was shelved.[46]

Fast forward two decades later, when the AIDS crisis hit.

The pharmaceutical company Burroughs Wellcome, based in North Carolina, started screening compounds for any that might work on cells infected with HIV in test tubes. Lo and behold, Compound S, a reformulated version of azidothymidine, appeared to block the virus' activity. Viruses, like cancer cells, depend on copying their genetic material to replicate themselves. AZT blocks the enzyme reverse transcriptase to prevent that from happening.[47]

The company sent samples of AZT to the National Cancer Institute, the FDA, and nearby Duke University for further testing. This time, unlike with the mice with cancer who were treated two decades earlier, AZT worked to prevent replication of the virus in the animals.[48]

On July 3, 1985, a six-week, Phase 1 clinical trial of four different doses of AZT conducted at the National Cancer Institute and Duke University enrolled its first of 19 patients, at the NCI. All of the patients were infected with HIV that had progressed to advanced AIDS-related complex (ARC) or outright AIDS—essentially, a death sentence in those days. Serious side effects to AZT included headaches and worsening of parts of the immune system. Yet, the component of the immune system that was affected by HIV—the T-cells—improved in 15 of the 19 patients. Two patients had resolution of infections; on average, these patients, who were wasted from the ravages of their disease, gained almost five pounds. The maximum tolerated dose was established for the next phase study.[49]

In February 1986, a follow-up study of zidovudine was opened at 12 medical centers across the United States.[50] In it, 145 patients with ARC or AIDS were randomized to receive AZT, while 137 ARC or AIDS patients received a placebo. In September of that year an independent data safety monitoring board, whose members were privy to which patients were receiving AZT and which got placebo—unlike the patients themselves and the doctors who were treating them—made a profound discovery: only a single person receiving AZT on the study had died, compared to 19 patients in the placebo arm. Patients receiving a placebo were also twice as likely as patients treated with AZT to develop the opportunistic infections like PCP, which occur in patients who have a compromised immune system.[51]

In a separate publication, the authors also noted the side effects with AZT, which were substantial. Many patients experienced nausea, muscle aches, insomnia, and crippling headaches. Bone marrow suppression could be severe, with patients taking AZT six times more likely to become anemic and five times as likely to require red blood cell transfusions as those who received a placebo. More patients on the AZT study arm than on the placebo arm actually had worsening of their immune system as a result of the drug.[52]

But recognizing the impressive decrease in deaths in patients receiving AZT during the 8-to-24-week observation period of the trial, the data safety monitoring board (DSMB) stopped the study, and patients who had previously been treated with placebos were switched over to receive AZT.[53]

DSMBs are tasked with reviewing the results from clinical trials—like the FDA, focusing mainly on drug toxicities, but also often on drug efficacy—in real time. They are careful in interpreting the data they see: whether afraid of either erroneously concluding that a drug is ineffective or dangerous based on early signals (which may reverse themselves as future patients are enrolled to the trial), thereby killing a drug; or wary of stopping a trial early based on signals that the drug is quite effective, for the same reason—that efficacy may be washed out with the experience of future patients. It is rare for a DSMB to halt a trial for either reason.

Burroughs Wellcome quickly submitted a new drug application to the FDA for zidovudine in December 1986. The FDA approved AZT without requiring a larger Phase 3 clinical trial on March 20, 1987—only 13 months after the trial had enrolled its first patient, and less than two years from when the first in-human trial had enrolled its initial patient.[54]

Compare that to the average 8-to-10-year period it usually took (at the time) for a drug to move from a laboratory to a person's medicine cabinet.

The breakthrough drug, and its rapid availability from a responsive, user-friendly FDA, was celebrated by advocacy groups and the regulatory agency alike. At the time, FDA officials explained one reason for the rapid approval of zidovudine: that FDA scientists were able to work closely with the drug's sponsor from the very beginning of the development process, and to provide advice on the best path forward to drug approval. This approach, of early phase meetings with the FDA and guidance about a potential playbook to get a drug across the finish line, would serve as a model for future expedited drug development legislation.[55]

But many scientists, advocates, and even the FDA itself recognized that AZT was not a panacea in AIDS treatment. In the words of Samuel Broder, MD, whose lab at the NCI led the seminal studies showing AZT's ability to control HIV in test tubes:

> We strongly believed then, as we do now, in Voltaire's maxim: *"Le mieux est l'ennemi du bien,"* which translated for the AIDS pandemic means, "The perfect is the enemy of the good." Rather than wait for the perfect antiretroviral drug to be developed, we decided to proceed with what we had in hand as rapidly as possible.[56]

Even in announcing the approval of AZT by the FDA, Dr. Robert E. Windom, an assistant secretary of Health and Human Services, was guarded in his comments:

> Today's approval marks an important step, but by no means a final victory, in our ongoing war against AIDS. Retrovir is not a cure for AIDS, but it has a demonstrated ability to improve the short-term survival of AIDS patients with recently diagnosed PCP and certain patients with advanced ARC.[57]

The Gay Men's Health Crisis expressed its satisfaction with the approval, but immediately castigated the manufacturer:

> We are, however, outraged at the extreme high cost of the drug and the fact that a person with AIDS may be forced to spend down all their assets in order to afford this excellent drug.[58]

That cost was estimated to be $8,000 to 10,000 per year: one-tenth the cost of Avastin 20 years later, or one-fifth when adjusted for inflation.[59]

Despite the clear need for something—anything—that might be effective against an unchecked pandemic, was the approval too rapid? The clinical trial had been hastily constructed and opened, and it didn't give clear guidance to investigators about how to manage some of the serious complications that accompanied ARC and AIDS, like life-threatening, atypical pneumonias or profuse diarrhea, which could have led to the higher death rates in patients receiving a placebo.

Additionally, anecdotes emerged about how patients enrolled in the trial would get together and pool their pills, so that if they had been randomized to receive a placebo, they would increase the likelihood of getting at least some AZT from someone who had been randomized to the drug. But that person, in turn, would be under-dosed.

Because they were that desperate for a treatment.

Of course, this would also compromise the accuracy of determining the balance of the drug's safety and efficacy.

Patients had to take the 250 milligram pills every four hours, around the clock.[60] This was about the same time that the Timex Ironman Triathlon watch came on the market, with its capacity to set multiple alarms. It and watches like it became a staple for AIDS patients who tried to take the drug religiously for as long as it was working.

Two years after the FDA approved zidovudine, a trial of 524 patients with HIV who had just experienced their first episode of PCP was carried out by the AIDS Clinical Trials Group. Patients were randomized to receive the standard dose of 1,500 milligrams per day of AZT or as little as 600 milligrams per day of the drug. The study found that, two years after starting on the drug, survival was 27 percent versus 34 percent.[61]

The results favored those who received the *lower* dose of AZT.

Not surprisingly, patients receiving the lower AZT dose were also less likely to have suppression of the immune system and anemia. If this had been known sooner, patients could have avoided those drug toxicities, lived longer, and even lived better, and many more would have been spared the unnecessary expense of the higher dose.

Five years later, in 1994, another study from the AIDS Clinical Trials Group would show that the lower dose of AZT, given for a discrete period of weeks to pregnant, HIV-positive women, cut the rates of transmission of HIV from mother to child by two-thirds, from 25 percent to 8 percent. Pregnant women hadn't been enrolled in the initial trials, similar to the way pregnant women are excluded from most drug studies, out of concern of an unapproved drug's effects on the fetus.[62]

The approval had been fast—very fast—by FDA standards. AZT represented a treatment that was good—even great—by the standards of what had been available previously: nothing. But it really wasn't that great a drug, and it had substantial side effects. People were still dying from AIDS, but living a few months longer than before AZT for some who took it. For others, there was no improvement in survival despite the drug's substantial side effects. As has been true throughout the history of the FDA, with increased speed of approval in response to a justifiably angry, terrified, and dying public came the risk of compromising that public's safety, safety, safety—the core value, and duty, of the FDA.

Had the AVADO and RIBBON-1 trials verified Avastin's effect, first seen in the E2100 trial, on mortality—on progression-free survival or overall survival? Or had Avastin's approval been too quick, also?

This question was actually first posed to the ODAC months before the 2011 hearings, on July 20, 2010. I was on that advisory panel, along with nine other ODAC members. Four of them—Ralph

Freedman, MD, PhD (the specialist is gynecology-oncology), Brent Logan, PhD (the statistician), Gregory Curt, MD (the non-voting industry representative), and Wyndham Wilson, MD (our chairperson)—would join me the following year at the Avastin hearing.

In all of the ODAC proceedings in which I had participated up until that point, the questions posed to our committee had to do with whether or not the balance of risk and benefit—safety and efficacy—should lead to a drug's being added to the nation's formulary.

This was the first time we were asked whether a drug's risks were dangerous enough, and its benefit so measly, that it should be pulled from the market for a specific disease, to safeguard the health of the public.

After listening to presentations about the AVADO and RIBBON-1 trial results from both Genentech and the FDA, and having the opportunity to ask questions of both, the agency asked ODAC members whether the data supported a favorable risk-benefit ratio for Avastin combined with chemotherapy drugs, or whether the side effects to the drug combination were too great given the paltry benefits. This is a standard question asked of ODAC members for almost any drug coming before us. But the FDA broke this down into more specific questions given the particular circumstances surrounding the so-called confirmatory AVADO and RIBBON-1 trials:[63]

Should Avastin progress from accelerated to full approval in combination with paclitaxel—do the current data support?

*We voted no, 13 to 0.*

If no, should Avastin's breast cancer indication be withdrawn from the label?

*We voted yes, 12 to 1.*

Should Avastin be approved in combination with docetaxel?

*We voted no, 13 to 0.*

Should Avastin be approved in combination with other drugs (the different types of chemotherapy used in the RIBBON-1 trial) being considered?

*We voted no, 12 to 1.*

A few months later, on December 15, 2010, in a memorandum written by Rick Pazdur, MD, to Janet Woodcock, MD, the director of the FDA's Center for Drug Evaluation and Research, and supported by the ODAC vote, he recommended (on behalf of the FDA's Office of New Drugs) withdrawing the approval of the breast cancer indication for Avastin, citing the failure of the two trials "to confirm the magnitude of benefit originally observed in the E2100 study" as well as concern for the "overall increase in serious adverse events" related to Avastin.[64]

Specifically, the FDA was troubled by:

1. The lack of improvement in progression-free survival or overall survival for those women treated with Avastin combined with chemotherapy in the AVADO and RIBBON-1 studies when compared to what was seen in the original E2100 study. [*The progression-free survival benefit actually shrank in the follow-up studies, and women with breast cancer who received Avastin did not live longer.*]

2. The lack of improvement in symptoms or patient-reported outcomes. [*Women enrolled on the AVADO trial who received Avastin were actually two-and-a-half times more likely to have bleeding events and in both the AVADO and RIBBON-1 trials were more likely than women not receiving Avastin to suffer other side effects rated as being serious, like high blood pressure, a suppressed immune system, and fevers. In fact, approximately 1 percent of deaths were attributed to* Avastin. *Women did not "live better," and some died sooner.*]

3. The difficulty in determining whether any benefit enjoyed by women receiving Avastin combined with chemotherapy was a result of the Avastin or the chemotherapy. [*This is always a challenge in trials that combine two or more drugs, when either drug individually could shrink a tumor.*]

4. The wimpy improvement in progression-free survival for women receiving Avastin across studies, especially as it was assessed using

CT scans, which can have subjective interpretations of progression. [*Recall that, when different radiologists and oncologists evaluate the exact same CT scan to determine if a patient's tumor has enlarged or has gotten smaller, they disagree almost one-third of the time.*]

5. That the progression-free survival for E2100 may have been exaggerated because the study was stopped early. [*At the time, investigators thought they had something really special with Avastin because of the progression-free survival benefit they were seeing, and they halted the study prematurely so all women could receive the drug. If the study had continued, and more women had been enrolled to it, the "benefit" seen with Avastin may have disappeared, eroding the "beginner's luck." This is the danger of a DSMB halting a trial based on early, promising results.*]

6. That there didn't appear to be any special benefits of adding Avastin to any of the chemotherapy combinations. [*It was a specious argument to say that Avastin may be a great drug, if only it was given along with Tumorminimab instead of paclitaxel.*]

7. Far more data now existed that Avastin did not provide much efficacy benefit but did add substantial toxicity.[*The ultimate assessment of whether or not a drug should be approved by the FDA— the vaunted ratio of risk to benefit—simply wasn't there.*]

The memo concluded with what was, for a government agency, a damning summary:

> The main goals of therapy for breast cancer are palliation of symptoms and prolongation of overall survival time without negatively impacting quality of life. After reviewing data from the studies, the Agency concluded that women who took Avastin did not live any longer than women who did not receive the drug, and yet were at risk of experiencing severe side effects, including side effects that are unique to this drug and death.
>
> Given the increase in toxicity, lack of direct clinical benefit, and failure to confirm the initial magnitude of improvement noted in E2100 . . . the Office of New Drugs proposes to *withdraw approval* of Avastin's breast cancer indication.[65]

Amid the AIDS crisis, other promising drugs—known as DDI and DDC for short—followed AZT in being developed to treat HIV, but that development appeared to have stalled in the regulatory process. Two events occurred in 1987 that raised hopes for a quicker path to drug approval for patients suffering from this life-threatening disease who had few, if any, other options.

The first was the presidential campaign of George Herbert Walker Bush, in which he ran on a platform that included faster action by the FDA to get drugs to market.[66]

The second was the formation of an activist organization called the AIDS Coalition To Unleash Power, or ACT UP, once again led by Larry Kramer. Kramer's goal was to create a political direct-action group to force governments, elected officials, public health agencies, the pharmaceutical and insurance industries, and religious institutions to act to protect those at risk of HIV, and those sick from AIDS.[67]

According to *Time* magazine, it would become the most effective health activist group in history. And it would write the playbook for health activist groups for decades to come.[68]

# 7
# Silence = Death

Hey, hey, FDA, how many people have you killed today?

—ACT UP protestors, 1988

Within two weeks of its formation in 1987, ACT UP staged a protest on Wall Street against Burroughs Wellcome, the manufacturer of AZT, lambasting their profiteering on the drug.[1] By this point, it was estimated that 5 to 10 million people worldwide were infected with HIV. The disease was running so rampant that it began to feel apocalyptic.[2]

A year later ACT UP returned to Wall Street, and this time garnered national news coverage for the event.[3]

The organization followed up in October 1988 with a protest at the FDA (which presaged the approach that would be taken 23 years later in support of Avastin for the treatment of breast cancer). ACT UP distributed press kits and made hundreds of phone calls to the media ahead of time, essentially constructing a story to circulate about an unfeeling government agency that wouldn't release drugs in early phase trials to dying patients.

Gathering outside the staid FDA building, more than 1,000 ACT UP protestors chanted "Hey, hey, FDA, how many people have you killed today?"[4]

And if that didn't spur enough drama to make their point, alongside an effigy of then president Reagan they hoisted a black banner that spelled out the FDA initials as "Federal Death Administration."[5] Protestors lay down, blocking the entrance to the agency while holding up cardboard tombstones inscribed with slogans like "R.I.P., Killed by the FDA" and "Dead from Lack of Drugs." Some protestors wore lab coats stained with bloody handprints.[6]

And of course they displayed the now-iconic black signs, designed by activist Avram Finkelstein, with a fuchsia triangle hovering over the words "Silence=Death."[7] Members of ACT UP demanded that the drug approval process be shortened, and that placebo-controlled randomized trials as a prerequisite for approval be eliminated. They also wanted to ensure that patients enrolled in trials be representative of those who had AIDS, and that insurance be required to pay for experimental therapies.[8]

FDA headquarters had to shut down that day. And within a week, members of the typically cloistered FDA agreed to meet with representatives of ACT UP.[9]

Eight days later Frank Young, MD, who had served as FDA commissioner since 1984, announced immediate implementation of a formal plan to reduce the time required for human testing of drugs for *serious conditions*—meaning life-threatening and severely debilitating diseases—such as AIDS, Parkinson's disease, and certain aggressive cancers.[10] The components of the new *fast-track* process would facilitate a dual agenda: earlier attention and consultation with the FDA regarding drugs with promise in treating such conditions, as occurred with AZT; and more efficient trial designs, potentially even eliminating the gold standard, randomized, Phase 3 clinical trials for drugs likely to improve survival or prevent irreversible morbidity. By planning the critical Phase 2 studies well, it was anticipated that the development and review process might be shortened by two to three years.

The victory must have been bittersweet for Larry Kramer, who had learned earlier in the year that he had contracted HIV. He lived more than 30 years longer, however, in large part because of drugs approved as a result of his own advocacy efforts, before dying of pneumonia in the midst of that other viral pandemic caused by COVID-19 in May 2020.[11]

One year later, in 1989, President Bush appointed Louis W. Sullivan as secretary of Health and Human Services and relieved Young of his job at the FDA. One contributing factor to Young's ouster concerned criticism from congressional leaders and consumer groups for his slow response to the AIDS crisis; another involved corruption uncovered within the agency, in which FDA employees took bribes from pharmaceutical companies.[12]

ACT UP and other advocacy groups wanted drugs to get approved faster, and it appeared that there might finally be movement in that direction from the FDA. But they didn't want to wait the years it would take to gain access to drugs that were still being investigated in clinical trials.

They also recognized that clinical trials had overly restrictive eligibility criteria. For example, the follow-up AZT trial exploring lower doses of the drug only included patients who were recovering from their first episode of PCP. For that study, those with a second infection with the pneumonia, or with certain other AIDS-defining illnesses, were excluded from the trial. ACT UP demanded a pathway that would allow patients to receive drugs *before* they were approved by the FDA, and not as part of a clinical trial—a parallel track for drug access, or what is now referred to more commonly as expanded access.[13]

Their demands no longer fell on deaf ears.

In truth, access to nonapproved drugs was not a new concept. From the passage of the Kefauver-Harris Amendment in 1962 into the

1980s, physicians who felt that a seriously ill patient might benefit from an experimental drug, when that person had no other treatment options available, could literally call the FDA and ask for the drug. Medical officers in the agency would evaluate each situation and either approve or deny the request, essentially depending on whether the proposed drug and indication were somewhat reasonable; and whether a manufacturer would supply the drug, a physician would prescribe it, and a patient agreed to take it. These drugs were intended for compassionate use under an investigational new drug (IND) protocol—essentially, a research clinical trial that would be written for a single person.[14]

But that protocol depended on several coinciding factors: finding a doctor who knew that a drug was under investigation; a treatment center equipped to handle and administer the experimental drug; a willing FDA medical officer on the particular day of that request, as the lack of written policies interfered with a uniform application of the compassionate use approach; and a leap of faith that the investigational agent wouldn't be too toxic.

After all, nobody wanted another thalidomide disaster.

The FDA had introduced a written policy in 1983, modified in 1987, clarifying the requirements for compassionate-use treatment INDs: As before, patients had to be suffering from a serious or life-threatening condition for which no satisfactory alternative therapy existed. The experimental drug had to be backed by clinical evidence showing it was relatively safe and may be effective, and the manufacturer had to be pursuing formal FDA approval of the drug with due diligence.[15]

Critics found the policy to be anything but clear. Who was to say that an alternative therapy was, in fact, not satisfactory? The phrase "may be effective" was too vague—did a requesting physician have to provide data that a drug worked, or that it had the potential of working? And how was "effective" defined?

The FDA countered that although critics found the existing policy vague, it seemed to work: by early 1990, 18 drugs had been provided under this mechanism to almost 20,000 patients. But most of those simply bridged the gap between the end of a clinical trial and full FDA approval, when a drug would become widely available on the market.[16]

There must be a way patients could get access to these drugs at earlier stages of drug development—an accelerated method— perhaps based on intermediate clinical endpoints likely to predict substantive outcomes, such as improved survival, in a future study: maybe a decrease in viral load for people with AIDS (meaning that an infection was receding) or tumor shrinkage in the case of cancer.

What type of fallout occurs when the FDA issues an edict to withdraw the approval of a drug that made it to the market in an accelerated fashion?

The December 15, 2010, memorandum written by Rick Pazdur to Janet Woodcock, the director of the FDA's Center for Drug Evaluation and Research (CDER), recommended withdrawing approval of the breast cancer indication for Avastin. Given that, as well as the concerns about safety and lack of efficacy, you might think that Avastin could no longer be prescribed for the treatment of metastatic breast cancer. You might even think that a manufacturer such as Genentech, out of respect for the FDA's authority, would quickly send notices to doctors that they shouldn't use Avastin for that indication. That's what the S. E. Massengill Company had done when reports started rolling in about the harm their drug sulfanilamide was causing 73 years earlier.

But that isn't what happened.

On December 16, 2010, the Center for Drug Evaluation and Research issued a NOOH (notice of opportunity for a hearing) to withdraw the marketing approval of Avastin for metastatic breast cancer. When CDER delivers a NOOH, a drug manufacturer has 30 days to respond, stating either that the company will voluntarily withdraw its drug from the market given the safety and efficacy concerns, or that it wants its day in court.

This wasn't the first time CDER had issued a formal communication about a drug that had made it onto the market under the accelerated approval mechanism but later flunked the risk-benefit analysis in the follow-up studies that were supposed to confirm that benefit.

A decade earlier the drug tongue-twistingly named gemtuzumab ozogamicin (Mylotarg) had been approved for older adults with acute myeloid leukemia whose cancer had initially gone into remission following regular chemotherapy, but who had later relapsed. (That was precisely what had happened with my patient Jimmy Petrarcha, who came from Philadelphia to Cleveland to enroll in a clinical trial.) Mylotarg received accelerated approval on May 17, 2000, based on studies in which 30 percent of 142 leukemia patients treated with the drug went into a remission—remission being a finding we know isn't the best predictor of a meaningful outcome in older adults with leukemia, as it does not always lead to improvement in overall survival.[17]

And in fact, the supposed follow-up confirmatory study, in which 637 leukemia patients were treated with Mylotarg combined with chemotherapy versus chemotherapy alone, failed to show a survival improvement for those receiving the Mylotarg (46 percent were alive five years after their diagnosis, compared to 50 percent of those who *didn't* receive the drug). After discussions with the FDA, Mylotarg's manufacturer, Pfizer, voluntarily withdrew their drug from the market on June 21, 2010, a year before the Avastin hearings, declining their right to a hearing.[18]

On May 5, 2003, the drug Iressa received accelerated approval for the treatment of advanced lung cancer that recurred or continued to grow following previous chemotherapy. Iressa, which acted on vascular endothelial growth factor (VEGF), was one of the drugs borne from Judah Folkman's remarkable research into the dependency of tumors on a good blood supply. The drug was initially approved based on a trial that enrolled just 142 lung cancer patients. Only 15 of those patients (11 percent) had shrinkage of their tumors that lasted an average of seven months. While most side effects to the drug were considered mild, approximately 1 percent of patients experienced severe lung disease on top of their lung cancer.[19]

In what was supposed to be the confirmatory trial, almost 1,700 patients with advanced lung cancer were randomized to receive Iressa or a placebo pill. The average overall survival for those treated with Iressa was 5.6 months, not significantly different from the 5.1 months for those taking the placebo. Once again, the FDA asked a manufacturer, in this case AstraZeneca, to remove a failed drug from the lung cancer market. And on June 17, 2005, with the exception of patients already receiving the drug who were benefiting from it or those enrolled on clinical trials, once again the manufacturer agreed voluntarily to stop marketing the drug.[20]

But on January 16, 2010, Genentech did not follow the precedent of either Pfizer or AstraZeneca: instead, the company refused to remove Avastin from the market for the treatment of metastatic breast cancer. They exercised their right to request a hearing and submitted the data and information about Avastin's safety and efficacy in metastatic breast cancer intended to justify such a hearing—essentially, the same data and information they had already submitted about the original E2100 study, and the follow-up AVADO, and RIBBON-1 trials for the ODAC meeting I attended in June 2010.[21]

Given the FDA's concerns, and the dearth of additional data to make a case for how Avastin really benefitted women with breast cancer more than it harmed them, why didn't Genentech voluntarily withdraw their drug from the market, too?

The company's chief medical officer and head of global product development, Hal Barron, MD, made the bland statement: "We believe Avastin is an important option for women with this disease and should remain an FDA-approved choice."[22]

Certainly, there were members of Genentech's highly successful research and clinical divisions who believed that statement—employees who genuinely believed they were developing and discovering drugs that made people's lives better. But I suspect it was also an important business decision. Recall that Avastin's use for breast cancer was a $1 billion per year money maker for the company. Exercising their right to a trial would keep the drug on the market for the treatment of breast cancer at least an additional six months—and by my calculation, $500 million in sales was more than enough to justify the legal fees it would cost the company to fight the FDA.

In June 1989 Anthony Fauci—who by then had already served five years as director of the National Institute of Allergy and Infectious Diseases—had an idea for getting drugs to AIDS patients faster. At a meeting in San Francisco, the man we still today call the nation's doctor (figure 7.1) discussed the concept of a "parallel track" protocol.[23]

This was not long after the irascible Larry Kramer had called him a "killer" and "an incompetent idiot" in the *San Francisco Examiner*.

The parallel track would make drugs available not only to HIV-infected patients who could not participate in conventional clinical trials—either because the eligibility criteria for those trials were too restrictive (what Abby Statler, PhD, would demonstrate for leukemia trials almost 30 years later), or because the trials were not open at a nearby medical center—but also to those who had no other treatment options. Trials would still be conducted rigorously, enrolling their "Olympic athletes" and strictly defining drug toxicities and drug efficacy, but other patients could receive the same drug in parallel to the trial without disrupting the progress of the

**Figure 7.1**
Larry Kramer's public health foil and the nation's doctor, Anthony Fauci, MD, director of the National Institute of Allergy and Infectious Disease, 2003. *Source*: Creative Commons, https://commons.wikimedia.org/wiki/File:Anthony_S._Fauci,_M.D.,_NIAID_Director_(26511521050)_(half_length_crop).jpg.

study. The parallel track protocols could be initiated for promising investigational drugs even when the evidence for effectiveness of those drugs was less than what was required for a compassionate-use application.[24]

Yet it took until April 1992 for the parallel track mechanism (which would later be combined with compassionate use and called "expanded access") to become an option for patients suffering from HIV/AIDS.[25] In October of that year d4T (subsequently called stavudine), would be the first drug patients could gain access to through the new mechanism. At the time only AZT and one other drug, Didanosine (DDI), which the FDA approved for AIDS patients who were intolerant of AZT or whose disease had worsened despite AZT, were on the market.

By June 27, 1994, the day stavudine became the fourth drug approved to treat AIDS and HIV infection, approximately 11,000 patients had been treated with the drug, either on clinical trials (which accrued patients rapidly) or using the parallel track mechanism. Scientists' concerns, that the parallel track would undermine the ability of clinical trials to recruit participants, had proven to be unfounded.[26]

Just imagine, though, how many people would have received the drug or another effective AIDS therapy if almost three years hadn't elapsed from the time of Fauci's announcement to the passage of the formal parallel track mechanism.

It had taken years, but part of ACT UP's mission had been fulfilled: the time it took for AIDS patients to access drugs that were still considered experimental, and still awaiting FDA approval, had decreased.

Yet there was still a good deal of risk in this approach. These drugs had to be shown to be *reasonably* safe, and to have *a promise* of effectiveness, for the parallel track to be invoked. As they were still being investigated in clinical trials, drugs that could be obtained under the parallel track mechanism had only been administered to a small percentage of the population of patients with the disease that needed a new treatment. Dangerous side effects could still emerge, and the drug could ultimately be shown to be no better than existing therapies, or no better (and perhaps worse) than nothing at all.

In 2011, at the Avastin hearings, the medical officer from the FDA's Center for Drug Evaluation and Research, Lee Pai-Scherf, MD, walked to the podium to discuss the agency's review of the drug's study results.[27]

We had already seen this information in several formats through the years: the regulatory history for Avastin and its approval in 2004 for metastatic colon cancer; the ODAC meetings in 2007 and 2010; and the many discussions Genentech had with the FDA, which led to conclusions about studies that would support a breast cancer indication. Lee acknowledged that the decision to grant accelerated approval to Avastin for the treatment of metastatic breast cancer in 2008—particularly when ODAC had voted against the approval—was a "difficult" one for the FDA.

We once again saw the progression-free survival graphs from the original E2100, and follow-up AVADO and RIBBON-1 trials, with less and less of an improvement in progression-free survival appearing from the first trial to the follow-up studies between women treated with Avastin, and those who weren't. The overall survival and quality of life graphs for each study continued to have no gap at all between the curves representing women treated with or without Avastin, as they lived equally long and reported no difference in how they felt whether or not they received the drug.[28]

And we once again saw the data about Avastin's side effects: the 20 percent increase in severe toxicities for women treated with Avastin and the increase in death attributed to the drug.[29] Many of us had heard about these high rates and types of toxicity to Avastin so often—across all of these trials and in our previous 2010 ODAC meeting—that they were now akin to the responsive prayer verses you might speak in church or temple, or as if we were reciting some of the 10 plagues:

Avastin—High blood pressure

Avastin—Bleeding

Avastin—Fever

Avastin—Suppression of the immune system

Avastin—Protein leakage into the urine

Avastin—Delayed wound healing

Avastin—Bowel perforation

Avastin—Death in 1 to 2 percent of those treated.

Safety, safety, safety.

In fact, the Avastin label was already forced to include a black box warning for bleeding, delayed wound healing, and bowel perforation.

Black box warnings, which take their name from the black border around the warning information on the label, were first implemented in the 1970s. They are the strictest labeling requirement that the FDA can mandate for prescription drugs, and further emphasize the serious side effects, injuries, or death that can occur with a drug by requiring that the information within the box be printed in boldface with a header that is entirely capitalized.[30]

But critics fault the usefulness of this extreme messaging for several reasons: the lack of physician compliance with the warnings (one study shows that physicians adhered to the warnings only 0.3 to 50 percent of the time); concern that the black boxes may inappropriately discourage patients from taking their medications; the FDA's lack of transparency regarding the criteria it uses to issue a black box warning requirement; and the likelihood that drugs coming to market quickly (such as those receiving accelerated approval) will lack black-box warnings until later, after more patients have been exposed to the drug.[31]

Dr. Pai-Scherf concluded her presentation deriding the AVADO and RIBBON-1 trials:

> The confirmatory studies . . . failed to verify clinical benefit in patients with metastatic breast cancer.
>
> They failed to substantiate the magnitude of progression-free survival in E2100.
>
> They failed to show any improvement in overall survival. . . .
>
> Avastin, in combination with chemotherapy has a modest effect on progression-free survival, balanced against its risks of serious and life-threatening toxicities.[32]

As she left the podium there was silence save for the clicking of cameras and the uncomfortable shuffling of people in their seats. The FDA appeared to be taking no prisoners.

What if, instead of taking the risks posed with unproven therapies under the parallel track mechanism proposed by Fauci, there was a way to get safe and effective drugs approved by the FDA at an accelerated pace, faster than the 8 to 10 years that was the standard at the time? Even if that method was based on a *surrogate marker* of efficacy—such as an improvement in the immune system in people with AIDS—that was reasonably likely to predict the drug's hoped-for benefit of improving survival?

The FDA was hesitant. It did seem logical that a surrogate marker like a blood test that measured improved immune function could reasonably predict prevention of those opportunistic infections that killed AIDS patients, such as PCP and CMV, and in turn lead to the hoped-for benefit of living longer. But how sure could they be that the benefit seen in some wouldn't be offset by serious risks in others, including death, as a result of the drug's side effects?

AIDS activists were not hesitant, and they didn't relent. In May 1990, a thousand ACT UP members protested at the National Institutes of Health for more clinical research trials of drugs to treat AIDS, setting off colored smoke bombs and deriding Fauci, who had done so much to advance their cause, by name.[33]

Fauci would comment later, at the time of Kramer's death, that the name calling and public castigation by Kramer wasn't personal. The two men respected each other, considered one another friends; and at one point, Fauci even became Kramer's doctor.[34]

But in 1990, again, the protests worked.

Before long, patient advocates were invited to join AIDS Clinical Trial Group committees, sitting shoulder-to-shoulder with the scientists designing the clinical trials.[35] From their perspective, many AIDS patients wanted new drugs regardless of the risks, because they wouldn't live long enough to see if a surrogate marker translated to a hoped-for-benefit anyway. Why not just let them take their chances on the drug? They were willing to accept more risk than some previous patient groups, because their disease was so deadly. Emphasizing their risk tolerance, some had even already joined black-market buying clubs (depicted in the Oscar-winning movie *Dallas Buyer's Club*) or had started to cook medicine for themselves.[36]

But the FDA has to think about the safety, safety, safety (and the efficacy) of a drug in the entire US population. What if that quickly approved drug (well, quickly by FDA standards—it still took years) turned out to be a dog? Would the FDA then have the authority to pull the drug from the market?

By January 1992, public and political pressure for the FDA to accelerate the drug development and approval process for people with life threatening diseases had reached a fevered pitch. Groups like ACT UP staged thousands of demonstrations from 1987 through 1996. Congress started looking into allegations of a "drug lag" at the FDA. Although the FDA continued to claim it was under-resourced to meet the nation's need for *new and guaranteed safe drugs* to be approved for marketing, the agency responded by amending its internal prioritization scheme. It gave drugs indicated for the treatment of AIDS or HIV-related disease an "AA" designation—its top category. First in line.

But while the FDA recognized the importance of drugs to treat AIDS, it still had to get them through their regulatory processes faster.

In 1992 Congress passed the Prescription Drug User Fee Act (PDUFA), legislation that could finally deliver on hastening the pace of approval and giving the FDA the funding it needed to make that process viable. PDUFA established a system of user fees, to be paid for by the pharmaceutical manufacturer when it applied for the New Drug Application (NDA), which the FDA required before considering a drug for marketing approval. In return, the FDA committed to a timetable for drug approval that would be quicker than before, and it created the accelerated approval mechanism for qualifying drugs.[37]

To be eligible for accelerated approval, a drug was required to meet three criteria; each are enumerated below, with explanatory text interspersed between no. 2 and no. 3.[38] See the summary of these criteria in table 7.1:

1. It had to treat a serious condition, defined by the FDA as:

   a disease or condition associated with morbidity [illness] that has substantial impact on day-to-day functioning. Short-lived and self-limiting morbidity [*e.g., pain from slamming your thumb in a car door*] will usually not be sufficient, but the morbidity need not be irreversible if it is persistent or recurrent [*e.g., recurrent, opportunistic infections such as PCP associated with HIV*]. Whether a disease or condition is serious is a matter of clinical judgment, based on its impact on such factors as survival, day-to-day functioning, or the likelihood that the disease, if left untreated, will progress from a less severe condition to a more serious one [*e.g., an HIV infection progressing to full-blown AIDS; or less advanced breast cancer progressing to metastatic breast cancer*].

2. It had to provide a meaningful advantage over available therapy. (*Recognize that these are two criteria rolled into one.*)

   *Meaningful advantage* can be seen differently through the eyes of the patient, the treating physician, the scientific investigator, or the drug manufacturer. A patient may find it meaningful that a new

**Table 7.1**
Requirements for Accelerated Approval

To qualify for accelerated approval, a drug has to meet the following three criteria:

1. It must treat a serious medical condition that has an impact on day-to-day functioning.
2. It must provide a meaningful advantage over available therapy.
3. It must demonstrate an effect on a surrogate endpoint that is reasonably likely to predict a clinically meaningful benefit.

drug does not cause nausea while visiting with his or her grand-children. A treating physician may find meaning in laboratory val-ues indicating improved immune system function, which may lower that patient's risk of developing a pneumonia. A scientific investigator may attribute a meaningful advantage to reduction in HIV viral load or tumor shrinkage. A drug manufacturer, with an eye toward drug approval, may give meaning to more subtle improvements in drug side effects or patient outcomes. The FDA is notoriously cagey in clari-fying this criterion, but generally defaults to "lives longer or lives better."

*Available therapy* refers to a drug already approved or licensed in the United States for the same indication being considered for the new drug, when the already approved drug is considered the current standard of care for the indication. It would thus not be considered appropriate to compare a new agent developed in the 2020s, let's say our mice lab investigator's Tumorminimab, to Hamlin's Wizard Oil from the nineteenth century.

3. It had to demonstrate an effect on a surrogate endpoint that is reasonably likely to predict clinical benefit, or on a clinical endpoint that can be measured earlier than irreversible morbid-ity (illness) or mortality—what's called an intermediate clinical endpoint.

This is probably the most complicated, and controversial aspect of accelerated approval.

*Clinical benefit*, in the eyes of the FDA, often boils down to *lives longer* or *lives better*. But what counts as a surrogate endpoint that can lead to a clinically meaningful outcome, but may not itself be immediately beneficial to a patient with a given disease?

For a person who has HIV/AIDS, a drug that lessens the viral load and improves the immune system (as measured by what's called a CD4 count) would not be experienced by that person as an immedi-ate benefit—he or she wouldn't necessarily feel any better because the amount of virus that can actively be measured in his or her blood stream decreased by 75 percent, or the CD4 count rose by 10 percent.

But a study conducted through the Veterans Affairs Cooperative Group in 270 HIV+ patients showed that those who achieved these viral load and CD4 count goals reduced their chances of dying by more than half.[39]

These patients *lived longer*. And in a clinical trial these surrogate endpoints of viral load and CD4 counts could be measured sooner than it would be possible to assess whether patients lived longer.

In fact, improvements in immune function and viral load could be seen, on average, in the first month or two of therapy. So a clinical trial of a new drug to treat HIV patients—such as stavudine, or d4T—with a surrogate endpoint of viral load reduction and CD4 count improvement could potentially be completed within a year or two. If the same study had survival as its endpoint—and on average, HIV patients at this time lived for four to eight years—the study may have taken a decade to determine whether or not the drug's benefits were meaningful.

For a person with a bloodstream infected by *staphylococcus aureus* or a pneumonia caused by *mycobacterium tuberculosis*, elimination of the *staph* infection from the bloodstream or of tuberculosis from the sputum are both reasonably likely to predict clinical resolution of both infections—either of which could cause *irreversible morbidity*, and possible *mortality*.

A pharmaceutical company that has developed a new antibiotic could study the drug in patients with either of these infections and attempt to gain FDA approval under the accelerated mechanism using these surrogate endpoints, without demonstrating complete resolution of the infections (which, for tuberculosis, could take a year or more), provided the other requirements of accelerated approval (treating serious conditions and demonstrating a meaningful advantage over available therapy) are satisfied.

As antibiotics are already used to treat *staph* infections and tuberculosis, one approach would be to design a study for patients with infections that are *resistant* to available antibiotics, thus defining a medical need for which existing therapies are inadequate.

Another medical condition for which surrogate endpoints are commonly used is cancer. Cancer is often easy to justify as being serious, as many cancers affect day-to-day function and can cause an early death. Additionally, as the cure rate for many cancers is nowhere near 100 percent, there are opportunities to demonstrate that available therapies are not cutting the mustard and thus can be improved upon.

It is particularly appealing to consider surrogate endpoints for so-called slow-growing cancers (acknowledging, of course, that cancer often thumbs its nose at any of our attempts to typify its course in an individual person).

Heraleen Broome, the 74-year-old woman who first approached the microphone at the FDA Avastin meeting in June 2011, was originally diagnosed with her breast cancer more than 10 years before that meeting. Almost by definition, her particular breast cancer could be considered slow-growing. Another slow-growing cancer is chronic myeloid leukemia.

A man in his 50s diagnosed today with chronic myeloid leukemia (CML) has a plethora of drugs—all of which are pills—to choose from for his initial therapy. Any one of these—imatinib, nilotinib, dasatinib, bosutinib, ponatinib—has a high likelihood not only of causing his leukemia to go into remission, but also of allowing him to enjoy a lifespan almost equivalent to any other man in his 50s.[40]

As if he never had a leukemia diagnosis at all.

Assuming he will live another 25 years, designing a trial today of a drug for CML based on whether or not that drug improves his survival would slow drug development for this type of leukemia to approximately the pace of natural human evolution!

Three or four decades ago, in the same era as the HIV pandemic, CML was just as deadly as AIDS, though.

CML is typified by a genetic mutation that a person acquires randomly involving chromosomes 9 and 22. The genetic basis for CML was first discovered in 1960 by a team of researchers, Peter Nowell and David Hungerford, in patients admitted to Philadelphia General Hospital with this type of leukemia. Consequently, it is referred to as the *Philadelphia chromosome*.[41]

Prior to the current millennium, the average survival for a person diagnosed with CML was about three-and-a-half years. The best available therapy was the drug interferon, which led to remissions in fewer than 10 percent of people and had awful side effects, even leading some to commit suicide rather than continue on the drug.[42]

Around the time when the accelerated approval regulations were codified, another scientist, Brian Druker, who had a laboratory at Oregon Health Sciences University, was working on a new type of drug to combat CML, called imatinib (later known as, Gleevec—one of those TKIs, or tyrosine kinase inhibitors). It actually targeted the Philadelphia chromosome genetic abnormality, worked incredibly well in mice, and had a dramatic effect in the first 83 people in whom the drug was tested in the late 1990s: in 98 percent of CML patients on that first trial, it restored their previously devastated blood counts (their red blood cells, white blood cells, and platelets) to normal, and even eliminated the Philadelphia chromosome—the root of the evil in CML—in almost one-third.[43]

Another study enrolled 532 CML patients who had previously been treated with interferon and showed similar impressive results for the wunderkind imatinib, with almost all patients enrolled on the trial achieving normal blood counts, and almost one-third having eradication of the Philadelphia chromosome. Neither study compared treatment with imatinib to interferon directly.[44]

But the stage was set to consider accelerated approval: CML was a serious condition that profoundly affected the survival of a person suffering from it; the standard therapy for that condition (interferon) was inadequate; and it had a measurable surrogate endpoint (the Philadelphia chromosome), the elimination of which could reasonably translate to the clinically meaningful benefit of improved survival.

In May 2001, considering the results of those clinical trials, the FDA granted accelerated approval to Gleevec. The agency based the decision not on survival but on elimination of the Philadelphia chromosome compared to what interferon has been able to achieve in the past, and on Gleevec's vastly superior side-effect profile.[45]

In a remarkable show of efficiency, the entire FDA review process took just 72 days—at the time, the fastest approval ever for a cancer drug.

CML is considered a "liquid tumor"—born and bred in the bone marrow, and circulating in the blood stream, but rarely invading solid organs.

Most cancers, though, like breast cancer, originate in an organ and grow in an unfettered fashion, creating a quickly expanding mass of cells that can cause pain, bleeding, or a lump. These symptoms are what often cause a person to seek medical attention and the eventual diagnosis of the "solid" cancer: first by detection, using either physical examination or a radiographic test such as an X-ray or computerized tomography (CT) scan; and then by a biopsy of the mass, when a pathologist examines the tissue under a microscope to identify what type of cancer is growing uncontrollably.

Once cancer treatment is started, the efficacy of that treatment is measured using follow-up radiographic tests, most commonly CT scans—as happened with my mom's lung cancer after she had surgery to remove it. Those scans can measure whether the cancer masses have shrunk from the surgery, radiation therapy, or chemotherapy used to treat the cancer; and if so, by how much. If the cancer has been eliminated entirely, the scans can detect whether it recurs.

When a tumor shrinks, it is referred to as a *response*, with specific criteria used across tumor types to standardize what that word really means. A tumor that has not changed in size is called *stable*, and a cancer that grows is unfortunately labeled *progressive*.

But how much shrinkage counts as a response? Is 5 percent enough? 10 percent?

And what counts as progressive cancer, which often means cancer that is resistant to chemotherapy, and is terrible news for the afflicted person? Should I tell a woman with 5 percent growth of her breast cancer mass—like one of the women treated on the Avastin trials—that it has progressed (meaning gotten worse) and we should stop treating her with chemotherapy because it is ineffective? Or does that assessment fall within the error of the CT scan technology (or the radiologist or oncologist interpreting the scan), and she actually has a cancer that is stable—it has neither improved, nor gotten worse. What about a 10 percent growth?

The system developed to standardize the assessment of tumor response and to eliminate the speculation about what constitutes response or progression, published in 2000, is called RECIST: Response Evaluation Criteria In Solid Tumors. Using this guidance, when a person is first diagnosed with cancer, and might have many cancer masses, for example in the lungs or the abdomen, the oncologist identifies *target lesions*—no more than five cancer masses to follow over time to determine if a therapy is effective.[46]

If the masses disappear entirely, this is called a *complete response*.

A decrease in size by at least 30 percent without disappearance is a *partial response*.

An increase in size by 20 percent or more constitutes *progressive disease*.

None of the above? *Stable disease*. So an increase or decrease in tumor size of 10 percent means the cancer isn't getting better or worse.[47]

Standardized response criteria for solid tumors have been important on so many levels: They gave a framework, and guidance, for evaluating the patients sitting in cancer center infusion chairs, and for knowing what to tell them about the success of the treatments they have been receiving. Results from one clinical trial of a cancer drug could be compared to results from another trial because both studies would use the same response definitions, allowing chemo apples to be compared to chemo apples. And regulatory agencies, like the FDA, could use those standardized response definitions to make decisions about the efficacy of a proposed new drug when compared to established drugs.

Response, and loss of response, could then be used as surrogate endpoints for accelerated approval.

This makes intuitive sense. Somebody who has a breast cancer that shrinks when treated with a drug like Avastin should have a reasonable likelihood of living longer than someone who has a cancer that shrugs off the chemo and continues to grow at a blistering speed: tumor *response* is often a good surrogate for improved survival, while tumor *progression* is a surrogate for worse overall survival.

Similarly, it seems logical that the longer a person has a breast cancer that does not worsen—let's say it has either responded to Avastin or remained stable—the more reasonably likely that person will live longer: a period of time called *progression-free survival*, which can also be used as a surrogate for the clinically meaningful overall survival.[48]

*Seems* logical. Makes sense. But unfortunately, cancer is a monster— a malignant Golem—and rejects our attempts at conventional wisdom.

Time and again clinical trials in older adults with acute myeloid leukemia (people like Jimmy Petrarcha, for whom the cancer was particularly nasty and recalcitrant to therapies), have shown that improvements in response rates—even complete response, the best of the best, and even a doubling of the response rates for a new drug approach versus the standard—lead to no differences in overall survival.

One such study was conducted in the United Kingdom and led by Alan Burnett, MD, at the time of Cardiff University, who has made a career of rigorously studying new treatment approaches in leukemia. In it, 406 patients with acute myeloid leukemia were randomized to receive either low-dose, standard chemotherapy, or a new drug called clofarabine, which had led to high response rates in patients treated in earlier studies. Sure enough, 22 percent of patients treated with clofarabine had a complete response, compared to only 12 percent of those treated with the low-dose chemotherapy. The overall response (complete and partial responses) was 38 percent for clofarabine versus just 19 percent for low-dose chemo. The overall survival at two years following study entry: 13 percent for patients treated with either drug. No difference.[49]

Why?

Patients treated with the low-dose chemotherapy who did not have a response actually lived longer than patients treated with clofarabine who did not have a response. Low-dose chemo patients were also less likely to die as a result of side effects to the drug. These two factors cancelled out any benefits that may have accrued to the higher response rate for the clofarabine.

The opposite can also occur. Since 2010 a number of cancers, particularly melanomas, lung cancer, and certain lymphomas, have been treated by a new class of drugs called checkpoint inhibitors—a type of immunotherapy. These harness the body's own immune system to attack the cancer, leading to remarkable improvements in overall survival in people who have advanced stages of these conditions.

One classic study, led by F. Stephen Hodi, MD, of the Dana-Farber Cancer Institute in Boston, randomized 676 patients with advanced melanoma to receive the checkpoint inhibitor ipilimumab, heralded as one of the greatest advances in melanoma treatment perhaps ever, or to receive another therapy.[50]

The complete response rate to the ipilimumab was just 0.6 percent: 3 patients out of 540 treated. The complete plus partial response rate rose to a whopping 7 percent.

Yet the average overall survival was 10 months for those treated with ipilimumab, compared to only 6.4 months for those treated with the other therapy, for a 32 percent reduction in risk of death. It turns out that response definitions—even those clearly defined by the RECIST criteria—don't work very well for this class of drugs, probably because they cause inflammation of tumors as they work. These tumors may enlarge on the CT scans used to determine whether a patient is responding to a drug as a result of that inflammation, tricking response assessments and even making it appear that a person's tumor is progressing when it is actually shrinking! For these patients, using response or progression-free survival for accelerated approval would undermine the purpose of the program. And in fact, based on these "lives longer" data, ipilimumab received full approval from the FDA to treat melanoma in March 2011.

Even the FDA acknowledges that "whether an endpoint is reasonably likely to predict clinical benefit is a matter of judgment."[51]

And even the FDA acknowledges that interpretations of cancer progression using CT scans may differ between a local site—by the oncologist or radiologist where a patient is getting treated—and central review of the same CT scan by a panel of experts almost one-third of the time.

Almost one-third of the time a patient's doctor says that the cancer has progressed, using these RECIST criteria, when other doctors say it hasn't, or vice-versa.

And these are the data used to determine if a surrogate marker to predict a clinically meaningful benefit, such as tumor progression or progression-free survival, is good enough to assume that patients will eventually live longer and should receive that drug in an accelerated time frame.

A drug like Avastin.

Since its inception in 1992, the FDA's accelerated approval mechanism was used to grant more than 275 marketing approvals for drugs (with some drugs receiving approval for multiple indications).[52] The very first, in June 1992, was zalcitabine, used in combination with AZT to treat patients with advanced HIV infection and significant deterioration in their health and/or immune system. The following year the antibiotic clarithromycin took advantage of this new regulatory mechanism for the treatment of mycobacterial infections—one of the opportunistic infections to which people with more advanced HIV were susceptible. The year after that, in 1994, stavudine (d4T—the drug that demonstrated the surrogate endpoint of viral load reduction and CD4-count improvement) received accelerated approval for HIV patients with advanced disease. And in 1995, five drugs were approved: three for HIV or complications of the virus, and for the first time two for cancer; Casodex for advanced prostate cancer; and zinecard to prevent heart failure from certain types of chemotherapy.[53]

From 1993 to 1995, 257,000 people in the United States were diagnosed with AIDS. Whereas previously the mortality rate had been 90 percent or higher, now 62 percent died.[54] New drugs, with better efficacy and fewer side effects, were getting to people with HIV/AIDS faster, and they were starting to have an impact on meaningful outcomes, like survival. And this could actually be seen on a population level.

AIDS activists desperately fought over the years for a treatment—any treatment—to combat this terrible disease that had laid waste to a generation, but use of the accelerated approval mechanism had been commandeered for the first time by pharmaceutical companies making drugs to treat the far vaster—and far more lucrative—cancer patient population.

In 1996, of the eight drugs receiving accelerated approval, four had a label directed to HIV or complications of AIDS and three were for cancer. By 1999 the ratio had shifted, with five drugs focusing on cancer or cancer prevention, and only one—Agenerase—on HIV. From that point through 2008, cancer drugs received accelerated approval at a ratio of three-to-one compared to drugs for HIV/AIDS.[55]

In 2008, the drug Etravirine was approved for the treatment of patients with HIV that was resistant to other HIV medications. It would be the last HIV medicine approved under the accelerated mechanism at the FDA until May 2020 when pomalidomide—a thalidomide derivative—was approved for that cancer associated with HIV, Kaposi's sarcoma.[56] That same year, in 2008, four drugs were approved for oncology indications, including one for lung cancer, another for a soft tissue cancer, one for leukemia, and another for breast cancer.[57]

The one for breast cancer, of course, was Avastin.

In total, for the three trials that we were considering at the 2011 Avastin hearings and across two additional trials, more than 3,500 women had been enrolled in studies before and after the 2008 accelerated approval to try to determine whether Avastin provided them, and future women with breast cancer, any benefit over being treated with just chemotherapy alone.

That number was breathtaking: 3,500 women who volunteered their time, who endured side effects, and who sometimes died to see if this new, exciting drug, which came in a vial decorated with a purple and teal label and was introduced at the dawn of a new millennium, worked better than chemotherapy that came of age in the twentieth century. Some enrolled on the trials for altruistic reasons, to help other women with breast cancer; some wanted to help themselves; some were maintaining their own hope; and some wanted to advance medical science.

Had they lived longer because they participated in those trials? Had they lived better?

What about the tens of thousands of women who followed them, who received Avastin as part of what had become a standard of care for metastatic breast cancer after its 2008 approval by the FDA?

Abigail Brandel, from the FDA's Office of Chief Counsel, came to the podium to explain the legal context for the hearing, taking us all through the particulars of the Public Health Service Act and the federal Food, Drug, and Cosmetic Act, under which the accelerated approval mechanism fell. The explanation sounded to me like an opening argument a lawyer might proffer to a jury in a criminal case. She reminded us that accelerated approval embodied "a delicate balance of two compelling and sometimes competing public health interests. The first . . . in providing patients with access to promising new therapies as soon as possible. . . . The tradeoff . . . however, was and is uncertainty about whether a drug's clinical benefit will be verified in the post-approval studies."[58]

If those studies didn't verify a drug's benefit, or the drug is not shown to be safe or effective, she offered an unofficial flipside to the coin of accelerated approval:

Accelerated withdrawal.

"It's a two-way street," she concluded.

> The balance of approval and withdrawal are needed to make
> the program work, and thereby protect patients and the public
> health. . . . If a post approval study fails to verify the drug's clinical
> benefit, or other evidence demonstrates that the drug is not shown
> to be safe or effective, [it is] grounds for withdrawal.

And then came Brandel's hard close: "Both of these criteria are met here. The legal standard for withdrawal has been met."[59]

By 2009, and for the next decade, medications that treated HIV or complications from the virus disappeared entirely from the list of drugs that received accelerated approval, which was now almost completely dominated by cancer therapies. By the end of that decade, cancer indications accounted for 17 out of 21 accelerated approvals in 2017; 16 of 18 approvals in 2018; 11 of 14 approvals in 2019; and 40 of 44 approvals (some involving one drug for multiple indications) in 2020.[60]

From the standpoint of accelerated approval, cancer was king.

A critical aspect of the accelerated approval program is the requirement for a post-marketing confirmatory trial to "verify and describe the anticipated effect on irreversible morbidity or mortality," and for this trial to be completed in a timely fashion. In other words, when a drug receives accelerated approval based on a surrogate marker of efficacy (such as a response rate) that is reasonably likely to translate to a clinically meaningful benefit (such as overall survival), the FDA wants to then see a confirmatory trial demonstrating that clinically meaningful benefit, or at least one that verifies the degree of improvement shown by the initial surrogate marker, to make sure it wasn't a fluke.

Gleevec—imatinib—had received accelerated approval based on the surrogate marker of elimination of the Philadelphia chromosome in almost one-third of patients with CML. The confirmatory, Phase 3 study for Gleevec, reported in March 2003, randomized over 1,100 CML patients to receive Gleevec or interferon combined with a chemotherapy, cytarabine. The results were equally dramatic as the initial studies that led to the drug's accelerated approval: After a year and a half of follow-up, 95 percent of patients treated with Gleevec had normalization of their blood counts, compared to 55 percent of those treated with interferon and cytarabine; 85 percent had some degree of eradication of their Philadelphia chromosome with Gleevec, compared to 22 percent with interferon and cytarabine. And side effects were again much more tolerable.

Based on the results of this study, Gleevec was granted full approval by the FDA in December 2003.[61]

Stavudine had received accelerated approval in 1994 for HIV patients based on reductions in viral load and improvements in the CD4 measure of the immune system. It gained full approval in December 1995, when a randomized study of 822 HIV-positive patients confirmed those initial benefits and showed a 15 percent reduction in HIV progression and 26 percent reduction in death, compared to patients treated with AZT.[62]

What happens, though, when a manufacturer is not able to actually confirm the initial benefit that led to accelerated approval, or fails to complete such a confirmatory trial?

Well, then the FDA can—and will—exercise its authority to withdraw that marketing approval. Just as Abigail Brandel promised.

# 8

# The FDA Makes Its Case

*I would not like them here or there.*
*I would not like them anywhere.*
                    —Dr. Seuss, *Green Eggs and Ham*, 1960

Next up for the agency at the 2011 hearings was Patricia Keegan, MD (figure 8.1), who at the time was the director of the Division of Biologic Oncology Products in the Center for Drug Evaluation and Research (CDER). She had been at the FDA since 1990, having spent the three years prior to that as an assistant professor at the University of North Carolina at Chapel Hill.

Dr. Keegan, the daughter of a Navy man and the second eldest of seven girls in her family, lived in different areas of the country before settling in Chicago, and remained in Illinois during her undergraduate and medical schools days. Her decision to pursue a career in medicine was influenced by her mother, in part because she nurtured Keegan's childhood interest in science books, and in part because she always told her daughters how well her female pediatrician—a rarity at the time—had cared for her after she contracted polio as an adolescent.

**Figure 8.1**
Patricia Keegan, MD, director of the Division of Biologic Oncology Products in the Center for Drug Evaluation and Research (CDER), 2012. *Source*: FDA photo by Michael J. Ermarth, https://commons.wikimedia.org/wiki/File:Patricia_Keegan,_M.D._ (8191494200).jpg.

Dr. Keegan would go on to become associate director for policy in the FDA's Oncology Center for Excellence in 2019. Her open, intelligent demeanor and no-nonsense approach to assessing the drug products under investigation during her tenure at the FDA seem a natural complement to the values and experience of working with a "down-to-earth" mentor in the oncology department during her residency.[1] As I was living in Cleveland at the time, I also wondered if her pragmatic approach reflected her Midwest upbringing.

During this hearing Keegan's job was to address four of Genentech's contentions that, if substantiated, should enable Avastin to stay on the market for its breast cancer indication:[2]

1. That the company should be allowed to conduct additional trials to try and demonstrate the same degree of efficacy for Avastin as in the original, E2100 trial;

2. That a new trial would finally pair Avastin with the right chemotherapy "partner" to establish its true efficacy.

3. That the trials it had conducted *were* actually successful, in that they showed an improvement in progression-free survival for women receiving Avastin, but that the FDA had thrown Genentech a curveball by changing how they measured success.

4. And, that the FDA had overstated Avastin's safety problems.

Dr. Keegan started by citing the multiple times the FDA had communicated with Genentech, in 2004, 2007, and 2008, to inform the company that the agency would be focusing on the *magnitude* of the progression-free survival benefit for women treated with Avastin. In other words, the FDA wanted to ensure that progression-free survival was statistically improved for women taking the drug *and* that the duration of survival improved by many months—like in the original E2100 trial—before it determined whether Avastin provided an actual clinical benefit to women: meaning, they lived longer or lived better.[3]

Why focus on magnitude of the difference in progression-free survival rather than on whether or not Avastin led to a statistically significant difference? A large enough study can make very small differences in efficacy seem significant. For example, a trial enrolling 1,000 woman with breast cancer would be able to show an improvement in efficacy of a study drug over standard therapy of 5 percent. A trial enrolling over 6,000 women could show an efficacy difference of as little as 2 percent! Neither of these, however, would likely represent a difference that was clinically meaningful to the majority of women receiving the drug, despite the statistical difference in drug efficacy.

A trial enrolling just 200 women, though, could miss identifying a drug that worked 10 percent better. Designing an appropriately sized trial that will demonstrate a difference in efficacy of one drug over another, and be meaningful to patients, requires a delicate (and judicious) balancing act. Keegan acknowledged that companies often gamed the statistics by designing very large trials to show miniscule differences in efficacy that would likely be irrelevant to patients.

"To be clear," she said, "CDER did not advise Genentech that *any* effect on progression-free survival, regardless of its magnitude, would be sufficient to demonstrate clinical benefit."[4]

She then very quickly dismissed Genentech's assertion that the FDA had changed the rules on them for what measure of efficacy would be acceptable for approval, by using Genentech's own presentation, made back in 2007, against them.

First, she quoted a breast cancer expert who spoke on behalf of Genentech at that first 2007 ODAC meeting when he stated that, for progression-free survival to equal benefit, for it to be meaningful, it had to be substantial in its magnitude.[5]

A handful of weeks wouldn't cut it.

Then, she showed a damning slide from the company's 2008 submission of its Avastin data to the FDA in which the results that Genentech experts thought showed a promising early trend in the AVADO trial—one of the two trials that was supposed to confirm Avastin's benefit, in which Avastin appeared to be improving overall survival in women who received the drug—were circled in red.[6] It was as if Genentech was agreeing with the FDA that progression-free survival in and of itself was not a meaningful endpoint—it only became meaningful if it *predicted that* (as a surrogate endpoint) women actually lived longer.

Recall, though, the AVADO trial enrolled its last participant in October 2007, just a few months earlier than that 2008 FDA submission. This trend for an improvement in overall survival for those receiving Avastin disappeared with additional follow-up, of course, and over time even slightly favored women who *didn't* receive Avastin in the study.

This also emphasized a couple of core caveats in the interpretation of early data coming from clinical trials—the pitfalls for data safety monitoring boards: First, such data might be incomplete—considering, for example, that not all centers where the trial was being conducted around the world had collected or submitted information about women participating in the trial to Genentech (including whether they were alive or dead). And second, because only a small number of "events" had occurred so soon after the trial had enrolled its last participant—an event, in this case, was defined as a woman dying—the results were extremely volatile; they could change markedly after a majority of "events" had occurred.[7] Think of trying to predict the outcome of an election with only 10 percent of precincts reporting.

As these technical terms were bandied about during the presentations that day—*subjects, participants, events, Kaplan-Meier curves, hazard ratios*—I constantly reminded myself that these weren't data points, or abstract statistical conclusions: these were women dealt a terrible hand of health cards in developing advanced breast cancer who were either living or dying. Some of them where in the audience at that very moment.

Genentech took issue with how the FDA was defining a drug's success. Dr. Keegan showed a slide of an advertisement for Avastin developed by Genentech that highlighted the exact same definition of success.[8]

Genentech felt that Avastin worked better than everyone thought, it just hadn't yet been paired with the right chemotherapy drug to show how wonderful it was. Dr. Keegan blasted that claim by emphasizing not only the lack of data developed pre-clinically (before the drug ever reached human trials) but also the lack of data from human trials showing that partner chemotherapies either helped, or hindered, Avastin's efficacy. Yet another clinical trial wouldn't clarify this or any of the other issues raised by the company or by the FDA.[9]

Finally, Genentech accused the FDA of overstating Avastin's safety risks. In my opinion—and given the FDA's sensitivity to its role in protecting the health of the public—this was a risky claim for the company to make. The bedrock of the FDA's existence, and indeed the precipitant for every major change in its regulatory history, has been a safety event in which tragic consequences of a drug's use had not been prevented.

Dr. Keegan cited Avastin's "serious and potentially fatal risks," including bleeding, bowel perforation, kidney injury, and severe hypertension. She mentioned milder toxicities, such as minor bleeding, neuropathies, and diarrhea. She cited a number of studies showing that the toxicities submitted to the FDA by Genentech may actually *underestimate* the true side effect profile of Avastin. She confirmed that the portion of the product label describing the "serious, irreversible, and life-threatening toxicities" caused by Avastin was accurate.[10]

Then, Dr. Keegan did something I had never before seen an FDA representative do at such a formal proceeding: she countered the stories we had heard during the open mike session with other patient stories:

> This morning we have heard from patients and their families describing how they feel they have benefited from Avastin. However, there are other voices that need to be heard. Those voices include a 53-year-old woman with metastatic breast cancer who suffered severe abdominal pain caused by gastrointestinal perforation that led to her death after 4 doses of Avastin; or an asymptomatic 33-year-old woman with metastatic breast cancer who suffered a massive fatal pulmonary hemorrhage after 11 doses of Avastin.[11]

These stories were moving, too. Keegan's entry into medicine was grounded in her own mother's experiences with polio. I suspected that, even in her role at the FDA, she thought a lot about individual patients. She concluded with a devastating assessment:

> Despite the hopes of everyone inside and outside this room, after conducting three trials enrolling more than 2,400 women receiving first-line treatment for metastatic breast cancer, there is no evidence that Avastin saves or extends lives.[12]

Again, the room was quiet as Dr. Keegan sat down, the solemnity of the trial interrupted only by a stray cough and some quiet murmuring.

The final presenter from the FDA was John Jenkins, MD, the director of the Office of New Drugs in the Center for Drug Evaluation and Research. Like Dr. Keegan, Dr. Jenkins had been at the FDA for about 20 years at the time of the hearings. But he would retire from the agency five years later, amid some controversy, after expressing his concern about drugs being considered for and receiving accelerated reviews, which could compromise the FDA's thorough evaluation of their safety, and drugs being considered for a special, new *breakthrough* designation when early signals of their efficacy were modest at best.[13] I wonder now how much the Avastin hearings influenced his future views on accelerated regulatory pathways and led to his decision to leave the FDA.

Jenkins again reviewed the trials that had been conducted in women with advanced breast cancer and the regulatory decisions that had been made along the way. Then he focused on the "rules" of accelerated approval. As of the date of the Avastin hearing, June 28, 2011, 49 cancer drugs had received accelerated approval in the history of the program. Clinical benefit had been confirmed in the majority of those drugs in subsequent trials, and where it hadn't, sponsors had *voluntarily* withdrawn the drugs or indications.[14]

Genentech was the only company that had not.

Failure to confirm benefit for a drug that had received accelerated approval, Dr. Jenkins emphasized, did not indicate a failure of the accelerated approval pathway:

> Rather, it is evidence that CDER is striking the right balance in making promising drugs available to patients while ensuring confirmation of clinical benefit following approval.[15]

He argued that a failed confirmatory trial, and withdrawal of drugs from the market, *actually* showed that the system was working. Pulling drugs with modest or no efficacy, but with substantial toxicities, was in fact how the FDA came into being. Dr. Jenkins finished by saying:

> In the end, CDER's decision must be based on the available scientific data from adequate and well-controlled trials. These data inform our assessment of the benefit-risk of the drug for the population of patients with breast cancer. That is our obligation under the law, and we take that obligation and our public health mission very seriously.[16]

With that, CDER and the FDA concluded its presentation, and we broke for lunch. That afternoon, Genentech would question the FDA presenters as the company started to make its case that Avastin should remain on the market for the treatment of breast cancer.

The room filled with noise as audience members stood and made a beeline for the tiny snack shop, which was quickly overwhelmed. The other members of ODAC and I lingered to collect our thoughts and wait for the lunch line to die down a bit; we would grab a sandwich and take it to the room reserved for our use during the breaks. The government did not provide us with food during the trial, the same as when Rick Pazdur conducted his interview with me; we purchased our own, just like other attendees at the proceedings.

We were given strict instructions to avoid discussions of the meeting or our impressions of what we had just heard with anyone, including each other, during the breaks.

I got up from the ODAC table and walked outside the Great Room with Natalie Compagni-Portis, ODAC's patient representative, and Ralph Freedman, the gynecologic oncologist. As we headed over to the lunch lines, we wanted desperately to talk about the FDA's presentation, to process the information and decompress from the heightened emotions of the morning. But we knew we shouldn't, and instead stood together in mostly awkward silence.

"Well, that was certainly interesting," Ralph eventually commented. Natalie and I chuckled at this understatement as our eyes met. Ralph laughed too. There was so much more to say.

I glanced around at the people waiting in the line, the ropes separating us from those in the audience now gone. There were a couple of reporters, and others I assumed were players in the finance sector. Nobody from Genentech was there, though. The company had reserved space in another part of the building where their own catered lunch would be served in what essentially had been turned into a war room. There they would spend the hour reviewing the points the FDA had just made, formulating their response, selecting appropriate slides, and gathering supporting data.

Then I saw two women, also waiting in line, who had bravely told their stories to us earlier in the morning. They stood next to each other and leaned close to chat, one talking, the other nodding. Perhaps they were friends prior to the day's events, or maybe new friends, bonded by a terrible disease and the drug being used to treat it. One woman glanced up and saw me staring, and the other followed her gaze. I smiled at them, and they started to smile back reflexively until spotting the name badge clipped to my sportscoat pocket. It identified me as a member of ODAC.

Their smiles slowly dissolved into expressions that were hard to read: Neutral? Angry? Scared? I couldn't tell. But I knew those looks were not warm. Not the same looks I received from my own patients. Not looks that conveyed trust in the people or the process of making decisions about the safety and efficacy of a drug they felt had saved their lives.

Natalie, Ralph, and I bought our sandwiches and took them to our small conference room, behind the Great Room. The other four ODAC members—the pediatric oncologist Frank Balis from Philadelphia, our statistician Brent Logan from Milwaukee, the ODAC chairperson Wyndham Wilson from the National Cancer Institute, and the industry representative Gregory Curt—were already there, quietly eating. We tried to focus the conversation on "safe" topics, asking each other about families, work, gossip within the oncology world, even upcoming summer vacations. But it was hard to avoid the elephant in the room.

Elephant? Hell, there was a herd—no, an entire reserve of large game mammals in the room.

"Those women who came up to speak were really something." Everyone agreed.

"Remember, some of them were paid by Genentech to be here." Murmured acknowledgment.

"I heard another member of ODAC was supposed to be here today, but he got a call from the FDA commissioner, Margaret Hamburg herself, a couple of days ago rescinding its request for him to serve because of a minor conflict of interest."

"This is big stakes. The FDA doesn't want even an *appearance* of a conflict when it makes its decision." More murmured acknowledgement.

"The FDA made a pretty convincing case this morning." Nods around the room.

"I'm sure Genentech will make a good case this afternoon." More nods.

The time had arrived to see just how good a case Genentech would make, and we returned to our table in the Great Room.

Representing Genentech, Paul Schmidt came to the microphone. He introduced himself, along with Phillipe Bishop, MD, who headed Genentech's development program for Avastin, and Jeff Helterbrand, PhD, the company's global head of biostatistics—Brent Logan's counterpart. Patricia Keegan and Rick Pazdur would be answering questions on behalf of the FDA—now playing the role of the "witnesses" to Schmidt's assuming the persona of defense attorney.

Schmidt started by discussing facts upon which the two sides could agree.

> When we talk about safety, am I correct that CDER agrees that the label fairly describes the safety for Avastin?[17]

Keegan said yes. Schmidt continued:

And that safety has not materially changed from the time of accelerated approval.[18]

Keegan said yes. Schmidt again:

Had the E2100 data replicated itself, in terms of magnitude of benefit, we wouldn't be having this discussion today. The benefit would outweigh the safety.[19] [*In other words, had the AVADO and RIBBON-1 trials (which were supposed to have confirmed Avastin's benefit seen in the original E2100 trial) shown the same degree of progression-free survival benefit of 5.9 months as the original E2100 trial, with the same side effects as seen in the original trial, the FDA would have transitioned the drug from accelerated approval to full approval for the treatment of breast cancer.*]

Keegan: "Correct." Schmidt followed up:

Does CDER stand behind those statements that progression-free survival can be an approvable endpoint and that overall survival is not always required?[20]

Rick Pazdur jumped in:

Yes we do; but it would have to be considered in the context of a risk-benefit assessment, and one would consider the magnitude of the effect in making a decision on that.[21] [*The totality of the data. Rick consistently preached about the* totality of the data—*that risks had to be weighed against benefits. And that all endpoints—response rates, progression-free survival, and overall survival—should complement each other, pointing in the same direction of benefit for a new drug, and that the benefit should be one that mattered to patients, and not just to a statistician.*]

Schmidt again:

Are we in agreement that there is an unmet medical need for HER2-negative metastatic breast cancer?[22] [*Schmidt referred to the genetic mutation that was identified in 1979 for which Genentech had developed the drug Herceptin almost 20 years later, in 1998. Women with breast cancers that contained the mutation were almost always treated*

*with Herceptin, or now with some close cousins of that drug. Those*
*whose breast cancer didn't have the mutation (they were HER2-negative)*
*had fewer treatment options at the time. If the breast cancer contained*
*hormone receptors for estrogen or progesterone, though, these women*
*could still be treated with hormonal therapy that blocked those receptors,*
*slowing the growth of the breast cancers.*]

Pazdur nodded: "In general, yes."

Then Schmidt asked to confirm certain facts I hadn't known:

> Am I correct that in the past 30 years, there has been only one other
> non-hormonal medication approved for HER2-negative metastatic
> breast cancer? . . . And that there has been no non-hormonal
> medication in the past 30 years that has shown a statistically
> significant improvement in overall survival?[23]

Wow. Avastin was one of only two treatments for women with
HER2-negative metastatic breast cancer approved over the past three
decades, and the other (gemcitabine, or Gemzar) was approved for
a variety of cancers.[24] Neither was able to demonstrate that women
with breast cancer taking the drugs lived any longer. Schmidt was
making the case that removing Avastin from the market would cut
in half the on-label treatment options for these women.

Dr. Keegan answered:

> Other than Avastin, there is no drug that carries that specific
> indication of HER2-negative metastatic breast cancer. So it's in a
> class by itself.[25]

Out of the corner of my eye I saw audience members turn to each
other and nod. Dr. Keegan was using the word "class" to mean a
drug classification—usually defined by what's called a *mechanism of
action*: how a drug works in the body—as with how the class of tyrosine kinase inhibitors like Gleevec work, all of which inhibit (block)
the enzyme tyrosine kinase in leukemia cells; or by a specific disease
subtype being treated. I think the audience members took her statement much more figuratively and assumed that she meant Avastin
was a great drug.

Schmidt changed gears:

> We'd like to ask some questions now about efficacy and specifically
> about the E2100 study. . . . We heard today many moving stories
> from patients of Avastin who used the phrase "super responder."
> Does CDER agree that there is some set of breast cancer patients for
> whom Avastin provides meaningful benefit?[26]

Keegan was definitive: "No, we do not agree."

A couple of audience members chuckled and I saw one woman point to herself, as if to say, *Here I am—living proof of a super responder.*

Schmidt then shifted gears again. He talked about the "missing data" issue from the original E2100 study, which had been called out as a concern by ODAC members, along with the quality (accuracy) of the data when they met in 2007 and voted *against* Avastin's approval. He wanted to demonstrate that the data irregularities didn't affect the study's results.

> Did CDER conclude that the amount of missing data [from the
> E2100 study] was in line with the amount seen in other trials?[27]

Keegan responded:

> We did *not* conclude that the amount of missing data or missing
> information and data issues were in line with other studies. We
> found this to be different.[28]

Schmidt then asked that a slide be shown that contained a memo *from the FDA* dated February 21, 2008.

> Let's look at the last two sentences. They say [that certain] "analyses
> corroborate the maintenance of a treatment effect in handling
> missing data. [*In other words, Avastin was judged to benefit women
> even if some of the study data were missing.*] Recent [drug] applications
> have had missing data *similar* to that observed in the current
> Avastin application." . . . Was that a correct statement when that
> was made?[29]

It seemed like a gotcha moment: taking one of the FDA's own justifications—that the original E2100 study data held up despite the missing data—and using it against the agency now to facilitate Avastin's accelerated approval.

Then Rick Pazdur jumped in.

> The problem that we had with this application were many issues that each in themselves perhaps were not unprecedented. However, when you took a look at all of the issues under consideration, we really felt that there was a need to repeat the study. [*Given the totality of the study's problems, but also the feeling that Avastin might benefit women, the FDA granted accelerated approval, which would necessitate a follow-up study that hopefully was cleaner.*]
>
> Those issues included a single study, . . . a lack of reliability in radiological reviews, almost a third of the patients not followed until a PFS [progression-free survival] event or [until the] end of [the] study, and missing scans in about 10 percent. [*The FDA didn't trust the CT scan results to determine whether or not a woman had worsening cancer, one-tenth had no scans at all, and for a substantial number of women enrolled in the trial, they weren't followed long enough to determine if their cancer worsened or if they died!*]
>
> Here, again, not one of these is unprecedented. However, once you start building a record here of multiple issues in an application, there is a problem which requires the study then to be replicated.[30] [*In this case the totality of data—data about study irregularities— played into the FDA's concerns about the original E2100 study, and its requirement for the AVADO and RIBBON-1 trials to be performed.*]

Pazdur handled the gotcha superbly. I could see why people referred to him as brilliant but also, at times, extremely hard to nail down.

The next line of questioning focused on some of the statistical nuances of analyzing survival.

We tend to focus on a median survival in cancer—the point at which half the patients on the study have died (or if you're more of an optimist, like me, the point at which half are still alive). For example, in the E2100 trial, the median progression-free survival for women treated with Avastin was 11.8 months.[31] (Earlier, in chapters 5 and 6, I called it an average for simplicity's sake, though an average refers to a mean survival, which may be similar to a median, or quite different depending on the rate of progression or death. I fully disclose this in an effort to skirt the slings and arrows from indignant statisticians!)

If you listed the time it took for the 347 women on the study treated with Avastin to have breast cancer that progressed, or who died—in order, from shortest time to longest—woman no. 174 would have a progression-free survival of almost 12 months. Woman no. 10 might have a progression-free survival of just three weeks, while woman no. 350 might not have progressed or died after three years.

Median survival is helpful because it's easy to communicate to other physicians and researchers. But more importantly, it's a number that patients and doctors can grasp and benchmark when making decisions about the benefits of a treatment. Let's say I hear that survival with a standard chemotherapy treatment for my cancer will be 6 months on average (there I go again with the sloppy use of this word!). But if I find out that with another drug—let's say our imaginary Tumorminimab—survival was 12 months in patients similar to me, I can weigh that 6-month survival advantage against the side effects of the drug I'll have to endure.

Another benchmark (also referred to as a landmark) is one-year survival: How many people are still alive one year after starting therapy with a drug? In the Tumorminimab example, since the average survival was 12 months, we can say that the one-year survival was 50 percent—half of the people treated with our fictitious drug are still alive a year after starting the drug. If 50 percent of people who did not receive Tumorminimab are alive only 6 months after enrolling in the trial (their average survival), then the one-year survival for them might only be 25 percent, or 13 percent, or maybe as high as 45 percent—because death rates don't always follow a regular pattern.

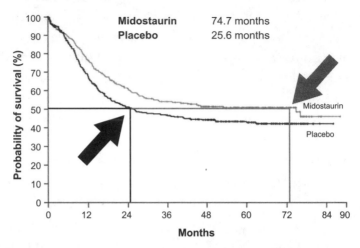

**Median overall survival**

**Figure 8.2**

An example of why reporting a median survival is not always accurate: Midostaurin. The median (approximately average) overall survival in this trial for patients with acute leukemia who received placebo (bottom line) was 25.6 months, but it was 74.7 months for those who received the drug midostaurin (top line)—an exaggerated difference because the median survival occurs at the inflection point of the midostaurin survival curve. In this case, it is more representative to say that midostaurin reduced the risk of death by 22 percent. *Source*: R. M. Stone, S. J. Mandrekar, B. L. Sanford, et al., "Midostaurin Plus Chemotherapy for Acute Myeloid Leukemia with a FLT3 Mutation," *New England Journal of Medicine* 377, no. 5 (August 3, 2017): 454–464.

But there's a problem with both these ways of measuring survival (see figure 8.2): they represent just one point in time, and that point may not reflect the experience of the majority of people being treated with a drug. And the survival measurements might even be ballyhooed by pharmaceutical companies to inflate the perception of how well their drug actually works.

A super example of this was a clinical trial conducted in patients with acute leukemia, like Jimmy Petrarcha. It tested a new drug called midostaurin, which "targets" a genetic abnormality called *FLT3* that occurs in about one-third of people with this type of leukemia.

Patients were randomized to receive midostaurin along with standard chemotherapy, or to receive the standard chemotherapy alone. The trial was a herculean, international effort in which over 3,000 patients were screened to identify the 717 who enrolled in the study. It took 10 years to complete, and was led by my mentor during the time I was training to be a hematologist/oncologist, Richard Stone, MD. And the trial was a success—patients randomized to receive midostaurin lived significantly longer than those who didn't. This is the trial that led to the drug's approval by the FDA on April 28, 2017.[32]

If you focused on the difference in median survival between those who were treated with midostaurin and those who weren't—wow! This drug seemed amazing: a median survival of almost 75 months for those who got midostaurin versus 26 months for those who didn't receive the drug! But the median occurred right at the inflection point of the survival curve, tremendously exaggerating the difference between those who got the drug and those who didn't. So, when my former mentor discussed the results, he was careful to refer instead to what's called a hazard ratio—the risk of dying that includes all deaths that occur over the course of the study in both treatment arms, and not just those at the halfway point or at one year. The hazard ratio still showed that midostaurin was beneficial, reducing the risk of death by 22 percent—a substantial reduction, but not quite the same wow factor.[33]

You can imagine, though, that when the drug's manufacturer discussed the results, it focused on the difference in median survival, because that seemed more impressive.

The opposite can occur, too: a drug's hazard ratio can seem more substantial than a difference in median survival. And a hazard ratio is really difficult for many people to grasp and apply to themselves in meaningful terms when making decisions about what treatment to receive—particularly when the term *progression-free survival* comes into play, in which case it would indicate a reduction (or increase) in risk of dying or of cancer getting worse.

In fact, the differences in median progression-free survival for women treated with Avastin versus those who weren't in the AVADO and RIBBON-1 trials were so puny—measured in just a few weeks— that Genentech wanted the FDA to focus instead on the hazard ratio for progression-free survival. In the Avado and RIBBON-1 trials, this showed a benefit for women treated with Avastin of about 35 percent.[34]

This was a tricky argument for Genentech to make, though. Because for *overall survival*, the hazard ratio seemed to indicate either no difference for women receiving Avastin versus those who didn't, or a slightly *higher* risk of death, by about 10 percent, for women getting Avastin.

Once again, Rick Pazdur used Genentech's selection of data against the company.

> If one wants to start taking a look at single points on a survival curve . . . it is tremendously treacherous to do so. If we take a look at your complete graph of the survival of all patients treated with Avastin from all of the trials, at three years, if I just pick that endpoint up, the placebo curve [*women not receiving Avastin*] is actually doing better.[35]

Genentech's statistician, Jeff Helterbrand, PhD, countered this by using the FDA's focus on median survival against the agency.

> In the Avastin case, CDER has chosen to emphasize the difference in medians [*of progression-free survival between women treated with Avastin and those who weren't*] as the measure of magnitude, as we saw with the presentation this morning.
>
> Now, would CDER agree that the outcomes of all patients are important, not just those of the median patients? And moreover, would CDER agree that the hazard ratio results from studies should not be ignored? [36]

Rajeshwari Sridhara, PhD, a statistician for the FDA, responded:

> Hazard ratio was certainly taken into consideration. Again, we
> don't look at it in isolation and we do look at the difference in
> medians.
> We have had applications [drug submissions for approval] where
> the hazard ratio was [a 50-percent reduction in death or a cancer
> worsening] and, in fact, the difference in progression-free survival
> was just two weeks. Where do we take that then?[37]

Good question. How does the FDA handle a drug for which two
valid measures of that drug's efficacy—hazard ratio and median
survival—show a major benefit for one and only a minor benefit for
the other? Or what happens if they contradict each other?

Rick Pazdur then chimed in. He sounded exasperated at having to
repeat himself.

> The decision to approve a drug is not based solely on a hazard ratio.
> It is not based solely on the median difference. It is not based on a p
> value [the statistical test measuring whether a difference in survival
> is significant]. But it is based on a risk benefit analysis.

He struck the same sing-song tone as Guy-Am-I, who—when pestered
by Sam-I-Am to eat green eggs and ham in the Dr. Seuss classic—
adamantly replies:

> I would not like them here or there.
> I would not like them anywhere.
> I do not like green eggs and ham.
> I do not like them Sam-I-Am.[38]

Helterbrand—as Sam-I-Am—pushed him again.

> Is it fair to say then that CDER is reluctant to communicate
> what measure of magnitude it's going to emphasize, such as the
> difference in medians or the hazard ratio, as well as what magnitude
> of improvement [a drug] will need to achieve for CDER to conclude
> it provides clinical benefit?[39] [*He emphasized the frequent criticism
> of the FDA that it is opaque when it comes to defining the bar for drug
> approval.*]

Pazdur stood firm:

> We are not reluctant to specify a specific number. . . . We do not
> approve a drug on a hazard ratio. We approve the drug on the
> clinical judgment of a risk-benefit decision.[40]

I have never heard the FDA publicly reveal a benefit in survival,
some arbitrary line in the sand, at which it will guarantee approval
of a drug, and Pazdur certainly wasn't going to do it during these proceedings. He wouldn't consume the green eggs and ham statistics
proffered by Helterbrand.

Why? Because as Pazdur consistently states, the FDA always considers the totality of data. A benefit without a risk is like a day without sunshine, and defining *benefit* was a moving target. Statistically,
all of the Avastin studies, and the application referenced by the
FDA's Sridhara, were successes. But to a patient, a drug that prevents
a tumor from worsening by a couple of weeks, and doesn't allow her
to live longer, can only be called a failure.

Right?

Paul Schmidt, playing the role of defense attorney, resumed his position at the podium for Genentech, and took a different tact. He
grilled Dr. Keegan about what the FDA did or didn't know regarding the results of the AVADO trial as the data were coming in, and
whether the paltry, three-week difference in progression-free survival between women receiving Avastin and those who didn't should
have been enough to gain the drug full approval status. Or did the
FDA know all along it wouldn't be enough?

With this line of questioning, it struck me that he was appealing
to our notions of fairness. If the FDA saw all long that the AVADO
trial was heading toward results that were inferior to the original
E2100 trial, why didn't the agency tell Genentech that Avastin's
approval for breast cancer was in trouble?

The company thought that AVADO [showed] clinical benefit. My question is, at any point in time, having this data in hand, having accepted AVADO as a confirmatory trial, did CDER say to Genentech that a 0.8-month median PFS difference will not be enough to support approval?[41]

Pazdur acknowledged that the FDA had not. Schmidt continued:

Thank you. I hope you have a sense from the comments and from some of our questions how the company has struggled to understand what the approval standard is.[42]

He portrayed Genentech as if the company were conducting these trials in good faith and meeting the FDA's standards for approval but had gotten no indication to the contrary from the agency. And he was hoping we would sympathize with their plight.

Pazdur had taught me that emotions—such as feeling bad for a company—shouldn't factor into any decisions about a drug's approval or its capacity to remain on the market. It should all be about the science.

But isn't it natural that emotions play some role? Does the FDA have a responsibility to warn companies that the trial results they're seeing won't be good enough to support a drug approval? Or should the drug manufacturer know better without having to be told by the agency?

Schmidt again changed his approach, asking about the legal standards for removing a drug from the market for a specific disease indication. He asked if the FDA had discretion to *not* remove a drug from the market, even if confirmatory studies were deemed inadequate.[43]

Abigail Brandel, from the FDA's Office of Chief Counsel, agreed that the FDA had discretion to not remove a drug from the market.[44]

Schmidt then reminded the audience that, though the FDA was proposing pulling Avastin from the market for the treatment of breast cancer, the FDA's equivalent in Europe, the European Medicines Agency or EMA, had retained full approval for Avastin. Why couldn't the FDA do the same?[45]

This time John Jenkins, the director of the Office of New Drugs and the man who would one day criticize the FDA for its accelerated review process, took the question.

> We acknowledge that we reached a different conclusion about the data than EMA. That's not unusual. We do occasionally reach different conclusions about drugs than the EMA does and, in fact, with Avastin, in particular, we approved Avastin for glioblastoma [a type of brain cancer], and the EMA looked at the same data and concluded that they would not approve it for that indication.[46]

Schmidt kept digging at him:

> Recognizing the EMA came out at a different place . . . does CDER recognize those as legitimate alternative views of the data?[47]

But Jenkins wouldn't budge:

> The EMA is a recognized regulatory body. We have a lot of interactions with EMA. We don't question that they reached a different decision than we did. As I said, we don't always reach the same decisions as EMA.[48]

This is the reason why some people of means fly to Europe to pursue what they think may be a life-saving drug they just can't obtain in the United States, and vice-versa. It's true—regulatory agencies in different parts of the world aren't bound by each other's decisions, and there are differences in access to drugs even in highly developed countries.

Schmidt closed by making the case that over years Genentech acted in good faith to address the concerns raised by the FDA about the use of Avastin in women with metastatic breast cancer: by conducting confirmatory studies following the original E2100 trial efficiently; by being open to changes in the medication's label; by looking at other "partner" drugs to combine with Avastin; and by emphasizing the unmet medical need for these women. He asked one final question of FDA:

> Is there any proposal that anyone on the panel can point us to that CDER has considered for keeping this medicine available for metastatic breast cancer patients?[49]

Dr. Keegan answered simply. "No."

Next, it was our turn to ask the FDA questions. In some ways, it was a strange position to be in, as we were an independent panel really beholden to nobody in the room except our own consciences. Yet we had been invited there by the FDA and had worked regularly with the agency for years as members of ODAC. So in other ways we had a relationship with FDA representatives that we didn't have with Genentech, and couldn't, by design, because of the conflict-of-interest screening.

Our chairperson, Wyndham Wilson from the National Cancer Institute, got us started. He focused on the point Schmidt had made, that there were only two drugs approved by the FDA for women who were HER2-negative, Avastin being one of them; that this was an unmet medical need for which 50 percent of the drugs that could treat it were about to be eliminated. Dr. Keegan from the FDA had said that Avastin "was in a class by itself."

> The recognition of HER2-negative breast cancer as a clinical entity has really only been known for approximately one decade. So how could FDA be approving drugs for a biologic entity that did not exist more than about 10 years ago?[50]

Wilson made a good point. Of course there weren't many drugs designated specifically for women with breast cancer whose cancer was HER2-negative—we only made the distinction about HER2 status in breast cancer after the drug Herceptin was approved by the FDA in 1998 to treat women whose cancers were HER2-positive. Prior to that, drugs to treat breast cancer were agnostic to HER2 status, and these drugs could work in women whose cancers were either HER2-positive or -negative. Dr. Keegan responded:

> That's why I said that this drug was in a class by itself because, in fact, this was . . . the first study that we had received where the eligibility criteria specifically excluded patients who were HER2 positive.[51]

Wilson then pointed out the obvious to anyone who hadn't been paying attention: that in truth, there were other drugs available to treat women with metastatic breast cancer, regardless of whether the tumors were HER2-positive or -negative:

> So just to be clear, then, the question that only one drug has been approved in the last 30 years isn't really relevant, because for most of that time, this has not been a recognized group.[52]

So much for the unmet-medical-need argument. I also had to wonder, given that Genentech also manufactured Herceptin, if they had designed the Avastin clinical trials to exclude women who were HER2-positive so that they wouldn't have two drugs competing with each other for the same patients.

Later in the Q&A session, Wilson asked about the "super responders" to the Avastin and paclitaxel chemo combination, alluding to the term mentioned by both the company and some of the folks who approached the microphone earlier, and also reminding us that in all of these studies, Avastin was never given alone—it was always combined with another type of chemotherapy.

> We've heard today, and we've heard it both from patients and we've heard it from treating doctors, as well, that they have seen what seems to be termed super responders to this drug, to these drug combinations. And I think that it was commented here that it's impossible to separate out the contribution of the Avastin from the chemotherapy simply because they're being given together.
>
> I will say that having been one of the original developers of Taxol [paclitaxel—the chemotherapy given with Avastin] back in the early 1990s, I saw numerous patients go on [survive] for numbers of

years on single-agent drug. . . . So I was just wondering what CDER's thought is about this.[53]

I had completely forgotten that, before focusing exclusively on treating lymphomas, Wilson had treated a variety of cancers, including breast cancer. Paclitaxel was actually discovered in 1962 as part of a National Cancer Institute initiative, in partnership with the US Department of Agriculture, to search for cancer cures from natural plant and animal products. The drug was derived from the bark of the Pacific Yew tree *Taxus brevifolia*, from which it derived its name.[54] Dr. Keegan again handled the question in her no-nonsense way:

[Breast cancer] is not like other diseases with very short and very predictable courses. . . . We're having a hard time identifying those [super responder] patients, and from the survival curves, from the progression-free survival curves, we're just not seeing that population. And I think the most compelling thing is . . . that in 2,400 patients, there doesn't seem to be a group emerging that's behaving differently.[55]

In reviewing the data from all of the Avastin trials, Keegan and others from the FDA didn't see any particular group of women they would call "super responders."

Ralph Freedman spoke up to question the FDA about the existing Avastin label, which was supposed to guide oncologists about the safety and efficacy of the drug.

Now you've got the results of the confirmatory trials that were supposed to be confirmatory, but they were not, so you do you think that the label indication is still accurate in terms of its presentation of efficacy and toxicity?[56]

Dr. Keegan again handled the question for the FDA:

No. We don't think it's accurate. It's listed as being safe and effective, and that is no longer our position.[57]

Wow. The FDA acknowledged that a label for a drug that still could have been prescribed on that date of June 28, 2011, did not reflect the drug's safety or efficacy. I wondered why they hadn't already changed the label based on the data they had, regardless of the outcome of these proceedings. Wouldn't that have been in the best interests of public health?

Gregory Curt, our industry representative who worked for the pharmaceutical company Astra-Zeneca, took his own crack at grilling the FDA. To help inform his company and others about trials they were conducting for future treatments, he often asked questions aimed at clarifying the FDA's standards for approving drugs. This was no exception:

> If an improvement in symptoms and a lack of alternative therapeutic options are two reasons for considering PFS [progression-free survival] as an approvable endpoint, does that mean that PFS is less robust in patients who are getting frontline therapy than in patients with refractory disease?[58]

In other words, did a company like Genentech have to show a larger improvement in progression-free survival for a drug like Avastin if it's part of the *first* treatment a woman sees for her initial breast cancer diagnosis than for a *second or third* round of treatment for a cancer that kept returning, where fewer and fewer treatment options existed? Pazdur took this one.

> When you have a first-line setting, we would expect a much more robust finding. Obviously, . . . when we're dealing with a very refractory disease population, with few therapeutic options available to them, there probably would be a greater degree of leniency in looking even at smaller progression-free survival values to consider truly an unmet medical need.[59]

Small improvements in progression-free survival, as were seen in the follow-up AVADO and RIBBON-1 trials, might have been okay for Avastin if it was a last-ditch treatment effort for women with metastatic breast cancer. But Avastin was approved as the first course of treatment, and an improvement in progression-free survival of just a few weeks wasn't good enough.

I was still bothered by that notion of fairness that Schmidt had raised earlier: that Genentech had acted in good faith and tried to meet the standards for approval the FDA had set, but that company officials claimed the FDA had changed those standards without telling them.

Yet between the time the FDA might first provide guidance to a company on standards for approval and the time when a trial is actually complete, those standards could change. I cautiously raised my hand to ask a follow-up question to the point Curt had made, and I gulped hard when Dr. Midthun recognized me. All eyes from the FDA, Genentech, and the audience turned to me.

> There's no line in the sand that the FDA can draw about what's an acceptable PFS [progression-free survival] or hazard ratio, because it's a risk-benefit analysis. . . . An unmet medical need and unavailability of other options for an at-risk population, like metastatic breast cancer, would also figure into that calculus, correct?

Rick Pazdur agreed. I went on:

> And that calculus then may change over time.

Again, Rick agreed. Me again:

> So, a bar [for approval] . . . that may have been acceptable 15 years ago or 7 years ago may change as other therapies become available and are studied, whether on label or off label?[60]

This time Pazdur gave a more expansive answer:

> We have attempted to give consistent advice to sponsors and our advice is the following: Everyone would prefer to see a survival advantage in patients with breast cancer. So we ask the sponsor to power [*design*] a trial [to be able to show an improvement in] overall survival, even if they plan on looking at progression-free survival. . . .
>     We are aware of the nuances that are associated with the interpretation of progression-free survival and they include, as we've had multiple discussions with the committee on, the

accuracy of measurement, missing scans, and the subjectivity of the interpretation of clinical benefit.

So to really have a trial that has the ability to look at both endpoints [progression-free and overall survival] is really what we're really advocating sponsors do at this time.[61]

The FDA's gold standard is and always will be to approve drugs for the public that allow people to live longer or live better. Pazdur was emphasizing that progression-free survival is messy, and that while the FDA will accept it as an approvable trial endpoint, they do so grudgingly, and really prefer an overall survival endpoint.

But what about if progression-free survival is associated with patients "living better?" I asked one final question:

We've discussed before on this committee when PFS can be an acceptable endpoint. In the absence of an overall survival advantage, if there is a PFS advantage and a patient-reported outcome [quality of life] advantage, then potentially you could demonstrate benefit to patients.

If . . . AVADO had shown some sort of magnitude of difference in patient-reported outcome, would that have been factored into the calculus for approval?[62]

Rick nodded.

Yes. . . . The bottom line for this drug is we wanted one positive trial. That trial could have shown an improvement in overall survival, . . . or it could have been some quality-of-life measurement. All we're asking for here is one trial that shows clinical benefit.[63]

The meeting adjourned for the day at about 3:30 p.m. The other members of ODAC and I gathered our computer bags slowly, partly waiting for the room to clear out before we took our leave, and partly lost in our own thoughts, replaying the presentations we had heard over the past seven-and-a-half hours. We walked as a quiet group down the long hallway outside the Great Room and wended our way through Building 1, out its front doors to our waiting shuttle.

The ride back to our rooms at the Hilton in Silver Spring was just as quiet. Usually, we arranged to grab dinner together during the evening bridging a two-day public service stint at the FDA.

But not that night—perhaps to prevent ourselves from discussing the hearing outside the public forum; and perhaps each of us craving solitude before the momentous decision we would have to make the following day.

# 9

# The Avastin Decision

A panel of six decided that we are statistically insignificant.
How do I explain that to my 4-year-old and 7-year-old?
—Crystal Hanna, 2011

I woke the following morning—June 29, 2011—at five-thirty, went for a quick workout in the hotel's cramped gym, showered, shaved, dressed, and packed my luggage. I then headed down to the hotel's lobby for breakfast before catching the shuttle back to the FDA.

Ralph Freedman was sitting at a table by the "grab and go" snack bar, as were Natalie Compagni-Portis and Brent Logan, all with their suitcases too; Gregory Curt and Frank Balis joined us soon afterward, their roller bags in tow, as the plan was to leave for the airport directly after the day's proceedings. More than a century had passed since itinerant troupes went town-to-town to hawk the likes of Hamlin's Wizard Oil and other unregulated drugs of its ilk. Now here we were, a modern-day traveling medical show charged with voting to approve—or remove—another drug whose safety and efficacy were under scrutiny.

As at lunch the previous day, we started the conversation by focusing on safe topics.

An initial, innocuous question—"How did you all sleep last night?"—elicited grumbles about the noise and general discomfort from bedding down in a hotel.

"What airport are you flying out from?" Some from Dulles, others from National, Frank from Washington Union train station.

"Do you think we'll finish on time today?" General accord that the FDA usually runs a tight ship.

Then, back to the elephant in the hotel lobby.

"The FDA seemed to handle Genentech pretty well yesterday." Cautious nods.

"The company will have to make a heck of a case today to keep their breast cancer indication." Weary acknowledgment.

"They still have their day in court." Universal agreement.

"What information can they present today that would change everyone's minds?" Silence, as we glanced at each other, unsure.

The shuttle driver appeared in the lobby, so we gathered our luggage and loaded it into the rear of the van for our return to the FDA's White Oak campus. As the vehicle pulled into the circular driveway, fewer protestors greeted us than on the previous day. We hopped out at our usual spot in front of Building 1.

Walking through the security area and over to the Great Room, we remarked on the lack of hubbub, compared to what we'd seen the day before. But the room would be no less crowded, and we were warned it would fill during the afternoon when we voted on our recommendation for Avastin.

We took the same seats at our table and waited for the hearing to resume. At precisely 8:00 a.m., Dr. Midthun approached the microphone again.

> Good morning and welcome to this, the second day of the Avastin hearing. Now we will proceed to the portion of the hearing where Genentech will make its presentation.[1]

**Figure 9.1**
Hal Barron, executive vice president of global product development and the chief medical officer for Genentech, photo taken in 2018. *Source*: GSK, https://www.gsk .com/en-gb/about-us/board-of-directors/dr-hal-barron/.

Hal Barron, MD, the executive vice president of global product development and the chief medical officer for Genentech (figure 9.1), stepped up to the microphone. He had joined the company as a scientist in 1996, at age 34, and climbed the ranks of power at Genentech over the ensuing 15 years. He usually evoked an open-collared, West Coast–style, nerdy-cool image, but for this occasion he had decided to dress more formally, in a suit and tie.

Earlier in the month, Barron had written a letter to the *New York Times* in which he extolled the large studies run by Genentech that showed "with high statistical confidence that adding Avastin to the first chemotherapy extends the time a woman lives before her breast cancer worsens" [progression-free survival] and that "withdrawing Avastin's breast cancer approval in the United States indisputably reduces options here, while European women still have it available."[2]

He started to speak, glancing toward our table.

I want to be clear about why we requested the hearing. We are here today for one purpose, to explain why we believe that women with metastatic breast cancer are better off if Avastin, in combination with paclitaxel, remains an approved treatment option.[3]

Barron described what Genentech and the FDA actually agreed upon: that the progression-free survival from the original E2100 study was meaningful, and that the FDA's authority to withdraw drugs from the market should be preserved. He then enumerated four points on which the company and the FDA disagreed:

The first point is that Avastin's safety profile has been broadly misunderstood based on how CDER [the Center for Drug Evaluation and Research at the FDA] has presented the data. Avastin has an acceptable risk profile for the indication for which it is approved.

Second, E2100 was a well-conducted clinical trial with robust results that are clearly clinically meaningful.

Third, the AVADO and RIBBON-1 studies met their prespecified primary endpoint . . . and as such do not invalidate the findings of E2100.

Fourth, the regulations around accelerated approval anticipated the current situation, a situation in which a definitive interpretation cannot be made. . . . In this situation, the regulations allow for accelerated approval to be maintained while subsequent studies are conducted to resolve important issues that remain.[4]

I scanned the audience, sparser now then at the beginning of the previous day's hearings. Women who had spoken yesterday, supporters of Avastin, were nodding. I looked over to the FDA's table, where expressions were neutral at best.

I fell somewhere in-between the audience's and the FDA's reaction. True, Avastin caused serious and at times deadly side effects. But so did a number of other chemotherapies that were used to treat even deadlier cancers. I agreed with Barron's first point.

But I disagreed with his second and third contentions. Was a progression-free survival benefit, in the absence of an improvement in overall survival or quality of life, really meaningful? If I had cancer, would I take solace in the fact that my cancer wasn't worsening—and would my friends and family be relieved that my cancer didn't grow— during my remaining days on this earth (which don't increase), if on those days I didn't feel any better with Avastin or without it?

I doubted it. But was my opinion reflective of the tens of thousands of women treated with Avastin?

The fourth point, about the follow-up AVADO and RIBBON trials having different study designs, was a tricky argument. Was he trying to make Genentech's case by saying that they conducted bad studies, but if the FDA gave them the chance, they would conduct a good one?

Barron continued:

> The scientific and regulatory issues at hand call for regulatory flexibility, a middle ground, if you will, of maintaining accelerated approval. I want to emphasize that this path forward is clearly allowed by law and supported by the science. Most importantly, this path forward is in the best interests of patients.[5]

He took his seat and Sandra Horning, MD, Genentech's global head of clinical development for hematology and oncology (figure 9.2), came to the microphone.

This would be interesting.

Having written or contributed to more than 300 scientific publications, Dr. Horning was incredibly respected in the cancer field. She grew up in the small town of Creston, Iowa, and attended the University of Iowa as an undergraduate. Soon after, her father developed metastatic cancer and died within six months, solidifying her decision to enter medicine. Before working for a pharmaceutical company, she was a professor at Stanford University for 25 years and president of the American Society of Clinical Oncology, the largest professional cancer organization in the world, with nearly 45,000 members, from 2005 to 2006.[6]

Dr. Horning also reminded us that she had been a member of ODAC herself in the early part of the past decade. She was one of us. Or had been.

**Figure 9.2**
Sandra Horning, MD, Genentech's global head of clinical development for hematology and oncology, photo taken in 2017. *Source*: Genentech, https://www.eurekalert.org/multimedia/pub/133191.php.

> Let's begin today's discussion in the clinic where an oncologist counsels her patient about the underlying disease, how it is behaving, and what the alternatives for treatment are. The clinical setting we are discussing is HER2-negative metastatic breast cancer.[7]

In 2010, 45,000 women had been handed this diagnosis, Horning said, reminding us that on average these women would live for one and one-half to two years.

Such a short period of time.

She reviewed what treatments might be offered to these women, including the Avastin and paclitaxel combination, and emphasized Barron's first point—that Avastin wasn't as toxic as the FDA was portraying it. More than 1 million people had already been treated with Avastin worldwide. Guidelines existed to help doctors manage those toxicities. Some of the toxicities attributed to Avastin—such as hypertension—were common in older adults, affecting 50 percent of those over age 60 in the United States, an age group that also makes up the majority of women who develop breast cancer. And she made the point that toxicities, including death, in the original E2100 study may have been *under-reported* in women who didn't receive Avastin, making Avastin *appear* more toxic than it actually was.

I hadn't known that. From the very first ODAC meeting about Avastin, there was concern about the quality of the data submitted to the FDA. And the results of a clinical trial, or any study, are only as good as the data upon which they are based. I had assumed the missing data were equivalent for women who did or did not receive Avastin. But maybe it was differentially missing, which would introduce a bias in the study to Avastin's detriment.

Horning then called into question the FDA's interpretation of deaths that were attributed to Avastin, versus those that weren't. This is always challenging in a clinical trial of a drug used to treat people with metastatic cancer because, unfortunately, so many people die from the cancer itself. Just as I tried to determine which of Jimmy Petrarcha's illnesses were caused—directly, indirectly, or not at all—by the immunotherapy clinical trial drug I used when leukemia was wreaking havoc on his body, so too in other trials, with other drugs, this was not an easy or straightforward assessment.

But members of the FDA are supposed to be experts at this, aren't they? Isn't that the core of their mission—safety, safety, safety?

Horning concluded:

> Avastin has serious side effects, as described in the product label, but it is not more or uniquely toxic compared to other [metastatic breast cancer] treatments.[8]

There was truth in that statement. We're willing to accept an awful lot of toxicity in drugs used to treat life-threatening illnesses like metastatic breast cancer—if they're effective.

She then discussed just that, emphasizing points that Hal Barron had made:

We have three areas of scientific disagreement with CDER regarding efficacy. First, we find the E2100 study to be well conducted with robust results. Second, AVADO and RIBBON 1 are both positive studies. They do not invalidate the E2100 study, and external experts endorse this position. Third, the chemotherapy partner [*the chemotherapy used with Avastin, most commonly paclitaxel*] may contribute to the greater magnitude of effect observed with paclitaxel and Avastin in E2100, and this can be studied in a confirmatory [*yet another*] trial.[9]

Next, Horning made the case that the original E2100 study (conducted by the esteemed National Cancer Institute) enrolled typical women with metastatic breast cancer (and not the "Olympic athletes" most trials enrolled). She stressed its global influence, as its results (that Avastin combined with paclitaxel led to improved progression-free survival for women with metastatic breast cancer) led to use of the drug in 84 countries.[10]

Hadn't known that either. We often forget, cloistered as we are in our own communities, or attending meetings only with other Americans, how treatment standards established in the United States can affect the rest of the world.

But then Horning did a statistical fast step that I didn't like.

For 10,000 women, the survival and PFS [progression-free survival] data [from the original E2100 study] would translate into 740 more women alive and 2,060 more alive and progression free at one year.[11]

This tactic was commonly referred to as *spinning the data*. The more derisive idiom that preceded it, *torturing the data*, originated with the British economist Ronald H. Coase, who wrote: "If you torture the data long enough, it will confess to anything."[12]

When making a case to the FDA, trying to spin the trial data to your advantage is considered one of the deadly sins (in addition to pride, perhaps, or maybe greed). The FDA employs talented statisticians who conduct their own analyses of clinical trial results and, like

Rajeshwari Sridhara, are hard to fool. Rick Pazdur and his team have themselves vetted hundreds of clinical trials and are quick to pick up on statistical slights of hand. As I looked over at my ODAC colleagues quietly listening to the presentation, I was reminded that each of them was a skilled clinical trial designer and investigator in his or her own right, and also hard to fool.

Just like the Farmers Insurance Group says in its slogan, *we know a thing or two because we've seen a thing or two.*

A presenter who spins data to the FDA and to ODAC compromises the trust we place in anything that person has to say and increases our suspicions, even when considering the quality of the information the pharmaceutical company submitted to the FDA.

None of the Avastin studies had shown a statistically significant improvement in how long women lived—meaning that even if survival *appeared* slightly higher for women treated with Avastin and paclitaxel compared to women treated with paclitaxel alone, that difference was likely due to chance. Similarly, in the follow-up AVADO and RIBBON trials, any appearance of improved survival for women who *didn't* receive Avastin was likely due to chance.

Horning had chosen one study (the original E2100 trial) and a single point in time during that study (one year from when a woman enrolled to the trial) to make her case. She had also inflated the number of women treated on the E2100 trial from 722 to 10,000 to increase the number of women she could say would be alive one year from enrollment to make her conclusions seem more impressive. If instead of one year she had chosen two years from when a woman enrolled in the E2100 trial, the number of "more women alive" out of 10,000 would have shrunk to 490. If she had chosen the three-year timepoint from enrollment, there would have been no difference in the number of women alive! If she had focused instead on the AVADO trial and the one-year time point for 10,000 women, about 600 *fewer* women who received Avastin would have been alive!

Out of the corner of my eye, I saw Pazdur shake his head in disdain. Horning next focused on findings from the follow-up AVADO and RIBBON studies that supported the results from the original E2100 trial, even if the progression-free survival advantage for women receiving Avastin was wimpier. She circled back to the notion of fairness, that the FDA knew all along where the results of those trials were headed but never told Genentech that those results would be insufficient. Moreover, these results were good enough for European regulatory agencies and US guideline panels composed of almost 30 breast cancer specialists. Why not for the FDA?

She concluded by revisiting the debate surrounding whether Avastin had been combined with the right chemotherapy drug.[13]

Genentech was eager for this point to hit home. It was an uphill battle to try and convince the FDA that the AVADO and RIBBON-1 follow-up trials had confirmed the advantages seen with Avastin in the original E2100 trial and thus had met the necessary condition for a drug receiving accelerated approval from the FDA to convert to full approval and remain on the market. The progression-free survival actually shrank (in my mind it was a questionable measure of efficacy to start with), and overall survival was not better for women receiving Avastin in the follow-up studies (it may have been even worse).

*Just give us one more chance*, Horning and Genentech seemed to be saying. *We know these weren't the right trials to show how Avastin can benefit women with breast cancer. Let us have another go at it—and keep Avastin on the market while we conduct the perfect trial!*

But they had their chance, didn't they? And with more and more clinical trials asking essentially the same question—does Avastin combined with chemotherapy benefit women with breast cancer more than chemotherapy alone—they run the risk of finding a difference between Avastin and chemotherapy by accident. This is similar to what occurs with a statistical error called *multiple testing*.

How does this work? It most commonly occurs within a single trial or set of data, but it can be applied to the above scenario.

Let's say you're conducting a trial of a new drug in patients with cardiac disease, Happyheartinib, in which you compare it to aspirin in its ability to prevent myocardial infarctions (heart attacks). In the trial, patients are randomly assigned to receive either Happyheartinib or aspirin. You look at how the two treatment groups are doing after 6 months and find no difference between them in their rates of myocardial infarctions at the standard statistical level (called a P-value) of 0.05 (this means you will accept that there is a 5 percent chance that you might erroneously find a difference in efficacy between the drugs when no difference actually exists). You look again at the two groups after one year—still no difference. Then again after 18 and after 24 months—no difference. But when you compare them at 30 months, patients receiving Happyheartinib have significantly fewer myocardial infarctions. Success! Quick, stop the trial!

Whoa, not so fast. The way statistics work, you are accepting a 5 percent chance that you erroneously find a difference between the drugs *every time you look at the data*, and to some extent that chance of error becomes cumulative. So by the time you have looked at the data five times, the chance of a false positive result, meaning that you find a difference in benefit between Happyheartinib and aspirin that doesn't actually exist, is actually now up to 23 percent![14]

Are you willing to treat your heart disease with an expensive drug that may have many side effects if there is an almost one-in-four chance that it works no better than an aspirin?

What about an expensive and toxic therapy for breast cancer?

The opposite can occur too—in which initial, highly influential clinical trial results are not substantiated, or worse yet are refuted, in follow-up studies.[15] One analysis of almost 50 such trials found that 16 percent had results that were *contradicted* by subsequent studies;

16 percent found effects that *weakened* in subsequent studies (similar to Avastin, in which the progression-free survival in the original E2100 trial was stronger than in the AVADO and RIBBON studies); and 24 percent remained completely *unsubstantiated* by follow-up studies. This phenomenon has been referred to as a reproducibility crisis in medicine—initial trials showing a benefit may be no more than a flash in the pan.

Dr. Horning concluded her presentation:

> In closing, based upon acceptable safety risks and demonstrated efficacy, we interpret the benefit risk for Avastin plus paclitaxel in MBC [metastatic breast cancer] to be favorable, and expert scientific bodies agree with this interpretation. In the context of an incurable disease and the available treatments, which we believe constitute an unmet need, and certainly this is what we heard from the testimonies yesterday, it is best for patients to continue to have this treatment option.[16]

As she stepped away from the microphone, scattered applause erupted from Avastin supporters in the audience who had returned on the trial's second day. This was Genentech's last chance to convince the FDA—and us—of their drug's benefits, or at least its lack of harm.

Joyce O'Shaughnessy, MD, another extremely well-respected clinical researcher in the oncology community, then came to the podium. She held the Celebrating Women Endowed Chair in Breast Cancer Research at Baylor University Medical Center, in Dallas, Texas. Like Horning, she was motivated to enter oncology by a family tragedy. When she was a 19-year-old freshman at Holy Cross College, in Worcester, Massachusetts, her younger sister died of leukemia at the nearby Dana-Farber Cancer Institute in Boston. After completing her internship and residency at the Massachusetts General Hospital, where I would complete my own internship and residency a decade later (and where Judah Folkman had completed his), she trained in oncology at the National Cancer Institute. She remained there for 10 years, focusing on breast cancer clinical trials, before moving to Texas.[17]

After explaining her credentials—and acknowledging that she had been paid by Genentech to attend the meeting—O'Shaughnessy stressed her commitment to furthering continued clinical research:

> I have been involved in developing and enrolling patients onto Avastin breast cancer clinical trials since 2000. I have come to speak to you today because, as a breast cancer specialist, I am very aware of where we still have gaping unmet medical needs that cause significant suffering. . . . [I am here] on behalf of the women in my practice who have aggressive metastatic breast cancer and those who I unfortunately will meet in the future who are best treated with tolerable and effective combination therapy.[18]

She spoke earnestly about breast cancer treatments as well as her experience with patients: not as abstract data points but as real people. I could imagine her looking them straight in the eye when explaining the treatment she would recommend—as I had done with Jimmy Petrarcha and countless other leukemia patients—when she said:

> Just last week alone, having carefully considered all of the available options, I recommended to three patients who have metastatic breast cancer and who are in need of rapid relief from severe bone pain, chest and arm pain, and liver pain that they begin treatment with Avastin.[19]

I believed her.

O'Shaughnessy talked about how well tolerated Avastin was compared to other chemotherapies she offered her patients. That might be true, depending on how she treated women with metastatic breast cancer. Her goals were to alleviate or prevent symptoms caused by the tumor (bone pain, liver pain) for as long as possible, with minimal toxicities from the treatment itself. She said that this could be accomplished by drugs that improved progression-free survival.

This part troubled me. Why didn't she mention using a drug that enabled women to live longer as a treatment goal? That's always my aim when I treat patients with leukemia. And if progression-free survival could measure improvement in symptoms, why then in all of the Avastin studies, was quality of life no better for women receiving Avastin?

O'Shaughnessy was followed by Michael Labson, an attorney specializing in food and drug regulation. Back in March, he wrote a letter on behalf of Genentech to the FDA hearing official, Karen Midthun, MD, requesting that Wyndham Wilson, Ralph Friedman, Gregory Curt, and I—those of us who has served on the 2010 ODAC that recommended removing Avastin's breast cancer indication—be excluded from these 2011 hearings. He made the point, knowing we had already voted against Avastin, that we would not be objective or fair. The FDA rejected the request, emphasizing that we were independent of the FDA.

At the 2011 hearing, Labson stated the FDA's position—that Genentech had its chance to conduct trials confirming Avastin's benefit to women as shown in the original E2100 trial and had failed—was too rigid and not required under the law. He reiterated Genentech's feeling that the subsequent AVADO and RIBBON-1 trials actually *did* confirm Avastin's benefit, as defined by the FDA itself, and that the FDA knew all along that these trials would not show the same magnitude of benefit as the original E2100 study. He quoted the FDA back to itself in statements made by Dr. Robert Temple during a 2003 ODAC meeting, to show that its proposal to withdraw Avastin was too rigid:

> "When a drug has proved active, you don't lightly remove it because a trial failed. You try to do other studies."[20]

He even went so far as to address Pazdur directly, turning something Pazdur had said during that same 2003 meeting, back at him:

"The withdrawal provision in the regulation gives us judgment so we don't [need] to have a reflex situation; you fail, therefore you must come off."[21]

Pazdur didn't react. It was a reminder that anything said during these proceedings—absolutely anything—was public record and could be used even years later to make the case for another drug. It felt like a gotcha moment, and again appealed to our notion of fairness in how the FDA interpreted its own rules.

Labson summarized these points:

This explains where we are now. CDER's thinking changed over time. . . . Genentech is not trying to undermine the accelerated approval program by gaining inappropriate multiple bites at the apple.[22]

Now that the rules for full approval had been established, Genentech just wanted a crack at conducting the right trial to show Avastin's benefit.

Hal Barron returned to the microphone.

We have seen many slides with many, many numbers; hazard ratios, response rates, confidence intervals, P-values, et cetera. But what we cannot lose sight of, though, is the many women behind these numbers.

We have heard moving testimonials from numerous women who have described their enormous hardships from being diagnosed with this devastating and incurable disease, how grateful they are for the simple pleasures in life, and how significant their unmet need truly is. . . . Our primary objective is to preserve . . . options for women with metastatic breast cancer.[23]

With that closing statement, Barron sat down. Dr. Midthun thanked him and called for a half-hour recess before the FDA's opportunity to question Genentech.

I stood up and looked out toward the audience. It seemed fuller than when we started earlier that morning, and I noticed more of the women who had come to the microphone the previous day. Some were talking to each other and nodding, as if approving of the case Genentech had just presented. I agreed, they had made good points. I still wasn't sure which way I would vote.

Carla Cartwright, an attorney with the FDA's Office of Chief Counsel, started things off after our break. She grilled Genentech's attorney, Michael Labson about whether the company was suggesting that the criteria for drug approval shift away from a pharmaceutical company's need to demonstrate a drug's safety and efficacy and move toward the FDA's responsibility for proving the drug is without benefit.[24]

Labson denied this.

She then asked if the company was proposing it be allowed to take an infinite number of "bites of the apple"—additional clinical trials—while Avastin remained on the market until one of those bites was a winner, finally supporting results from the original E2100 study.

Nope. Genentech wanted just one more trial but clarified that what defined success in such a trial would be up for debate.[25]

John Jenkins, MD, the director of the Office of New Drugs and the man who would one day criticize the FDA for its accelerated review process, took over the questioning. Genentech had made the point repeatedly over the past day-and-a-half that Avastin was used to treat breast cancer worldwide—in 84 countries according to Dr. Horning.[26] Given this, Jenkins commented:

> Patients are reluctant to agree to be randomized to not receive what's an approved treatment for their serious and life-threatening condition. So if this [breast cancer] indication remains in the [Avastin] label, can you help me understand the feasibility of conducting this trial in those countries?[27]

Jenkins emphasized a truism of conducting clinical trials, particularly in the United States: patients don't like to participate in clinical trials in which there's a chance they won't receive a new drug, when they could receive that drug outside of a clinical trial anyway.

How would Genentech be able to complete such a study with Avastin remaining on the market?

Horning responded that there was enough scientific debate about interpreting the data from the multiple Avastin trials that patients and physicians might still be willing to enroll on another Avastin study, even if there was a 50/50 chance of not receiving the drug.[28]

I had my doubts, though.

Over the years, we had seen a number of clinical trials for cancer drugs come before ODAC in which patients—not from the United States or other developed countries, where some of these drugs were already available, but from less developed countries where cancer drugs and even more basic medications like antibiotics were in short supply—had incentives to enroll.

Were these trials able to be conducted with the same rigor as trials in countries where CT scans for example—the crux of assessing cancer progression—weren't a precious resource? And did patients who enrolled on these trials do so with the same free will and considerations of, for example, altruism as patients in developed countries like the United States? Or did they enroll because if they didn't, they wouldn't be able to receive any treatment whatsoever for their cancers?

As someone who conducts clinical trials, time and again I had seen studies grind to a halt when a drug being tested in the trial got approved by the FDA based on results from another study.

How long would it take for the results of just such a trial to come in?

Genentech anticipated three-and-a-half years from the start of the study for an interim analysis, four and a half years for a final analysis, and they didn't expect the trial to begin until 2012.

This, of course, begged the question of whether it was safe for women to remain on Avastin in the United States until 2016, thus allowing Genentech to take one more bite from the apple, when that bite might be rotten?

Cartwright returned to the microphone to address this:

Just so we're clear, we're looking at approximately 2016/2017, and we could potentially be right back here having another proceeding to determine whether or not you've confirmed clinical benefit?[29]

A statistician with Genentech made the point that there were a number of drugs that had received accelerated approval from the FDA that took up to 11 years, while awaiting confirmatory follow-up studies, before receiving full FDA approval.[30] Thus, this time frame, which seemed long to probably everyone listening, was not unprecedented.

In fact, one analysis found that, for drugs approved by the FDA under its accelerated approval program between 1992 and 2008, over one-third of confirmatory studies were never actually completed. Half of these uncompleted studies took an average of five years to even begin!

A similar review from the FDA itself focusing on hematology and oncology drugs reported that 64 drugs for 93 indications received accelerated approval from 1992 to 2017. Of these, only 55 percent fulfilled their post-marketing requirement and verified the benefit seen in the initial study that led to accelerated approval (the equivalents of the initial E2100 trial for Avastin, but with their version of AVADO and RIBBON-1 actually substantiating the initial trial results). On average, it took about three-and-a-half years for these follow-up trials to verify the initial benefit—right in line with the AVADO and RIBBON-1 trials for Avastin, but far quicker than the additional three-and-a-half years Genentech was now proposing.[31]

Cartwright from the FDA and Horning from Genentech tousled over whether or not the FDA had explicitly or implicitly indicated that early results from the follow-up AVADO trial—the one with a progression-free survival advantage of only about three weeks, shown at the time of Avastin's accelerated approval—would be enough for full approval.

I sided with Genentech on this point—the FDA could be opaque when it came to setting its bar for approval, and it would be nice for the agency to provide more concrete guidance.

Finally, the FDA's Jenkins and Genentech's Labson sparred about whether it was more important to focus on the median progression-free survival (the time point at which half the patients on the study have died or have tumors that have worsened) or the hazard ratio (the risk of dying or of cancer getting worse that includes all deaths and worsening cancer that occur over the course of the study in both treatment arms, and not just those at the halfway point). Jenkins even made the point that a hazard ratio (the endpoint Genentech wanted to focus on, because it made results from the AVADO and RIBBON-1 follow-up trials seem more impressive) could be misleading to a patient:

> If we're just looking at the hazard ratio, how do I put that into a benefit-risk assessment of looking at the toxicities of a drug? If I have a 0.5 hazard ratio [meaning, the risk of dying is 50 percent less for one drug versus another], that could mean the difference [in survival] between 1 week and 2 weeks or 12 weeks and 24 weeks.[32]

In the end, both the FDA and Genentech agreed that all measures of a drug's efficacy should be considered, despite what each side had been focusing on in its respective presentations.

Back to the totality of the data.

Recognizing the benefits and flaws of each approach, though, I still couldn't wrap my head around how I could communicate a hazard ratio meaningfully to a patient.

Cartwright and Jenkins sat down, and Dr. Midthun announced it was now time for ODAC members to question Genentech. Once again, all eyes were on us. And once again, our chairperson, Wyndham Wilson, started things off.

I'd like to turn to the toxicity that actually is reported in the
[original] E2100 trial. There is a very clear signal of increased
toxicity in the [Avastin] arm. In fact, if we look at [high grade]
infection, it's 9.3 percent versus 2.9 percent for the control [non-
Avastin] arm. . . . If we look at hypertension, it's 14.5 percent
versus zero percent. . . . Cardiovascular ischemia [angina] was
1.9 percent in the [Avastin] arm versus zero percent in the
control arm. Hemorrhage was .5 percent versus zero percent in
the control arm. And gastrointestinal perforation was .5 percent
versus zero percent. . . .

Perhaps you could comment on that in light of your summary
data. . . . It seemed like there [were] a lot of statements [by
Genentech] that these sorts of toxicities were seen on both arms
equally. At least, that's the kind of general sense I got.[33]

Me too. When Dr. O'Shaughnessy had talked about the bone and
liver pain her patients felt, and how these were relieved with Avastin, she and Genentech representatives made it seem as if the drug's
side effects were really not that bad, particularly given the seriousness of a metastatic breast cancer diagnosis.

O'Shaughnessy acknowledged the side effects and said there was
a "learning curve" to giving Avastin safely to certain patients.

I had trouble with that answer—nobody had presented any information about how only certain women should get Avastin, or about
how to select those women. Nobody was suggesting changing Avastin's label to indicate that women less likely to perforate a bowel, or
at a lower risk of getting a heart attack, let's say, could safely take it.

Frank Balis, the pediatrician from Philadelphia, was next up.

I'd like to ask whether you think that finding a statistically
significant difference equates to a clinically significant outcome.[34]

This simple question was, of course, the crux of why the FDA was
not accepting the follow-up AVADO or RIBBON-1 trials as being
confirmatory. Sure, the statistics said that patients who received
Avastin went a longer period of time, either without their breast
cancer worsening or without dying. But women didn't actually live

any longer, and their progression-free survival dwindled compared to the original E2100 study.

Genentech representatives fell over themselves trying to answer.

James Reimann, Genentech's head of oncology biostatistics, answered no.

Dr. Horning, their global head of clinical development for hematology and oncology, wouldn't respond directly, but reminded Balis that breast cancer doctors had designed the studies, and *they* had felt it was a good study.[35]

Dr. O'Shaughnessy made the case that Avastin changed the natural history of breast cancer, but she acknowledged that they couldn't assess any potential improvement in quality of life very well.[36]

And Hal Barron, Genentech's chief medical officer, tried to shift the discussion from the paltry improvement in average progression-free survival of just a few weeks to the improvement in the hazard ratio (the reduction—or increase—in risk of dying or of cancer getting worse)—which of course seemed more impressive than the average, but is difficult to explain to patients in a meaningful way.[37]

Dr. Midthun called on me to ask the next question. When sitting on an ODAC panel, in front of an audience that included high-ranking officials in the FDA, reporters, investors, company chief officers, and most importantly people affected by the cancer for which a drug is being considered, I always worried about imposter syndrome: Did I really deserve to be there? I looked out at the brave women who had come to the microphone the previous day—I owed it to them to ask questions about whether this drug really helped them. I took a deep breath—and plunged ahead.

> Progression-free survival . . . paired with patient-reported outcomes that were also positive, may be a beneficial effect to patients. In the absence of that, the gold standard for effect is an improvement in overall survival. A progression-free survival without improved

patient-reported outcome or quality of life improvement and
without overall survival may just be a Pyrrhic victory.[38]

I still couldn't quite understand how a woman who went a longer
period of time without her cancer worsening, but who didn't feel
any better or live any longer, was helped. But that's how Genentech had constructed all of their studies: with a goal of improving
progression-free survival. I went on:

> Are you saying it would be impossible to design a study that showed
> on overall survival benefit for women with metastatic breast cancer?[39]

Genentech's statistician, James Reimann, answered:

> First, we believe that a large magnitude of PFS [progression-free
> survival] benefit is a clinical benefit [meaningful to women] in this
> setting. . . . I think a four-month prolongation in overall survival
> would be very important. . . . In order to detect that magnitude
> of benefit, we would need studies on the order of 1,500 to 2,300
> patients. It's doable. It's just they're very big studies.[40]

*What?* I was incensed. They could design the right study—one that
would actually be able to show whether or not Avastin enabled women
to live longer. I suspected they just didn't want to because they were
shooting for the lowest achievable bar for approval—an improvement
in progression-free survival—which would require fewer participants,
and thus would cost the company less, too. I continued:

> Conducting a study of 2,000 women powered on overall survival
> when, as you pointed out, there are 45,000 women diagnosed
> with this in the US each year and many-fold more than that
> internationally, doesn't seem impossible. To me, it seems like the
> right thing to do.[41]

Ralph Freedman, our gynecologic oncologist from Houston, followed up on the lack of improvement in quality of life for women
treated with Avastin:

> Dr. O'Shaughnessy mentioned the fact that . . . [metastatic breast
> cancer] is highly symptomatic in most patients. I think that's correct.

And also that improving or decreasing patient symptoms with the least amount of [drug] toxicity is a major objective. And yet we didn't see any of this in the studies. I just wondered . . . what do you feel about that, [having] these results without [their showing] clinical benefit?[42]

Dr. O'Shaughnessy took this one:

When you see nice benefits in PFS [progression-free survival] in those patients and higher response rates, you can be pretty certain that that's translating into clinical benefit in those patients.[43]

Ralph, ever polite, didn't get upset that O'Shaughnessy dodged his question. But I saw his eyes narrow a bit as he persisted.

Were you disappointed not to see any symptom improvement in this subgroup of patients presented from this trial?[44]

Dr. Horning took over, and blamed inadequate quality-of-life questionnaires for not being able to show a benefit for Avastin. Her contention was that women did have an improved quality of life, but the ways in which we measured that—the questionnaires themselves—were flawed. Again, I had trouble with this answer—the blame for choosing questionnaires that didn't adequately assess quality of life should fall squarely on Genentech's shoulders.

Natalie Compagni-Portis, our patient representative from Oakland, was next up. I was again reminded of how insightful she could be:

I very much appreciate the testimony we received yesterday from patients, but I want to remind us all that we are not hearing from patients who discontinued treatment due to adverse effects, and we're not hearing from people who died due to Avastin. . . .
Would you say that you then consider that [the original] E2100 was a success despite the fact that there is missing data, there's discrepancy of interpretations of the scans, there is no quality-of-life data, and there is no improvement in overall survival? I hear people keep talking about no *impairment* of overall survival, but what matters to patients is improvement in overall survival.[45]

Wow—she summed up my concerns with the first trial, never mind the follow-up studies, far more concisely and eloquently than I could have. I heard some murmuring from the audience, but I couldn't tell if it supported or disparaged Natalie's comment.

Reimann answered for Genentech:

> Yes, we do feel that the study was a big success that has led to labeling for the medication.[46]

Yikes! That was a huge blunder and another deadly sin—placing regulatory and business objectives ahead of making people's lives better. The company seemed to be showing its true stripes. Product labeling may be how success is defined to stockholders. But not to cancer patients. They want to live longer and feel better!

The chief medical officer Hal Barron jumped in to clarify Reimann's statement:

> It's absolutely true that there was no statistically significant improvement in overall survival. . . . One of the people who made a testimonial yesterday . . . said something that I think we need to remember, which is, the absence of evidence is not evidence of absence.[47]

I had heard a variation of the phrase before: lack of evidence is not evidence of lack. In other words, just because a study doesn't support a treatment approach in medicine, that doesn't mean the treatment won't work. It always struck me as a convenient justification to practice medicine outside the boundaries of rigorous science. It also struck me as undercutting over 50 years of FDA standards. I saw members of the agency sitting at their table, shaking their heads incredulously.

Compagni-Portis continued, undaunted:

> Are you saying that you're comfortable with a risk for patients in continuing to administer Avastin, especially if [the additional study Genentech was proposing to conduct] wouldn't be completed until at least 2016? And are you comfortable with women continuing

to bear those risks and the deaths that may come about with that much more time studying this drug?[48]

Horning answered for Genentech:

Absolutely. We're very comfortable with this.[49]

After we concluded our questioning, an awkward silence descended on everyone in the room as Dr. Midthun approached the microphone again. We knew what was coming next.

It was time to vote.

We took a short break while more chairs were brought to accommodate the steady stream of people entering the Great Room. The noise level in the room rose. As the number of audience members swelled, the chaos approached what we'd seen at the start of the previous day.

None of us left the ODAC table. We didn't converse with one another or even make eye contact. I suspect that each of us was deep in thought about the decision we were about to make. I also suspect that, knowing we would be under particular public scrutiny right now, none of us wanted to tip our hat to the way we were thinking of voting or be accused of colluding by talking to each other.

People took their seats as Midthun came to the microphone again. She spoke to those in the audience and then addressed us at the ODAC table, explaining what was about to happen. She asked us to vote yes or no on three questions; the first would ask us to verify the clinical benefit of Avastin regarding the breast cancer indication for which it was approved.

Again, a yes vote means that you find that the AVADO and RIBBON 1 trials *failed* to verify the clinical benefit of Avastin for the breast cancer indication at issue in this hearing. CDER [FDA] asks for a yes vote. Genentech asks for a no vote, and I'll ask you to vote simultaneously.[50]

That was it, without further preamble. There was no acknowledgment of the heated testimonies over the past two days, of the brave women who told their moving stories, of the thousands of women who participated in the Avastin breast cancer trials.

There was no recognition of the implications of our vote on public trust of FDA decisions, or of what it would mean to the tens of thousands of women with breast cancer receiving Avastin for us to tell them that we felt the drug's danger outweighed any benefit.

There were no assurances that a "yes" vote would still preserve the sanctity of the accelerated approval mechanism, born from AIDS activists in response to what they saw as an uncaring, tone deaf, and homophobic government.

There were no assurances that a "no" vote would keep women safe while Avastin remained on the market for breast cancer.

I looked over to Natalie, Wyndham, and Ralph, and I caught them looking at me. Our mutual glances confirmed the inevitable: it was, actually, time to vote. We cautiously reached toward our microphones, where we would push "yes" or "no" buttons to register our votes.

After a few seconds of tense silence, the vote was displayed on the screens around the room.

Yes    6

No     0

I heard a rush of disappointed murmuring from the audience.

Midthun asked each of us to state our names and explain how we voted and why we voted that way.

Wyndham Wilson started:

> I believe, based on the results of those trials, in the absence of a survival benefit or improvement of quality of life, that delaying progression on a CT scan for just a month or two, given the toxicity of this agent . . . I did not feel that these two studies confirmed clinical benefit.[51]

Ralph Freedman, Natalie Compagni-Portis, and Brent Logan essentially echoed Wyndham's thoughts. Then it was my turn:

> I also voted yes. Unfortunately, the follow-up trials, which were supposed to have been confirmatory, did not confirm the magnitude of progression-free survival, and in my mind, didn't validate that as a clinical endpoint by demonstrating any improvement in overall survival or quality of life.[52]

Frank Balis agreed, and Greg Curt, our industry representative who could not vote, declined to offer a statement.

Dr. Midthun moved on to Question 2(a):

> Does the available evidence on Avastin demonstrate that the drug has *not* been shown to be *effective* for the breast cancer indication for which it was approved? CDER asks for a yes vote. Genentech asks for a no vote.[53]

Again, we reached for the buttons on our microphones. And again, after a few seconds of silence that seemed to last for minutes, the vote was displayed on the screens around the room.

Yes     6

No      0

When asked to justify our votes, our statistician, Brent Logan, summed it up best for the rest of us:

> The totality of the data suggests no survival benefit, a very modest improvement in progression-free survival, which has questionable clinical relevance, and no evidence of a benefit in quality of life.[54]

Midthun then explained the terms for our vote on Question 2(b):

> Does the available evidence on Avastin demonstrate that the drug has *not* been shown to be *safe* for the breast cancer indication for which it was approved and that Avastin has *not* been shown to present a clinical benefit for this that justifies the risk associated with use of the product for this indication? CDER asks for a yes vote. Genentech asks for a no vote.[55]

The pressing of the buttons, the silence, the display on the screens:

Yes    6

No     0

I looked out to the audience. Sitting side by side I saw a couple of women who had approached the microphone the previous day. They quietly sobbed as they comforted each other.

When we cast our votes, we were considering the science, the data, the thousands of women who enrolled in these trials, and the studies themselves that did not convincingly show that Avastin was better than chemotherapy alone, and in fact caused harm.

The two sobbing women in the audience were probably thinking, "But what about us?"

Our patient representative Natalie Compagni-Portis further explained her yes vote, in part by invoking the women who were no longer alive to present their testimony:

> We have heard repeatedly that the risks involved are usual, and that they're manageable, and even that they're similar to other drugs that are given for metastatic breast cancer, but it seems to me that the adverse effects of Avastin are significant, and the studies do show this; that the risks even include death without any demonstrated benefit. . . . We're not hearing from patients who have really suffered because of the drug. . . . And I think we can only ask patients to take on this risk when there is significant benefit to them.[56]

Dr. Midthun spoke again:

> We'll now go onto the last issue. Question 3. If the Commissioner agrees with the grounds for withdrawal set out in [Question] 1, [Question] 2(a), or [Question] 2(b), should FDA nevertheless *continue the approval* of the breast cancer indication while the sponsor designs and conducts additional studies intended to verify the drug's clinical benefit?
> Genentech asks for a yes vote. CDER asks for a no vote.[57]

We voted a final time:

Yes    0

No    6

I couldn't help but notice that seven women in the audience rose from their seats and linked arms. They stood silently, glaring at us, weeping, like the chorus in a Greek tragedy. The vote was in, and the proceedings continued. Ralph Freedman verbalized what many of us were thinking:

> I voted no. I have to say that I struggled with this and struggled with this until just before the meeting. I don't know that people would believe me, but that's true. And, eventually, I felt that the lack of clarity on the risk-benefit assessment, the fact that the label no longer adequately represents the [risks] in light of the subsequent studies, and also whether it's feasible to conduct [another] study is certainly in doubt.[58]

I considered those women in the audience again, what this meant to them, when I made my statement:

> It gave me pause to continue to make available a drug for an indication when that drug hasn't demonstrated the type of efficacy that women with breast cancer deserve and [it will still] expose them to serious toxicities.
>
> We have tried to slice this pie in a lot of different ways to try to find some kind of benefit for this drug in combination with chemotherapy for a desperate breast cancer population. And no matter which way we look at it, all we're left with is crumbs.[59]

I heard some mixed reactions from the now overflowing audience as Wyndham Wilson prepared to make the final comment on behalf of ODAC:

> I voted no. I feel the confirmatory trials were extremely well done, used the same agents, and did not show any clinically meaningful improvement in progression-free survival or in overall survival.

I would encourage the company, if they are in fact convinced that there is a clinical benefit here, to do this follow-up trial as quickly as possible.

I would say to, also, patients out there with breast cancer that I think these have been extremely important trials. . . . I hope that they . . . see that, in very large, randomized studies . . . there was no evidence that this drug was of help to them and [they won't] come away feeling as though an important drug that is going to make them feel better or make them live longer is being taken from them.[60]

What follows is the official transcript of the proceedings, as Dr. Midthun tried to make her closing statement:

[Audience comments off mic—inaudible.] Dr. Midthun: I thank you for your comments. I would now like to—[Audience comments continued—inaudible.][61]

But those comments were clearly audible to me. Angry shouts and protests erupted from members of the audience who claimed injustice, and voiced disappointment and disbelief.

"No!"

"You can't!"

"I have children! I have four children!"

"What would you like us to take instead?"

"This is a sham!"

"Do we look terminal?"

Midthun pressed on:

Thank you for your participation and your attention during this proceeding. This administrative hearing, provided for under our regulations, is a means to prepare a record that will form the basis for the final decision by Commissioner Hamburg.

The hearing has also provided an opportunity for the public to observe and participate in the type of difficult decision-making process that the FDA engages in each day as it considers the approval or the withdrawal of approval of drug products.

As illustrated by the public presentations at the beginning of the hearing, FDA's focus is always on the effect that our decisions will have on patients who will use those products, including those patients who may be benefited by them and those who may also be harmed by them. . . .

We very much appreciate the significant efforts that so many people have put into the presentations at this hearing and the high level of discussion that has prevailed. The hearing is now adjourned. Thank you.[62]

The official transcript then ends, indicating it was 3:15 p.m.

As we closed our laptops, stashed the cords into our computer cases, and reached for our luggage, armed security guards rushed to the ODAC table. The decibel level in the room had suddenly doubled, then tripled. Behind the guards, members of the audience, including the seven women of the Greek chorus, pressed toward our table, having circumnavigated the rope cordons that had separated us.

They linked arms again as they swayed back and forth, sobbing.

Others screamed at us, "You should be ashamed of yourselves! Killers!"

One woman held up a photo album right in front of me. I could make out images of her with her husband, both of them dressed casually, both of them smiling, as if photos could testify on Avastin's behalf .

"You want to see my quality of life on Avastin?" she shouted. "Here's my quality of life! Look at my life! Look at my quality of life!" She jabbed her finger at the pages.

Another woman had positioned herself near Natalie Compagni-Portis and yelled at her, "I hope your breast cancer comes back so you know how we all feel!"

Natalie's face lost all color as she looked away, crestfallen. She knew how it felt: that awful day, that moment, when a doctor tells you that you have breast cancer. She was one of them. She represented them on our committee. And she had cast her votes because she thought Avastin didn't help women, and in fact could hurt them.

Security guards escorted us out of the room quickly and down a back hallway. The jeering slowly faded as the guards hustled us through a heavy door and then through an emergency exit to a back lot. Three limousines waited, their engines running, their dark-tinted windows promising refuge if any protesters had figured out our escape route. I threw my luggage into the trunk of one car and piled into the backseat with Ralph Freedman and Brent Logan, who were also heading to National Airport. The moment we shut our doors the car sped off, taking back roads as it headed toward the highway.

We were quiet, the three of us, again lost in our own thoughts, replaying moments from the day. We had voted unanimously on every question, unequivocally recommending that Avastin's breast cancer label be removed. The FDA would likely follow suit, and it would then withdraw Avastin's marketing approval for breast cancer.

But the reaction of the women, still alive with breast cancer, still receiving Avastin, had shaken me. One of those women, Crystal Hanna, would later make the comment:

> A panel of six, none of which specialize in metastatic breast cancer, decided that we are statistically insignificant. How do I explain that to my 4-year-old and 7-year-old?[63]

I had to wonder. Had we just participated in the greatest demonstration of how the FDA's accelerated approval program works, fulfilling its purpose to get promising drugs for life-threatening conditions to market fast, but to withdraw those drugs when confirmatory trials fail?

Or had we shown how it doesn't?

# Epilogue

FDA representatives had recommended to members of ODAC, off the record, that we unlist our personal phone numbers to help protect us from threatening phone calls after the hearing. I hadn't bothered, and none of those phone calls came to my home.

Plenty came to my office, though, and my administrative assistant back in Cleveland became adept at determining which calls were coming from my own patients, asking for help with their medications, chemotherapy treatments, or management of symptoms, and which came from people pretending to be patients so they could instead lambast me for the decision that our "Panel of Six" had made. She didn't send the latter calls through to me, but I asked her to keep track of them and let me know what was said, to remind myself of the people affected by our regulatory recommendations.

Four and a half months later, on November 18, 2011, the FDA commissioner, Margaret A. Hamburg, MD, issued her 70-page decision on the accelerated approval of Avastin for the treatment of metastatic breast cancer.[1] To almost no one's surprise, the FDA withdrew its approval for the breast cancer indication.

In a section of the document provided as an explanation to patients and those who support them, Hamburg addressed a number of questions a woman with breast cancer might ask regarding the impact of the FDA's decision on treatment for her breast cancer:

Could patients still use Avastin for the treatment of breast cancer? Yes. The FDA does not regulate the practice of medicine, and Avastin remained on the market for the treatment of other cancers, such as cancers of the colon, lung, brain, and kidney. Use of Avastin to treat breast cancer would now constitute "off-label" use.[2]

Will insurance cover the cost of Avastin for breast cancer if its use is now considered off-label? Maybe, but maybe not. That was up to insurance companies, as the FDA's decisions have no direct effect on what they cover.[3] While regulatory agencies in other parts of the world include drug cost in their decisions, the FDA does not. As Hamburg stated:

> Ultimately, my responsibility, and the Agency's responsibility, is to put aside preconceived beliefs that I, or patients or physicians may hold, and take a hard look at the objective evidence.[4]

Did Avastin receive a fair hearing? Yes. The Center for Drug Evaluation and Research (CDER) made the decision to approve Avastin initially, and then it withdrew that approval. Hamburg, as commissioner of the FDA, explained how she separated herself from those decisions, and then listened to arguments from CDER and Genentech during the hearing to inform her decision to withdraw the approval in November 2011.[5]

How can the FDA make a different decision about Avastin than European regulatory authorities? Different countries have different standards and different decision-makers.[6]

Is it possible Avastin will be approved again to treat women with metastatic breast cancer? Yes. This would require another trial showing clear benefit, defined as unequivocally improving survival, quality of life, or a long progression-free survival.[7]

Hamburg went on to say:

> Sometimes, despite the hopes of investigators, patients, industry
> and even the FDA itself, the results of rigorous testing can be
> disappointing. This is the case with Avastin when used for the
> treatment of metastatic breast cancer.[8]

She then ended the document by stating simply:

> I conclude that the currently available data do not support
> accelerated approval of this drug for this indication.[9]

Whatever did happen with the follow-up trial Genentech was proposing, the one that was supposed to be conducted while Avastin remained on the market? The same one that would vindicate the progression-free survival results from the original E2100 trial?

It never materialized. One subsequent study, however, enrolled women with breast cancer and randomized them to receive chemotherapy only, chemotherapy with Avastin, or chemotherapy with Avastin, followed by long-term Avastin therapy. The number enrolled—almost 5,000 women—was more than double what the Genentech statistician James Reimann had told us would have been necessary to design a trial to show whether or not Avastin improved overall survival. It, too, was a loser—no advantage to women receiving Avastin in terms of how long they lived without their breast cancer returning, or in how long they lived. In the words of the study's authors, "We have no choice but to conclude that the underlying hypothesis, namely that inhibiting vascular endothelial growth factor [Judah Folkman's life's work, with Avastin] would be effective, is simply wrong."[10]

Another subsequent study, RIBBON-2, enrolled 684 women with metastatic breast cancer who had already received one treatment regimen and randomized them to receive chemotherapy combined with Avastin or chemotherapy alone. The results? For the women receiving Avastin, the improvement in progression-free survival was only about two months, with no improvement in overall survival.[11]

Following the FDA's formal decision to withdraw Avastin's breast cancer indication, the drug went on to get approved for the treatment of cervical cancer in 2014 and for different types of ovarian cancer in 2014 and 2016.[12]

Sales of Avastin in 2009 for breast cancer were $900 million. That figure dropped by $125 million, to $775 million, in 2010—the year ODAC made its initial recommendation to the FDA to withdraw the breast cancer indication.[13] But considering its global sales for all cancer indications of $5.5 billion, Avastin remained the world's best-selling cancer drug.[14]

In 2011, the year of the hearing and of Dr. Hamburg's formal withdrawal of the breast cancer indication, Avastin's breast cancer sales dropped about another 10 percent. But worldwide sales for all cancer indications increased to $6.3 billion—largely on the backs of ovarian cancer patients. Avastin sales reached $7.12 billion by 2019, although sales are actually expected to drop precipitously in years to come.[15]

Why? Because in 2017 the FDA approved the first Avastin biosimilar drug—essentially, a generic Avastin, and a second one in 2019. Biosimilars, as the name implies, are nearly identical to a brand name drug (called a reference product) in structure, purity, and activity within the body. They have no clinically meaningful differences in safety or potency from the brand drug. By July 2020, the FDA had approved 28 biosimilars for conditions ranging from cancer to rheumatologic disorders, thus introducing increased market competition and a drop in prices for these costly drugs. Marketing of these Avastin biosimilars began in 2019—the year Avastin's marketing exclusivity expired.[16]

Meanwhile, the FDA went on a juggernaut of drug approvals during the Trump administration, following guidance (particularly from the 21st Century Cures Act) for the FDA to remove barriers to approval, make more drugs available, and allow market forces to dictate which drugs are used preferentially in patients. These goals aligned not only with the wishes of the executive branch, but also with the objectives of Scott Gottlieb, MD, the FDA commissioner who served for about two years during this period. Several years before his nomination he had commented, "In so heavily prioritizing one of its obligations—the protection of consumers—the FDA has sometimes subordinated and neglected its other key obligation, which is to guide new medical innovations to market."[17] Gottlieb advocated for an FDA that would allow greater access to drugs that had yet to prove conclusive results of their efficacy, as long as they provided strong clues to indicate that they might actually work.[18]

In a similar move toward deregulation, Gottlieb criticized one randomized study that used a placebo arm, saying it was invasive and unnecessary: that particular study ultimately failed to show an advantage of the study procedure over the placebo.[19]

To be fair, though, the trend of the FDA's approving more drugs based on non-comparative trial data, or on endpoints that did not include an improvement in survival, existed prior to and continued beyond the Gottlieb era.

By 2019, the FDA Center for Drug Evaluation and Research (CDER) had a five-year rolling approval average of 44 new drugs per year—double the nadir of 22 new drugs per year in 2009. In 2019 alone, these included drugs for postpartum depression, multiple sclerosis, muscular dystrophy, cystic fibrosis, psoriasis, schizophrenia, porphyria, osteoporosis, narcolepsy, insomnia, hypoactive sexual desire, acne, anemia, urinary tract infections, tuberculosis, macular degeneration, migraines, Parkinson's disease, heart disease, and of course, a variety of cancers.[20] Most of what CDER approved (58 percent) were what's referred to as priority review products—those therapies expected to offer significant improvements over what's already on the market. *Breakthrough* designated drugs—those thought to offer substantial improvements over available therapies—accounted for 27 percent of approvals, while about one in five drugs received accelerated approval, similar to Avastin.

The fast rate of cancer drug approvals may also be directly attributed to a tragic occurrence in the personal life of Rick Pazdur, the director of FDA's Office of Oncology Drug Products. When Rick interviewed me to be a member of Oncologic Drug Advisory Committee, he had reminded me that ODAC's decisions, and those of the FDA, were based purely on the science, and should be separated from emotions. But in 2015, Rick lost his wife, Mary Pazdur, to ovarian cancer. Her three-year cancer struggle played a role in changing the oncology chief's approach to cancer drug approval at the FDA. As he told one reporter:

> I have a much greater sense of urgency these days. I have been on a jihad to streamline the review process and get things out the door faster. I have evolved from regulator to regulator-advocate.[21]

One of those drugs that received both priority and breakthrough approval was for the treatment of sickle cell disease—a crippling, lifelong condition that primarily affects blacks in America and for which there previously existed almost no therapies.[22] This was a triumph.

Other drugs that harness a person's own immune system to attack cancer—known as checkpoint inhibitors—have been an unequivocal success in multiple cancers, even markedly improving survival in previously hopeless cases. One of the most profound examples of this is in the treatment of melanoma. Until 2011, people with this skin cancer had only a 16 percent chance of being alive five years after their diagnoses. Then, the first checkpoint inhibitor, ipilimumab, was approved by the FDA for patients with end-stage melanoma, in whom the new drug led to an average survival of about 10 months, compared to 6.4 months in patients receiving just chemotherapy.[23] Another checkpoint inhibitor, pembrolizumab, approved by the FDA in 2014, led to an average survival of 33 months and a five-year survival of almost 40 percent in patients with advanced melanoma.[24] This is the drug used to treat former president Jimmy Carter for his melanoma.

Other approvals for drugs targeting the genetic basis for disease, particularly cancer, were also exciting. Decades of work exploring the basis for cancer have identified the genetic defects that cause cells to go rogue and wreak havoc on the body. Now, finally, drugs have been designed to latch on to those defects and be the undoing of the cancer. As we identify more and more genetic mutations that cause cancer, how we define cancer becomes increasingly refined, though, and the population of patients who might benefit from a particular drug shrinks dramatically.

For example, acute myeloid leukemia is diagnosed in approximately 20,000 people per year in the United States. Among those affected by the cancer approximately 5 percent, or 1,000 patients, will have leukemia with a genetic mutation called *IDH1*. A trial testing a drug that targets that mutation would take years, or even more than a decade, to enroll the 5,000 patients who were included in that subsequent Avastin trial for women with breast cancer!

That means smaller clinical trials for drugs that target genetic mutations affecting only a sliver of a cancer population. And many of these trials don't have a comparator arm, leaving us wondering whether the new, exciting, genetic mutation eliminating drug is really any better than our old standards.

The drug targeting *IDH1*—called ivosidenib—was approved by the FDA based on a trial enrolling just 258 patients, all of whom received the new drug. I was one of the investigators on that trial. One out of every five of these patients had a complete response to ivosidenib that lasted, on average, about eight months.[25]

Was this better than the efficacy of regular old chemotherapy? Was it less toxic? Hard to tell without a comparison treatment.

Another of those approvals was for gemtuzumab ozogamicin—that mouthful of a name given to a drug treating acute myeloid leukemia. Although the drug had received accelerated approval in 2000, it was withdrawn from the market in 2010 because the confirmatory trial was a failure. Additional studies using the drug were conducted in patients with leukemia; some of those studies were also failures, but one conducted in 237 older patients showed that gemtuzumab ozogamicin could improve overall survival when compared to no chemotherapy at all—by an average of only about five weeks.[26]

This re-approval was a head-scratcher, and it may have undercut some of the trust placed in the FDA to safeguard the public against drugs with high toxicity rates and limited clinical benefit. It's hard for me to believe—when compared to no active therapy, and even though other therapy *does* exist for these patients—that an improvement in survival of five weeks (for a drug that was approved, withdrawn for lack of efficacy, and then approved again) met the bar Margaret Hamburg set for Avastin's reinstatement as a breast cancer therapy by requiring "another trial showing clear benefit, defined as unequivocally improving survival, quality of life, or a long progression-free survival."

The coin of the realm for the FDA is the trust the public holds in the agency—trust that it will safeguard our health while approving the drugs necessary to fight disease effectively. That trust can be bolstered when drugs like checkpoint inhibitors that work really, really well, with acceptable side effects given the diseases they're treating, are brought to market quickly.

But that same trust is eroded when drugs with accelerated approval are yanked in the setting of worrisome toxicities or lack of efficacy—even if the removal is also safeguarding the health of the public. This is particularly true when the initial approval occurred despite a negative vote from an independent panel of experts on a committee such as ODAC.

In 2021, just such a committee voted overwhelmingly against the Alzheimer's drug aducanumab. The drug had been studied in two randomized trials: one was felt to demonstrate a modicum of clinical benefit to patients by Biogen, the manufacturer; the other trial was a failure. Aducanumab was associated with reduction of the amyloid plaques that typify Alzheimer's, though other analyses showed no correlation between plaque reduction and improvement in cognition. The drug also was associated with significant side effects, including bleeding into the brain.[27]

Despite the committee's vote and the study results, the FDA granted accelerated approval to aducanumab, based largely on the plaque reduction. The agency likely felt pressure to grant the approval as the first new therapy for Alzheimer's in 18 years. Immediately, three members of that committee resigned, and reprobation from the scientific community was swift.[28] Some hospitals have refused to allow the drug on their formularies, as its use remains controversial despite the approval.[29]

An even quicker method than accelerated approval to get drugs to patients faster is by allowing patients access to medications that have not yet been approved.

On May 30, 2018, the "Trickett Wendler, Frank Mongiello, Jordan McLinn, and Matthew Bellina Right to Try Act" was signed into law. This law provided a pathway for patients who have been diagnosed with life-threatening diseases or conditions—and who have tried all approved treatment options and were unable to participate in a clinical trial—to access certain unapproved treatments.[30] Right to Try was born from the efforts of Frank Burroughs, cofounder of the Abigail Alliance on behalf of his daughter Abigail, who was denied access under the FDA's "compassionate use exception doctrine" to treat her squamous cell carcinoma of the head and neck with a drug available at the time only for use by colon cancer patients in clinical trials.

Right to Try was designed to speed patient access to investigational drugs, and to provide liability protection to the pharmaceutical company providing the drug and the doctor prescribing it. One criticism of this program was that it fed the ongoing political drama surrounding FDA regulatory practices more than it served the needs of patients trying to obtain drugs prior to their approval.[31] Another FDA program, expanded access (also known as compassionate use) has been in place since 1987. As expanded access essentially requires that a clinical trial be developed—sometimes to treat only one person—it includes information about drug side effects and stipulates dosing regimens, and it requires that insurance companies cover drug costs. During the ten-year period from 2005 to 2014, the FDA received almost 11,000 expanded access requests and approved 99.7 percent of them. For emergency expanded access requests, average turnaround time by FDA was less than one day; for regular requests, about a week.[32]

Writing a trial for one person and getting it approved through institutional review boards and the FDA can take time (estimated to be 30 hours of physician and staff time) and resources.[33] Right to Try was intended to avoid those hurdles, but it left in place perhaps the biggest obstacle to patients receiving drugs prior to their approval: the pharmaceutical company's willingness to provide the drug. Data have not been reported about how many patients have taken advantage of Right to Try, but the numbers are estimated to be quite low.

Let's return to the question that started this book: Was the FDA's decision to revoke Avastin's breast cancer approval the ultimate demonstration of how the FDA's system of checks and balances really works? Or, in how it doesn't?

I believe it actually shows that our drug regulatory structure—forged from tragedy and beholden to a myriad of medical, political, economic, and societal pressures—functions well. And the key to its success is the tension between the agency and the many people to whom it must answer.

This tension, between getting patients access to drugs for life-threatening conditions as quickly as possible and ensuring the safety, safety, safety, and efficacy of those drugs, will never go away.

This human need to offer succor to dying patients—in the form of a medication that has a chance of working, no matter how small, if only for a short period of time—and to offer some kind of hope, but not false hope, will never go away.

This drive to manufacture the drugs that patients need—this moral, scientific, and financial imperative to rid humankind of disease—will never go away.

Which is a good thing, and perhaps the only way we will be able to continue to improve on the safety and efficacy of the drugs that patients need.

# Acknowledgments

I am blessed to have been counseled, comforted, and buoyed by a number of magnificent people throughout my life, which has taken the twists, turns, and eventual migration down south that a lot of lives do. These are but a few of those special individuals.

First, my mentors: Brian Strom, MD, MPH, who taught me in medical school how to think critically, conduct clinical research, and evaluate the regulatory aspects of drug development; Stephanie Lee, MD, MPH, who honed my critical evaluative skills during my fellowship and led the American Society of Hematology with such intellect, grace, and dignity during that most awful of pandemic years; Richard Stone, MD, who taught the fine art of treating people with leukemia, conducting clinical trials, and thoughtfully analyzing the findings from those studies; and Ilene Galinsky, MSN, ANP, and Barbara Tripp, RN, CNS, who never let me forget the people behind the numbers.

Next, my friends: Doug Neu, Noam Neusner, and Shoshana Landow, MD, MPH, my oldest and dearest, who have been steadfastly supportive for decades; David Steensma, MD; Joseph Porcelli; Jeffrey Algazy, MD, MPH; Timothy Gilligan, MD; Hetty Carraway, MD, MBA; Aaron Gerds, MD, MS; Jaroslaw Maciejewski, MD, PhD; Nate

Pennell, MD; Alison Loren, MD; Joe Mikhael, MD; Jay Baruch, MD; Erin Kobetz, PhD; Anastasia Santiago, DNP, APRN; Jenifer Hamilton; Maria (Ken) Figueroa, MD; Davis and Amy Shumaker, PharmD, my midlife friends, colleagues, writing buddies, cycling companions, and the people I turn to when my insecurities rear their ugly heads. And to Stephen Nimer, MD; Craig Moskowitz, MD; and Roy Weiss, MD, PhD: thanks for your faith in recruiting me to the Sylvester Comprehensive Cancer Center | University of Miami and for modeling such extraordinary leadership skills.

Thanks also to Toby Bilanow and Roberta Zeff, my editors at the *New York Times*, who have been so encouraging of me and my essays for years, and so exquisitely skilled at transforming them into readable stories.

My indefatigable agent, John Thornton, of The Spieler Agency, still believes in me after all of these years and has been a constant source of wisdom and calm. I can't wait to see what the next few years will bring.

Robert Prior, my editor at the MIT Press, has this wonderful ability to identify the compelling story and a Yoda-like talent to guide me to see it, too! Bob, you believed in me from the very beginning and I am forever grateful. Thanks also to Nicholas DiSabatino, my publicist at the MIT Press, for being a great editor, having an infectious enthusiasm, and for being infinitely patient with me! And thank you, thank you, thank you Mary Bagg for joining me again in the intimate process of copyediting, for your quick wit, willingness to debate grammar, and for your ability to calm the occasional rough waters of my prose.

My wife Jennifer and my kids are my oasis, the people I want to spend every day with forever. You are the loves of my life. And I still don't care if that sounds cringey.

And finally, thank you to all of my patients, you are my inspiration.

# Appendix

*Sample Clinical Trial Eligibility Criteria*

(From a Phase 2 clinical trial of two drugs to treat myelodysplastic syndromes, a type of bone marrow cancer)

## Inclusion Criteria

1. Subject is ≥18 years of age the time of signing the informed consent form (ICF).
2. Subject must understand and voluntarily sign an informed consent form prior to any study-related assessments/procedures being conducted.
3. Documented diagnosis of myelodysplastic syndromes according to World Health Organization classification that meets International Prognostic Scoring System classification (Greenberg et al., 2012; Appendix D) of very low, low, or intermediate risk disease; intermediate patients must have a blast percentage <5% to be enrolled.
4. Refractory or intolerant to, or ineligible for, prior erythropoiesis stimulating agent (ESA) treatment, as defined by any one of the following:

- Refractory to prior ESA treatment—documentation of non-response or response that is no longer maintained to prior ESA-containing regimen; ESA regimen must have been either:

  —recombinant human erythropoietin (rHu EPO) ≥40,000 IU/wk for at least 8 doses or equivalent;

OR

  —darbepoetin alpha ≥200–500 μg Q1–3W for at least 4 doses or equivalent;

- Intolerant to prior ESA treatment—documentation of discontinuation of prior ESA-containing regimen, at any time after introduction due to intolerance or an adverse event
- ESA ineligible—Low chance of response to ESA based on endogenous serum erythropoietin level >200 U/L for subjects not previously treated with ESAs

5. If previously treated with ESAs, agents must have been discontinued ≥4 weeks prior to date of Cycle 1, Day 1 of study treatment.

6. Requires red blood cell (RBC) transfusions, as documented by the following criteria:

   - Average transfusion requirement of ≥2 units/8 weeks of RBCs confirmed for a minimum of 16 weeks immediately preceding Cycle 1, Day 1.
   - Hemoglobin levels at the time of or within 7 days prior to administration of a RBC transfusion must have been ≤10.0 g/dL for the transfusion to be counted towards meeting eligibility criteria. Red blood cell transfusions administered when hemoglobin levels were >10.0 g/dL and/or RBC transfusions administered for elective surgery will not qualify as a required transfusion for the purpose of meeting eligibility criteria.
   - No consecutive 56-day period that was RBC transfusion-free during the 16 weeks immediately preceding Cycle 1, Day 1.

7. Eastern Cooperative Oncology Group (ECOG) performance status score of 0, 1, or 2

8. Females of childbearing potential (FCBP), defined as a sexually mature woman who: (1) has not undergone a hysterectomy or bilateral oophorectomy or (2) has not been naturally postmenopausal (amenorrhea following cancer therapy does not rule out childbearing potential) for at least 24 consecutive months (i.e., has had menses at any time in the preceding 24 consecutive months), must:

   • Have two negative pregnancy tests as verified by the Investigator prior to starting study therapy (unless the screening pregnancy test was done within 72 hours of C1D1). She must agree to ongoing pregnancy testing during the course of the study, and after end of study treatment.

   • If sexually active, agree to use, and be able to comply with, highly effective contraception without interruption, 5 weeks prior to starting investigational product, during the study therapy (including dose interruptions), and for 12 weeks after discontinuation of study therapy.

9. Male subjects must:

   • Agree to use a condom, defined as a male latex condom or nonlatex condom NOT made out of natural (animal) membrane (for example, polyurethane), during sexual contact with a pregnant female or a female of childbearing potential while participating in the study, during dose interruptions and for at least 12 weeks following investigational product discontinuation, even if he has undergone a successful vasectomy.

10. Subject is willing and able to adhere to the study visit schedule and other protocol requirements.

## Exclusion Criteria

The presence of any of the following will exclude a subject from study enrollment:

1. Prior therapy with (Drug A).

2. Prior therapy with (Drug B).

3. Myelodysplastic Syndromes associated with deletion 5q cytogenetic abnormality

4. Known clinically significant anemia due to iron, vitamin B12, or folate deficiencies, or autoimmune or hereditary hemolytic anemia, or gastrointestinal bleeding

   • Iron deficiency to be determined by serum ferritin ≤15 µg/L and additional testing if clinically indicated (e.g., calculated transferrin saturation [iron/total iron binding capacity ≤20%] or bone marrow aspirate stain for iron).

5. Prior allogeneic stem cell transplant

6. Known history of diagnosis of acute myeloid leukemia

7. Abnormal kidney function (defined as creatinine >1.5 times upper limit of normal)

8. Abnormal hepatic function (defined as alanine transaminase or aspartate aminotransferase (ALT/AST) levels >2.5 times upper limit of normal)

9. Abnormal cardiac function (Ejection fraction <40%)

10. Use of any of the following within 4 weeks prior to Cycle 1, Day 1:

    • Anticancer cytotoxic chemotherapeutic agent or treatment

    • Other red blood cell hematopoietic growth factors (eg, Interleukin-3)

    • Investigational drug or device, or approved therapy for investigational use. If the half-life of the previous investigational product is known, use within 5 times the half-life prior to Cycle 1, Day 1 or within 5 weeks, whichever is longer is excluded.

11. Uncontrolled hypertension, defined as repeated elevations of diastolic blood pressure (DBP) ≥100 mmHg despite adequate treatment.

12. Prior history of malignancies, other than myelodysplastic syndromes, unless the subject has been free of the disease (including completion of any active or adjuvant treatment for prior malignancy) for ≥1 year. However, subjects with the following history/concurrent conditions involving in situ cancer (or similar) are allowed:

- Basal or squamous cell carcinoma of the skin
- Carcinoma in situ of the cervix
- Carcinoma in situ of the breast
- Incidental histologic finding of prostate cancer (T1a or T1b using the tumor, nodes, metastasis [TNM] clinical staging system)

13. Major surgery within 4 weeks prior to Cycle 1, Day 1. Subjects must have completely recovered from any previous surgery prior to Cycle 1, Day 1

14. History of stroke, deep venous thrombosis (DVT), pulmonary or arterial embolism within 6 months prior to Cycle 1, Day 1

15. Pregnant or breastfeeding females

16. Subject has any significant medical condition, laboratory abnormality, psychiatric illness, or is considered vulnerable by local regulations (e.g., imprisoned or institutionalized) that would prevent the subject from participating in the study.

# Notes

## Chapter 1

1. US FDA, "White Oak Campus Information," April 20, 2020, https://www.fda .gov/about-fda/buildings-and-facilities/white-oak-campus-information.

2. GSA, "FDA White Oak Campus, January 12, 2017, https://www.gsa.gov/about -us/regions/welcome-to-the-national-capital-region-11/buildings-and-facilities /maryland/fda-white-oak-campus; Eugene L. Meyer, "FDA Consolidates at Former Navy Site," *New York Times*, February 24, 2009, https://www.nytimes.com/2009/02 /25/business/25labs.html.

3. Paul Goldberg, "With Flashing Lights, Heckling and Folk Song Avastin Sets New Tone for FDA Debates," *Cancer Letter* 37, no. 26 (July 1, 2011): 1.

4. "Protest Organizer Terry Kalley Speaks . . . ," video, YouTube, June 28, 2011, https://www.youtube.com/watch?v=8aE0Jghm2hw.

5. "The Avastin Protest Anthem," video, YouTube, June 28, 2011, https://www .youtube.com/watch?v=AoiHDNGt6C8.

6. Felipe Ades, Konstantinos Tryfonidis, and Dimitrios Zardavas, "The Past and Future of Breast Cancer Treatment-from the Papyrus to Individualised Treatment Approaches," *Ecancermedicalscience* 11, no 746 (June 8, 2017).

7. Denise Gellene, "Dr. Bernard Fisher, Who Revolutionized Breast Cancer Treatment, Dies at 101," *New York Times*, October 21, 2019, https://www.nytimes.com /2019/10/19/science/dr-bernard-fisher-dead.html.

8. "Oldest Evidence of Breast Cancer Found in Egyptian Skeleton," March 24, 2015, Reuters, https://in.reuters.com/article/egypt-antiquities-cancer/oldest-evidence -of-breast-cancer-found-in-egyptian-skeleton-idINKBN0MK1ZW20150324.

9. Michael K. Keng, Candace M. Wenzell, and Mikkael A. Sekeres, "A Drug's Life: The Pathway to Drug Approval," *Clinical Advances in Hematology & Oncology* 11, no. 10 (2013): 646–665, https://www.hematologyandoncology.net/archives/october -2013/a-drugs-life-the-pathway-to-drug-approval/.

10. "Hamlin's Wizard Oil: The Cancer Curing Liniment," CulinaryLore.com, January 19, 2019, https://culinarylore.com/other:hamlins-wizard-oil-the-cancer-curing -liniment/.

11. Ben Panko, "Where Did the FDA Come From, and What Does It Do?" Smithsonian.com, February 8, 2017, https://www.smithsonianmag.com/science-nature /origins-FDA-what-does-it-do-180962054.

12. Panko, "Where Did the FDA Come From?"

13. NIH, "A Short History of the National Institutes of Health: Biologics," n.d., https://history.nih.gov/display/history/Biologics; Thomas A. Hayes, "The Food and Drug Administration's Regulation of Drug Labeling, Advertising, and Promotion: Looking Back and Looking Ahead," *Clinical Pharmacology & Therapeutics* 63, no. 6 (1998): 607–616; Suzanne White Junod, "Biologics Centennial: 100 Years of Biologics Regulation," n.d., fda.gov, https://www.fda.gov/files/Biologics-Centennial--100 -Years-of-Biologics-Regulation.pdf.

14. Junod, "Biologics Centennial."

15. Arlene Finger Kantor, "Upton Sinclair and the Pure Food and Drugs Act of 1906," *American Journal of Public Health* 66, no. 12 (December 1976): 1202–1205; Constitutional Rights Foundation, "Upton Sinclair's *The Jungle*: Muckraking the Meat-Packing Industry," *Bill of Rights in Action* 24, no. 1 (Fall 2008), https://www.crf-usa .org/bill-of-rights-in-action/bria-24-1-b-upton-sinclairs-the-jungle-muckraking-the -meat-packing-industry.html.

16. Bob McCoy, "Overview: Great American Fraud," MuseumofQuackery.com, http://www.museumofquackery.com/ephemera/overview.htm.

17. E. Fee, "Samuel Hopkins Adams (1871–1958): Journalist and Muckraker," *American Journal of Public Health* 100, no. 8 (2010):1390–1391.

18. "Muckraker: 2 Meanings," *New York Times*, April 10, 1985, Section D, 27.

19. Samuel Hopkins Adams, *The Great American Fraud* (New York: P. F. Collier & Son, 1906), 13.

20. Bob McCoy, "Overview: Great American Fraud."

21. John Swann, "100 Years of the 1906 Food and Drugs Act," *Apothecary's Cabinet* 9 (Fall 2005), fda.gov, https://www.fda.gov/media/72065/download.

22. Adams, *The Great American Fraud*, 3.

23. Kantor, "Upton Sinclair and the Pure Food and Drugs Act of 1906," 1203.

24. Kantor, "Upton Sinclair and the Pure Food and Drugs Act of 1906," 1203.

25. US FDA, "Milestones in US Food and Drug Law History. Part I. FDA's Evolving Regulatory Powers," January 31, 2018, https://www.fda.gov/about-fda/fdas-evolving -regulatory-powers/milestones-us-food-and-drug-law-history.

26. Nicola Davies, "FDA Focus: The Sherley Amendment," *The Pharmaletter*, October 11, 2014, https://www.thepharmaletter.com/article/fda-focus-the-sherley-amendment.

27. C. E. Terry, "The Harrison Anti-narcotic Act," *American Journal of Public Health* 5, no. 6 (June 1915): 518.

28. Steven H. Woolf and Heidi Schoomaker, "Life Expectancy and Mortality Rates in the United States, 1959–2017," *Journal of the American Medical Association* 322, no. 20 (2019): 1996–2016.

29. "Leading Causes of Death, 1900–1998," cdc.gov, https://www.cdc.gov/nchs/data /dvs/lead1900_98.pdf.

30. Carol Ballentine, "Sulfanilamide Disaster," *FDA Consumer*, June 1981, https:// www.fda.gov/files/about%20fda/published/The-Sulfanilamide-Disaster.pdf.

31. Ballentine, "Sulfanilamide Disaster."

32. Ballentine, "Sulfanilamide Disaster."

33. Jef Akst, "The Elixir Tragedy, 1937," *The Scientist*, June 1, 2013, https://www.the -scientist.com/foundations/the-elixir-tragedy-1937-39231.

34. Ballentine, "Sulfanilamide Disaster."

35. Ballentine, "Sulfanilamide Disaster."

36. "Chemist of Death Elixir is Suicide," *Madera Tribune* 73, no. 64, January 18, 1939, 1.

37. "'Death Drug' Hunt Covered 50 States," *New York Times*, November 26, 1937, 42, https://timesmachine.nytimes.com/timesmachine/1937/11/26/94467337.html ?auth=login-email&pageNumber=42.

38. "'Death Drug' Hunt," 42.

39. John Parascandola, "Dinitrophenol and Bioenergetics: An Historical Perspective," *Molecular and Cellular Biochemistry* 5 (1974): 69–77.

40. US FDA, "Basics of Drug Ads," June 19, 2015, https://www.fda.gov/drugs /prescription-drug-advertising/basics-drug-ads#product_claim.

41. US FDA, "Basics of Drug Ads."

42. Woodie M. Zachry III, Marvin D. Shepherd, Melvin J. Hinich, et al., "Relationship between Direct-to-Consumer Advertising and Physician Diagnosing and Prescribing," *American Journal of Health System Pharmacy* 59, no. 42 (2002): 42–49.

43. S. Gilbody, P. Wilson, and I. Watt, "Benefits and Harms of Direct-to-Consumer Advertising: A Systematic Review," *British Journal of Medicine Quality and Safety* 14, no. 4 (2005): 246–250; Geert W. Jong, Bruno H. Ch. Stricker, Miriam C. J. M. Sturkenboom, "Marketing in the Lay Media and Prescriptions of Terbinafine in Primary Care: Dutch Cohort Study," *British Medical Journal* 328 (2004): 931.

44. Robert Peter Gale and Hillard M. Lazarus, "Physicians, New Drugs, and Pharma," *ASCO Post*, August 10, 2020, https://ascopost.com/issues/august-10-2020/physicians -new-drugs-and-pharma/#.XzZwlYMfPCI.mailto.

45. US FDA, "Milestones in US Food and Drug Law History. FDA's Evolving Regulatory Powers," https://www.fda.gov/about-fda/fdas-evolving-regulatory-powers /milestones-us-food-and-drug-law-history.

46. Theodore G. Klumpp, "The New Federal Food, Drug, and Cosmetic Act," *Journal of the American Medical Association* 113, no. 25 (1939): 2233–2235.

47. "Proposal to Withdraw Approval for the Breast Cancer Indication for Bevacizumab (Avastin): FDA Public Hearing" (transcript of minutes), part 1, *A Matter of Record*, Tuesday, June 28, 2011, 6.

## Chapter 2

1. "Proposal to Withdraw Approval for the Breast Cancer Indication for Bevacizumab (Avastin): FDA Public Hearing" (transcript of minutes), part 1, *A Matter of Record*, Tuesday, June 28, 2011, 10–12.

2. "Proposal to Withdraw Approval," part 1, 19.

3. Nicholas Rasmussen, "America's First Amphetamine Epidemic 1929–1971: A Quantitative and Qualitative Retrospective with Implications for the Present," *American Journal of Public Health* 98, no. 6 (2008): 974–985.

4. "The Durham-Humphrey Amendment," *Journal of the American Medical Association* 149, no. 4 (1952): 371.

5. "Drug Ads Gallery, 1950–1959," https://prescriptiondrugs.procon.org/background -resources/drug-ads-gallery-1950-1959/.

6. "This Child's Life May Depend on the Safety of 'Distaval,'" advertisement, *British Medical Journal* (June 24, 1961).

7. "About Us: Where We Come From," Grunenthal.com, https://www.grunenthal.com/about-us/history#.

8. Michael Winerip, "The Death and Afterlife of Thalidomide," *New York Times*, September 23, 2013, https://www.nytimes.com/2013/09/23/booming/the-death-and-afterlife-of-thalidomide.html; Joanne Cavanaugh Simpson, "Pregnant Pause," *Johns Hopkins Magazine*, September 2001, https://pages.jh.edu/~jhumag/0901web/pregnant.html.

9. Winerip, "The Death and Afterlife of Thalidomide."

10. Linda Bren, "Frances Oldham Kelsey: FDA Medical Reviewer Leaves Her Mark on History," *FDA Consumer* 34, no. 2 (March–April, 2001): 24–29, https://web.archive.org/web/20080113102840/https://www.fda.gov/fdac/features/2001/201_kelsey.html; Frances Oldham Kelsey, "Autobiographical Reflections," fda.gov, https://www.fda.gov/media/89162/download.

11. Peter Dreier, "Frances Kelsey: The Government Bureaucrat Who May Have Saved Your Life," *The American Prospect*, August 10, 2015, https://prospect.org/environment/frances-kelsey-government-bureaucrat-may-saved-life/.

12. Bren, "Frances Oldham Kelsey."

13. Bren, "Frances Oldham Kelsey."

14. Bren, "Frances Oldham Kelsey."

15. A. Leslie Florence, "Is Thalidomide to Blame?" *British Medical Journal* 2 (December 16, 1960): 1954.

16. Bren, "Frances Oldham Kelsey."

17. F. Vogel, "Widukind Lenz," *European Journal of Human Genetics* 3 (1995): 384–387, https://www.nature.com/articles/000472329?proof=t%3B.

18. "Linde Schulte-Hillen—Parent of Thalidomider Jan Schulte-Hillen," *NO Limits*, http://thalidomidestories.com/story/other-notables/other/linde-schulte-hillen/; for the Greek root of *phocomelia*, see Helen B. Taussig, "The Thalidomide Syndrome," *Scientific American* 207, no. 2 (1962): 29–35.

19. Taussig, "The Thalidomide Syndrome."

20. Jerry Avorn, "Learning about the Safety of Drugs—A Half Century of Evolution," *New England Journal of Medicine* 365 (2011): 2151–2153; Widukind Lenz, "The History of Thalidomide," from a lecture given at the 1992 UNITH Congress, https://www.thalidomide.ca/wp-content/uploads/2017/12/Dr-Lenz-history-of-thalidomide-1992.pdf.

21. William G. McBride, "Thalidomide and Congenital Abnormalities," *Lancet* 1358 (December 16, 1961): 278.

22. Avorn, "Learning about the Safety of Drugs."

23. Simpson, "Pregnant Pause."

24. Nigel Armstrong, Steve Ryder, Carol Forbes, Janine Ross, and Ruben G. Quek, "A Systematic Review of the International Prevalence of BRCA Mutation in Breast Cancer," *Clinical Epidemiology* 11 (2019): 543–561; NIH National Cancer Institute, BRCA Gene Mutations: Cancer Risk and Genetic Testing," https://www.cancer.gov /about-cancer/causes-prevention/genetics/brca-fact-sheet.

25. "Proposal to Withdraw Approval," part 1, 20.

26. "Proposal to Withdraw Approval," part 1, 22.

27. Valarie Blake, "The Terminally Ill, Access to Investigational Drugs, and FDA Rules," *Virtual Mentor* 5, no. 18 (2013): 687–691.

28. "Proposal to Withdraw Approval," part 1, 23.

29. "Proposal to Withdraw Approval," part 1, 24–26.

30. Bren, "Frances Oldham Kelsey."

31. Morton Mintz, quoted in Bren, "Frances Oldham Kelsey."

32. Peter Dreier, "Frances Kelsey: The Government Bureaucrat Who May Have Saved Your Life," *The American Prospect*, August 10, 2015, https://prospect.org/environment /frances-kelsey-government-bureaucrat-may-saved-life/.

33. Avorn, "Learning about the Safety of Drugs."

34. Jeremy A. Greene and Scott H. Podolsky, "Reform, Regulation, and Pharmaceuticals—The Kefauver-Harris Amendments at 50," *New England Journal of Medicine* 367, no. 16 (2012): 1481–1483; "Kefauver-Harris Amendments Revolution- ized Drug Development," FDA Consumer Health Information, October 2012, https:// www.gvsu.edu/cms4/asset/F51281F0-00AF-E25A-5BF632E8D4A243C7/kefauver -harris_amendments.fda.thalidomide.pdf.

35. "Kefauver-Harris Amendments Revolutionized Drug Development."

36. Greene and Podolsky, "Reform, Regulation, and Pharmaceuticals."

37. Lee Kennedy-Shaffer, "When the Alpha Is the Omega: P-Values, 'Substantial Evidence,' and the 0.05 Standard at FDA," *Food And Drug Law Journal* 72, no. 4 (2017): 595–635.

38. "Kefauver-Harris Amendments Revolutionized Drug Development."

## Chapter 3

1. Suzanne White Junod, "FDA and Clinical Drug Trials: A Short History," n.d., US FDA, https://www.fda.gov/media/110437/download.

2. Mikkael Sekeres, *When Blood Breaks Down: Life Lessons from Leukemia* (Cambridge, MA: MIT Press, 2020).

3. Courtney D. DiNardo, Keith Pratz, Vinod Pullarkat, Brian A. Jonas, Martha Arellano, et al., "Venetoclax Combined with Decitabine or Azacitidine in Treatment-Naive, Elderly Patients with Acute Myeloid Leukemia," *Blood* 133, no. 1 (January 3, 2019): 7–17.

4. DiNardo et al., "Venetoclax Combined with Decitabine or Azacitidine."

5. Heraleen Browne, quoted in "Proposal to Withdraw Approval for the Breast Cancer Indication for Bevacizumab (Avastin): FDA Public Hearing" (transcript of minutes), part 1, *A Matter of Record*, Tuesday, June 28, 2011, 73.

6. Browne, quoted in "Proposal to Withdraw Approval," part 1, 73.

7. Patricia Edwards, quoted in "Proposal to Withdraw Approval," part 1, 27–28.

8. Michael W. N. Deininger, John M. Goldman, and Junia V. Melo, "The Molecular Biology of Chronic Myeloid Leukemia," *Blood* 96, no. 10 (2000): 3343–3356.

9. Hideki Makishima, Tetsuichi Yoshizato, Kenichi Yoshida, Mikkael Sekeres, et al., "Dynamics of Clonal Evolution in Myelodysplastic Syndromes," *National Genetics* 49, no. 2 (2017): 204–212.

10. Sudipto Mukherjee, Chandana A. Reddy, Jay P. Ciezki, May Abdel-Wahab, . . . Mikkael A. Sekeres, "Risk for Developing Myelodysplastic Syndromes in Prostate Cancer Patients Definitively Treated with Radiation," *Journal of the National Cancer Institute* 106, no. 3 (March 2014).

11. CDC, "History of the Surgeon General's Reports on Smoking and Health," Centers for Disease Control and Prevention, Smoking & Tobacco Use, https://www.cdc.gov/tobacco/data_statistics/sgr/history/index.htm.

12. American Cancer Society. "Key Statistics for Prostate Cancer," https://www.cancer.org/cancer/prostate-cancer/about/key-statistics.html; Janet Farrar Worthington, "Treatment for Prostate Cancer: External-Beam Radiation Therapy," Prostate Cancer Foundation, https://www.pcf.org/c/treatment-for-prostate-cancer-external-beam-radiation-therapy/.

13. Worthington, "Treatment for Prostate Cancer."

14. Mukherjee et al., "Risk for Developing Myelodysplastic Syndromes in Prostate Cancer Patients."

15. Mukherjee et al., "Risk for Developing Myelodysplastic Syndromes in Prostate Cancer Patients."

16. Michael Schaapveld, Berthe M. Aleman, Anna M. van Eggermond, Cecile P. Janus, Augustinus D. Krol, et al., "Second Cancer Risk Up to 40 Years after Treatment for Hodgkin's Lymphoma," *New England Journal of Medicine* 373, no. 26 (December 24, 2015): 2499–2511.

17. Nancy Haunty, quoted in "Proposal to Withdraw Approval," part 1, 32.

18. Crystal Hanna, quoted in "Proposal to Withdraw Approval," part 1, 35.

19. Junod, "FDA and Clinical Drug Trials."

20. See Robert Bazell, *HER-2: The Making of Herceptin, a Revolutionary Treatment for Breast Cancer* (New York: Random House, 1998).

21. Patty Delaney, book review, "HER-2: The Making of Herceptin, a Revolutionary Treatment for Breast Cancer," *Journal of the National Cancer Institute* 19, no. 15 (August 4, 1999): 1329–1330.

22. Sujata Gupta, "Trials and Tribulations," *Nature Index* (2017): 528–531.

23. Delaney, "HER-2: The Making of Herceptin."

24. Gupta, "Trials and Tribulations."

25. Junod, "FDA and Clinical Drug Trials"; Conor Hale, "New MIT Study Puts Clinical Research Success Rate at 14 Percent," *CenterWatch*, February 5, 2018, https://www.centerwatch.com/articles/12702-new-mit-study-puts-clinical-research -success-rate-at-14-percent.

26. David P. Steensma, "What's In a (Drug's) Name," *ASH Clinical News*, April 17, 2018, https://www.ashclinicalnews.org/viewpoints/whats-drug-name/.

Chapter 4

1. Anroop B. Nair and Shery Jacob, "A Simple Practice Guide for Dose Conversion between Animals and Human," *Journal of Basic Clinical Pharmacy* 7, no. 2 (March 7, 2016): 27–31; Pawel Szymański, Magdalena Markowicz, and Elzbieta Mikiciuk-Olasik, "Adaptation of High-Throughput Screening in Drug Discovery-Toxicological Screening Tests," *International Journal of Molecular Sciences* 13, no. 1 (2012): 427–452.

2. Chi Heem Wong, Kien Wei Siah, and Andrew W. Lo, "Estimation of Clinical Trial Success Rates and Related Parameters," *Biostatistics* 20, no. 2 (April 2019): 273–286.

3. Tony H. Truong, Jane C. Weeks, E. Francis Cook, and Steven Joffe, "Altruism among Participants in Cancer Clinical Trials," *Clinical Trials* 8 (2011): 616–623.

4. Troung et al., "Altruism among Participants."

5. Rebecca A. Hazen, Stephen J. Zyzanski, Justin Baker, Dennis Drotar, and Eric Kodish, "Communication about the Risks and Benefits of Phase I Pediatric Oncology Trials," *Contemporary Clinical Trials* 41 (March 2015): 139–145.

6. Hazen et al., "Communications about Risks and Benefits."

7. American Cancer Society, "Key Statistics for Lung Cancer," https://www.cancer.org/cancer/lung-cancer/about/key-statistics.html.

8. Genzeme Corporation, "What Is Gaucher Disease," GaucherCare website, https://www.orpha.net/consor.

9. Hajime Asahina, Ikuo Sekine, Hidehito Horinouchi, Hiroshi Nokihara, Noboru Yamamoto, et al., "Retrospective Analysis of Third-Line and Fourth-Line Chemotherapy for Advanced Non-Small-Cell Lung Cancer," *Clinical Lung Cancer* 13, no. 1 (January 2012): 39–43.

10. Mikkael A. Sekeres, "When the Doctor's Mother Has Cancer," *New York Times*, October 31, 2017, https://www.nytimes.com/2017/10/31/well/live/when-the-doctors-mother-has-cancer.html.

11. Elihu H. Estey, Robert Peter Gale, and Mikkael A. Sekeres, "New Drugs in AML: Uses and Abuses," *Leukemia* 32 (2018): 1479–1481.

12. Michal Kicinski, David A Springate, and Evangelos Kontopantelis, "Publication Bias in Meta-Analyses from the Cochrane Database of Systematic Reviews," *Statistics in Medicine* 34, no. 20 (2015): 2781–2793.

13. Helen Schiff, quoted in "Proposal to Withdraw Approval for the Breast Cancer Indication for Bevacizumab (Avastin): FDA Public Hearing" (transcript of minutes), part 1, *A Matter of Record*, Tuesday, June 28, 2011, 82–83.

14. CDRMP, "In Honor of Christine Brunswick, Breast Cancer Advocate," n.d., https://cdmrp.army.mil/cwg/stories/2013/brunswick_profile.

15. Christine Brunswick, quoted in "Proposal to Withdraw Approval," part 1, 91.

16. Brunswick, quoted in "Proposal to Withdraw Approval," part 1, 92.

17. Kimberley Jewett, quoted in "Proposal to Withdraw Approval," part 1, 93.

18. For the exclusion criteria protocols I explain to Abby Slater, see Estey, Gale, and Sekeres, "New Drugs in AML: Uses and Abuses."

19. Abby Statler, T. Radivoyevitch, C. Siebenaller, A. T. Gardis, . . . Mikkael Sekeres, et al., "The Relationship between Eligibility Criteria and Adverse Events in Random Controlled Trials of Hematologic Malignancies," *Leukemia* 31, no. 8 (2017): 1808–1815.

20. Abby Statler, Meghan Otheus, Harry B. Erba, Thomas A. Chauncey . . . Mik-kael Sekeres, et al., "Comparable Outcomes of Patients Eligible vs. Ineligible for SWOG Leukemia Studies," *Blood* 131, no. 25 (2018): 2782–2788.

21. G. Montalban-Bravo, X. Huang, E. Jabbour, G. Borthakur, C. D. DiNardo, et al., "A Clinical Trial for Patients with Acute Myeloid Leukemia or Myelodysplastic Syndromes Not Eligible for Standard Clinical Trials," *Leukemia* 31 (2017): 318–324.

22. Katie Reilly, "Muhammad Ali's Wit and Wisdom: 6 of His Best Quotes," *Time*, June 4, 2016, https://time.com/4357493/muhammad-ali-dead-best-quotes/.

23. Terry Kalley, quoted in "Proposal to Withdraw Approval," part 1, 87–88.

24. Kalley, quoted in "Proposal to Withdraw Approval "Proposal to Withdraw Approval," part 1, 89.

**Chapter 5**

1. Gardiner Harris, "Where Cancer Progress Is Rare, One Man Says No," *New York Times*, September 15, 2009, https://www.nytimes.com/2009/09/16/health/policy/16cancer.html?ref=todayspaper.

2. Harris, "Where Cancer Progress Is Rare, One Man Says No."

3. Richard Pazdur, quoted in "Proposal to Withdraw Approval for the Breast Cancer Indication for Bevacizumab (Avastin): FDA Public Hearing" (transcript of minutes), part 1, *A Matter of Record*, Tuesday, June 28, 2011, 126–127.

4. Richard Pazdur, quoted in Harris, "Where Cancer Progress Is Rare."

5. Harris, "Where Cancer Progress Is Rare."

6. D. Gospodarowicz, G. Neufeld, L. Schweigerer, and G. Neufeld, "Molecular and Biological Characterization of Fibroblast Growth Factor, an Angiogenic Factor which also Controls the Proliferation and Differentiation of Mesoderm and Neuro-ectoderm Derived Cells," *Cell Differentiation* 19, no. 1 (July 1986): 1–17.

7. Patricia K. Donahoe, "Judah Folkman: 1933–2008, A Biographical Memoir," National Academy of Sciences, 2014, http://www.nasonline.org/publications/biographical-memoirs/memoir-pdfs/folkman-judah.pdf.

8. Judah Folkman, "Tumor Angiogenesis," *New England Journal of Medicine* 285 (November 18, 1971): 1182–1186.

9. F. Esch, A. Baird, N. Ling, N. Ueno, J. Hill, et al., "Primary Structure of Bovine Pituitary Basic Fibroblast Growth Factor (FGF) and Comparison with the Amino-Terminal Sequence of Bovine Brain Acidic FGF," *Proceedings of the National Academy of Sciences* 82 (1985): 6507–6511; Gospodarowicz et al., "Molecular and Biological Characterization of Fibroblast Growth Factor."

10. Napoleone Ferrara and William J. Henzel, "Pituitary Follicular Cells Secrete a Novel Heparin-Binding Growth Factor Specific for Vascular Endothelial Cells," *Biochemical and Biophysical Research Communities* 161, no. 2 (June 15, 1989): 851–858.

11. Donahoe, "Judah Folkman."

12. Donahoe, "Judah Folkman"; A. P. Adamis, D. T. Shima, M. J. Tolentino, E. S. Gragoudas, N. Ferrara, et al., "Inhibition of Vascular Endothelial Growth Factor Prevents Retinal Ischemia-Associated Iris Neovascularization in a Nonhuman Primate," *Archives of Ophthalmology* 114 (1996): 66–71.

13. Donahoe, "Judah Folkman."

14. R. J. D'Amato, M. S. Loughnan, and E. Flynn, "Thalidomide Is an Inhibitor of Angiogenesis," *Proceedings of the National Academy of Sciences* 91 (1994): 4082–4085.

15. S. Singhal, J. Mehta, R. Desikan, D. Ayers, . . . B. Barlogie, "Antitumor Activity of Thalidomide in Refractory Multiple Myeloma," *New England Journal of Medicine* 341, no. 21 (1999): 1565–1571.

16. K. J. Kim, B. Li, J. Winer, M. Armanini, . . . N. Ferrara, "Inhibition of Vascular Endothelial Growth Factor-Induced Angiogenesis Suppresses Tumour Growth in Vivo," *Nature* 362, no. 6423 (April 29, 1993): 841–844.

17. Laurie Goodman, "Persistence—Luck—Avastin," *Journal of Clinical Investigation* 113, no. 7 (2004): 934.

18. M. S. Gordon, K. Margolin, M. Talpaz, G. W. Sledge Jr, E. Holmgren et al., "Phase I Safety and Pharmacokinetic Study of Recombinant Human Anti-Vascular Endothelial Growth Factor in Patients with Advanced Cancer, *Journal of Clinical Oncology* 19, no. 3 (February 1, 2001): 843–850.

19. K. Margolin, M. S. Gordon, E. Holmgren, J. Gaudreault J, W. Novotny, et al., "Phase Ib Trial of Intravenous Recombinant Humanized Monoclonal Antibody to Vascular Endothelial Growth Factor in Combination with Chemotherapy in Patients with Advanced Cancer: Pharmacologic and Long-Term Safety Data," *Journal of Clinical Oncology* 19, no. 3 (February 1, 2001): 851–856.

20. Fairooz Kabbinavar, Herbert I. Hurwitz, Louis Fehrenbacher, Neal J. Meropol, William F. Novotny, et al., "Phase II, Randomized Trial Comparing Bevacizumab Plus Fluorouracil (FU)/Leucovorin (LV) with FU/LV Alone In Patients with Metastatic Colorectal Cancer," *Journal of Clinical Oncology* 21, no. 1 (January 1, 2003): 60–65.

21. David H. Johnson, Louis Fehrenbacher, William F. Novotny, Roy S. Herbst, John J. Nemunaitis, et al., "Randomized Phase II Trial Comparing Bevacizumab Plus Carboplatin and Paclitaxel with Carboplatin and Paclitaxel Alone in Previously Untreated Locally Advanced or Metastatic Non-Small-Cell Lung Cancer," *Journal of Clinical Oncology* 22 (2004): 2184–2191.

22. J. C. Yang, L. Haworth, R. M. Sherry, P. Hwu, D. J. Schwartzentruber, et al., "A Randomized Trial of Bevacizumab, an Anti-Vascular Endothelial Growth Factor Antibody, for Metastatic Renal Cancer," *New England Journal of Medicine* 349, no. 5 (July 31, 2003): 427–434.

23. Pazdur, quoted in "Proposal to Withdraw Approval," part 1, 127–128.

24. Pazdur, quoted in "Proposal to Withdraw Approval," part 1, 128–129.

25. Herbert Hurwitz, Louis Fehrenbacher, William Novotny, Thomas Cartwright, John Hainsworth, et al. "Bevacizumab plus Irinotecan, Fluorouracil, and Leucovorin for Metastatic Colorectal Cancer," *New England Journal of Medicine* 350 (2004): 2335–2342.

26. Guillaume Dighiero, Karim Maloum, Bernard Desablens, Bruno Cazin, Maurice Navarro, et al., for the French Cooperative Group on Chronic Lymphocytic Leukemia, "Chlorambucil in Indolent Chronic Lymphocytic Leukemia," *New England Journal of Medicine* 338 (1998): 1506–1514.

27. Josep M. Llovet, Sergio Ricci, Vincenzo Mazzaferro, Philip Hilgard, Edward Gane, et al., for the SHARP Investigators Study Group, "Sorafenib in Advanced Hepatocellular Carcinoma," *New England Journal of Medicine* 359 (2008): 378–390.

28. Hurwitz et al., "Bevacizumab plus Irinotecan, Fluorouracil, and Leucovorin."

29. Hurwitz et al., "Bevacizumab plus Irinotecan, Fluorouracil, and Leucovorin."

30. "Avastin Approval History," Drugs.com, https://www.drugs.com/history/avastin.html.

31. Alan Sandler, Robert Gray, Michael C. Perry, Julie Brahmer, Joan H. Schiller, et al., "Paclitaxel–Carboplatin Alone or with Bevacizumab for Non–Small-Cell Lung Cancer," *New England Journal of Medicine* 355 (2006): 2542–2550.

32. Kabbinavar, "Phase II, Randomized Trial."

33. Alex Berenson, "A Cancer Drug Shows Promise, at a Price That Many Can't Pay," *New York Times*, February 15, 2006, https://www.nytimes.com/2006/02/15/business/a-cancer-drug-shows-promise-at-a-price-that-many-cant-pay.html.

34. William H. Burns, quoted in *Congressional Record—Extensions of Remarks*, Hon. Dennis J. Kucinich, House of Representatives, April 6, 2006, E235.

35. Kathy Miller, Molin Wang, Julie Gralow, Maura Dickler, Melody Cobleigh, et al., "Paclitaxel plus Bevacizumab versus Paclitaxel Alone for Metastatic Breast Cancer," *New England Journal of Medicine* 357 (2007): 2666–2676.

36. Ronald Piana, "The Evolution of US Cooperative Group Trials: Publicly Funded Cancer Research at a Crossroads," *ASCO Post*, March 15, 2014.

37. Miller et al., "Paclitaxel plus Bevacizumab versus Paclitaxel Alone."

38. Miller et al., "Paclitaxel plus Bevacizumab versus Paclitaxel Alone."

39. D. F, Cella, D. S. Tulsky, G. Gray, B. Sarafian, E. Linn, et al., "The Functional Assessment of Cancer Therapy Scale: Development and Validation of the General Measure," *Journal of Clinical Oncology* 11, no. 3 (April 1993): 570–579.

40. "FACT-B: For Patients with Breast Cancer: Overview," Facit.org, https://www.facit.org/measures/FACT-B.

41. US FDA, Summary Minutes of the Oncologic Drugs Advisory Committee, 2007, part 1, 19, https://wayback.archive-it.org/7993/20170404050554/https:/www.fda.gov/ohrms/dockets/ac/07/transcripts/2007-4332t1-part1.pdf.

42. US FDA, Summary Minutes of the Oncologic Drugs Advisory Committee, 2007, part 2, 102, https://wayback.archive-it.org/7993/20170404050555/https:/www.fda.gov/ohrms/dockets/ac/07/transcripts/2007-4332t1-part2.pdf.

43. US FDA, Summary Minutes of the Oncologic Drugs Advisory Committee, 2007, part 2, 101.

44. R. Ford, L. Schwartz, J. Dancey, et al., "Lessons Learned from Independent Central Review," *European Journal of Cancer* 45 (2009): 268–274.

45. Ford, et al., "Lessons Learned."

46. US FDA, Summary Minutes of the Oncologic Drugs Advisory Committee, 2007.

47. John Simons, "Genentech's Silver Lining: The FDA's Rejection of Avastin as a Treatment for Breast Cancer Was Certainly a Setback, but the Drug Giant May Yet Prevail," *CNN Money*, December 6, 2007, https://money.cnn.com/2007/12/06/news/companies/simons_genentech.fortune/index.htm?postversion=2007120611.

48. Pam Belluck, Sheila Kaplan, and Rebecca Robbins, "How an Unproven Alzheimer's Drug Got Approved." *New York Times*, July 19, 2021, https://www.nytimes.com/2021/07/19/health/alzheimers-drug-aduhelm-fda.html.

49. Andrew Pollack. "FDA Extends Avastin's Use to Breast Cancer," *New York Times*, February 23, 2008, https://www.nytimes.com/2008/02/23/business/23drug.html.

50. Pollack, "FDA Extends Avastin's Use to Breast Cancer."

51. Pollack, "FDA Extends Avastin's Use to Breast Cancer."

52. Pollack, "FDA Extends Avastin's Use to Breast Cancer."

53. Daniel Costello, "Avastin OK'd for Breast Cancer," *Los Angeles Times*, February 23, 2008, https://www.latimes.com/archives/la-xpm-2008-feb-23-fi-cancer23-story.html.

## Chapter 6

1. Worldometer, "COVID-19 Coronavirus Pandemic," April 1, 2022, https://www.worldometers.info/coronavirus/.

2. Centers for Disease Control and Prevention, "1918 Pandemic (H1N1 virus)," https://www.cdc.gov/flu/pandemic-resources/1918-pandemic-h1n1.html.

3. Jay Baruch. "You Are Waiting for the Surge," *Stat News*, April 21, 2020, https://www.statnews.com/2020/04/21/you-are-waiting-for-the-surge/.

4. M. S. Gottlieb, H. M. Schanker, P. T. Fan, A. Saxon, J. D. Weisman, I. Pozalski, "Pneumocystis Pneumonia—Los Angeles," *Morbidity and Mortality Weekly Reports* 30 (June 5, 1981): 1–3.

5. "A Timeline of HIV/AIDS," HIV.gov, https://www.hiv.gov/sites/default/files/aidsgov-timeline.pdf.

6. J. M. Cohen and S. Burgin, "Moritz Kaposi: A Notable Name in Dermatology," *JAMA Dermatology* 151, no. 8 (2015): 867.

7. Gottlieb et al., "Pneumocystis Pneumonia—Los Angeles."

8. Lawrence Altman, "Rare Cancer Seen in 41 Homosexuals," *New York Times*, July 3, 1981, https://www.nytimes.com/1981/07/03/us/rare-cancer-seen-in-41-homosexuals.html.

9. Avert, "History of HIV/AIDS Overview," Avert.org website, https://www.avert.org/professionals/history-hiv-aids/overview.

10. Lawrence Altman, "Five States report Disorders in Haitians' Immune Systems," *New York Times*, July 9, 1982, https://www.nytimes.com/1982/07/09/us/five-states-report-disorders-in-haitians-immune-systems.html.

11. Lawrence Altman, "Clue Found on Homosexuals' Precancer Syndrome," *New York Times*, June 18, 1982, https://www.nytimes.com/1982/06/18/us/clue-found-on-homosexuals-precancer-syndrome.html.

12. HIV.gov, "A Timeline of HIV/AIDS."

13. Stonewall National Museum and Archives, "AIDS/HIV Major Events," https://www.stonewallnma.org/aids1.

14. Anthony S. Fauci, "The Acquired Immune Deficiency Syndrome The Ever-Broadening Clinical Spectrum. *Journal of the American Medical Association* 249, no. 17 (1983): 2375–2376.

15. B. L. Evatt, "The Tragic History of AIDS in the Hemophilia Population, 1982–1984," *Journal of Thrombosis and Haemostasis* 4, no. 11 (2006): 2295–2301.

16. "Case Closed: Famous Royals Suffered from Hemophilia," *Science Magazine*, October 8, 2009, https://www.sciencemag.org/news/2009/10/case-closed-famous -royals-suffered-hemophilia.

17. Evatt, "The Tragic History of AIDS in the Hemophilia Population, 1982–1984."

18. FACT, "A Brief Timeline of AIDS," https://www.factlv.org/timeline.htm.

19. CDC. "HIV and AIDS—United States 1981–2000," *Morbidity and Mortality Weekly Reports* 50 (June 1, 2001): 430–434.

20. CDC, "HIV and AIDS—United States 1981–2000."

21. "A Timeline of HIV/AIDS."

22. Paul M. Krawzak and Andrew Siddons, "White House Seeks $1.25 Billion More for Coronavirus Response," *Roll Call*, February 24, 2020, https://www.rollcall.com /2020/02/24/white-house-seeks-1-25-billion-more-for-coronavirus-response/.

23. CDC, "Current Trends Update: Acquired Immunodeficiency Syndrome (AIDS)— United States," *Morbidity and Mortality Weekly Reports* 32 (September 9, 1983): 465–467.

24. Paul Monette, *Love Alone: Eighteen Elegies for Rog* (New York: Open Road Integrated Media, 1988).

25. Phillip Shenon, "A Move to Evict AIDS Physician Fought by State," *New York Times*, October 1, 1983.

26. "Who We Are," Lambda Legal, https://www.lambdalegal.org/about-us.

27. The New York Public Library Archives & Manuscripts, The Gay Men's Health Crisis Records, http://archives.nypl.org/mss/1126.

28. The New York Public Library Archives & Manuscripts, The Gay Men's Health Crisis Records.

29. FACT, "A Brief Timeline of AIDS."

30. Larry Kramer, "1,112 and Counting," *New York Native* 59, March 14–27, 1983, xxxi.

31. "A Timeline of HIV/AIDS."

32. Jerry Falwell, quoted in Eric Zorn, "22 Years Later, The Follow-Up Question," *Chicago Tribune*, March 31, 2005, https://blogs.chicagotribune.com/news_columnists _ezorn/2005/03/22_years_later_.html.

33. "A Timeline of HIV/AIDS"; R. C. Gallo and Luc Montagnier, "The Discovery of HIV as the Cause of AIDS," *New England Journal of Medicine* 349, no. 24 (December 11, 2003): 2283–2285.

34. Larry Altman, "AIDS Studies Hint Saliva May Transmit Infection," *New York Times*, October 9, 1984, C1, 21.

35. John Balzar, "The Times Poll: Tough New Government Action on AIDS Backed," *Los Angeles Times*, December 19, 1985, https://www.latimes.com/archives/la -xpm-1985-12-19-mn-30337-story.html.

36. "Avastin Approval History," Drugs.com, https://www.drugs.com/history/avastin .html.

37. Kathy Miller, Molin Wang, Julie Gralow, Maura Dickler, Melody Cobleigh, et al., "Paclitaxel plus Bevacizumab versus Paclitaxel Alone for Metastatic Breast Cancer," *New England Journal of Medicine* 357 (2007): 2666–2676.

38. US FDA, "Summary Minutes of the Oncologic Drugs Advisory Committee," 2007, part 2, 127, https://wayback.archive-it.org/7993/20170404050555/https:/www.fda .gov/ohrms/dockets/ac/07/transcripts/2007-4332t1-part2.pdf.

39. Miller et al., "Paclitaxel plus Bevacizumab versus Paclitaxel Alone."

40. Miller et al., "Paclitaxel plus Bevacizumab versus Paclitaxel Alone."

41. Nicholas J. Robert, Veronique Diéras, John Glaspy, Adam M. Brufsky, Igor Bondarenko, et al., "RIBBON-1: Randomized, Double-Blind, Placebo-Controlled, Phase III Trial of Chemotherapy with or without Bevacizumab for First-Line Treatment of Human Epidermal Growth Factor Receptor 2-Negative, Locally Recurrent or Metastatic Breast Cancer," *Journal of Clinical Oncology* 29, no. 10 (2011): 1252–1260.

42. Robert et al., "RIBBON-1: Randomized, Double-Blind, Placebo-Controlled, Phase III Trial."

43. FDA-NIH Biomarker Working Group, "BEST (Biomarkers, EndpointS, and other Tools) Resource," Entry for "accelerated approval," https://www.ncbi.nlm.nih .gov/books/NBK338448/.

44. US FDA, "The History of the FDA's Role in Preventing the Spread of HIV/ AIDS," US FDA Virtual Exhibits of FDA History, https://www.fda.gov/about-fda /virtual-exhibits-fda-history/history-fdas-role-preventing-spread-hivaids.

45. "A Failure Led to Drug Against AIDS," *New York Times*, September 26, 1986, https://www.nytimes.com/1986/09/20/us/a-failure-led-to-drug-against-aids.html.

46. Alice Park, "The Story behind the First AIDS Drug," *Time Magazine*, March 19, 2017, https://time.com/4705809/first-aids-drug-azt/.

47. Eve Nichols and Institute of Medicine (US) Roundtable for the Development of Drugs and Vaccines Against AIDS, *Expanding Access to Investigational Therapies for HIV Infection and AIDS: March 12–13, 1990 Conference Summary* (Washington DC: National Academies Press, 1991), 1; "Historical Perspective," https://www.ncbi.nlm .nih.gov/books/NBK234129/; Park, "The Story behind the First AIDS Drug."

48. Park, "The Story behind the First AIDS Drug."

49. Richard Yarchoan, Raymond W. Klecker, Kent J. Weinhold, Phillip D. Markham, H. Kim Lyerly, et al., "Administration of 3'-azido-3'-deoxythymidine, an Inhibitor of HTLV-III/LAV Replication, to Patients with AIDS or AIDS-Related Complex," *Lancet* 1, no. 8484 (March 15, 1986): 575–580.

50. "A Failure Led to Drug Against AIDS."

51. Douglas D. Richman, Margaret A. Fischl, Michael H. Grieco, Michael S. Gottlieb, Paul A. Volberding, et al., "The Toxicity of Azidothymidine (AZT) in the Treatment of Patients with AIDS and AIDS-Related Complex," *New England Journal of Medicine* 317 (1987): 192–197.

52. Nichols, "Expanding Access to Investigational Therapies for HIV Infection and AIDS"; Margaret A. Fischl, Douglas D. Richman, Michael H. Grieco, Michael S. Gottlieb, Paul A. Volberding, et al., "The Efficacy of Azidothymidine (AZT) in the Treatment of Patients with AIDS and AIDS-Related Complex," *New England Journal of Medicine* 317 (1987): 185–191.

53. S. Broder, "The Development of Antiretroviral Therapy and Its Impact on the HIV-1/AIDS Pandemic," *Antiviral Research* 85, no. 1 (2010): 1–18, table 2.

54. Broder, "The Development of Antiretroviral Therapy," table 2.

55. Broder, "The Development of Antiretroviral Therapy."

56. Broder, "The Development of Antiretroviral Therapy."

57. Irwin Molotsky, "US Approves Drug to Prolong Lives of AIDS Patients," *New York Times*, March 21, 1987, Section 1, 1.

58. Quoted in Molotsky, "US Approves Drug to Prolong Lives of AIDS Patients."

59. Molotsky, "US Approves Drug to Prolong Lives of AIDS Patients."

60. Margaret A. Fischl, Corette B. Parker, Carla Pettinelli, Michael Wulfsohn, Martin S. Hirsch, et al., "A Randomized Controlled Trial of a Reduced Daily Dose of Zidovudine in Patients with the Acquired Immunodeficiency Syndrome," *New England Journal of Medicine* 323 (1990): 1009–1014.

61. Fischl et al., "A Randomized Controlled Trial."

62. Edward M. Connor, Rhoda S. Sperling, Richard Gelber, Pavel Kiselev, Gwendolyn Scott, et al., "Reduction of Maternal-Infant Transmission of Human Immunodeficiency Virus Type 1 with Zidovudine Treatment," *New England Journal of Medicine* 331 (1994): 1173–1180.

63. FDA Center for New Drug Evaluation and Research, "Memorandum to the File BLA 125085 Avastin (Bevacizumab)," December 15, 2010, https://www.fda.gov/media/79525/download.

64. FDA Center for New Drug Evaluation and Research, "Memorandum to the File."

65. FDA Center for New Drug Evaluation and Research, "Memorandum to the File," 8.

66. Martin Delaney, "Accelerated Approval: Where Are We Now?" *TheBodyPro for the HIV/AIDS Workforce*, June 1, 2002, https://www.thebodypro.com/article/accelerated-approval-now.

67. ACT UP, "ACT UP Accomplishments, 1987–2012," https://actupny.com/act-up-chronology-in-brief/.

68. Park, "The Story behind the First AIDS Drug."

**Chapter 7**

1. ACT UP, "ACT UP Accomplishments, 1987–2012," https://actupny.com/act-up-chronology-in-brief/.

2. Nurith Aizenman, "How to Demand a Medical Breakthrough: Lessons from the AIDS Fight," National Public Radio, February 9, 2019, https://www.npr.org/sections/health-shots/2019/02/09/689924838/how-to-demand-a-medical-breakthrough-lessons-from-the-aids-fight.

3. ACT UP, "ACT UP Accomplishments, 1987–2012."

4. United Press International, "Police Arrest AIDS Protesters Blocking Access to FDA Office," *Los Angeles Times*, October 11, 1988, https://www.latimes.com/archives/la-xpm-1988-10-11-mn-3909-story.html.

5. United Press International, "Police Arrest AIDS Protesters Blocking Access to FDA Office."

6. Aizenman, "How to Demand a Medical Breakthrough:

7. Eric Westervelt, "ACT UP at 30: Reinvigorated for the Trump Fight," *All Things Considered*, National Public Radio, transcript, April 17, 2017.

8. Douglas Crimp, "Before Occupy: How AIDS Activists Seized Control of the FDA in 1988," *Atlantic*, December 6, 2011, https://www.theatlantic.com/health/archive/2011/12/before-occupy-how-aids-activists-seized-control-of-the-fda-in-1988/249302/.

9. United Press International, "Police Arrest AIDS Protesters Blocking Access to FDA Office."

10. Philip J. Hilts, "FDA Commissioner Reassigned in Aftermath of Agency Scandals," *New York Times*, November 14, 1989, https://www.nytimes.com/1989/11/14/us/fda-commissioner-reassigned-in-aftermath-of-agency-scandals.html.

11. Daniel Lewis, "Larry Kramer, Playwright and Outspoken AIDS Activist, Dies at 84," *New York Times*, May 27, 2020, https://www.nytimes.com/2020/05/27/us/larry -kramer-dead.html.

12. Hilts, "FDA Commissioner Reassigned."

13. US Department of Health and Human Services, *Expanding Access to Investigational Therapies for HIV Infection and AIDS: March 12–13, 1990*, Conference Summary, https://www.ncbi.nlm.nih.gov/books/NBK234129/.

14. US Department of Health and Human Services, *Expanding Access.*

15. US Department of Health and Human Services, *Expanding Access.*

16. US Department of Health and Human Services, *Expanding Access.*

17. Eric L. Sievers, Richard A. Larson, Edward A. Stadtmauer, et al., "Efficacy and Safety of Gemtuzumab Ozogamicin in Patients with CD33-Positive Acute Myeloid Leukemia in First Relapse," *Journal of Clinical Oncology* 19, no. 13 (2001): 3244–3254.

18. "FDA: Pfizer Voluntarily Withdraws Cancer Treatment Mylotarg from US Market," Fierce Pharma.com, June 21, 2010, https://www.fiercepharma.com/pharma /fda-pfizer-voluntarily-withdraws-cancer-treatment-mylotarg-from-u-s-market.

19. Martin H. Cohen, Grant A. Williams, Rajeshwari Sridhara, Gang Chen, and Richard Pazdur, "FDA Drug Approval Summary: Gefitinib (ZD1839) (Iressa) Tablets," *Oncologist* 8, no. 4 (2003): 303–306.

20. US FDA, "FDA Statement on Iressa," *ScienceDaily*, December 24, 2004.

21. "FDA Grants Genentech a Hearing on Avastin's Use for Metastatic Breast Cancer in the United States," *Business Wire*, February 24, 2011, https://www.businesswire .com/news/home/20110224006786/en/FDA-Grants-Genentech-Hearing-Avastin's -Metastatic-Breast.

22. "FDA Grants Meeting on Avastin for Breast Cancer," February 4, 2011, *6abc Action News*, https://6abc.com/archive/7978605/.

23. Marie-Amelie George, "The Fight against AIDS Has Shaped How Potential COVID-19 Drugs Will Reach Patients," *Washington Post*, April 29, 2020, https:// www.washingtonpost.com/outlook/2020/04/29/fight-against-aids-has-shaped-how -potential-covid-19-drugs-will-reach-patients/.

24. US Department of Health and Human Services, *Expanding Access.*

25. George, "The Fight against AIDS Has Shaped How Potential COVID-19 Drugs Will Reach Patients."

26. US Department of Health and Human Services, "FDA Approval of Stavudine (d4T)," *AIDSinfo*, June 27, 1994, accessed May 10, 2020, https://aidsinfo.nih.gov/news /116/fda-approval-of-stavudine--d4t-.

27. Lee Pai-Sherf, quoted in "Proposal to Withdraw Approval for the Breast Cancer Indication for Bevacizumab (Avastin): FDA Public Hearing" (transcript of minutes), part 1, *A Matter of Record*, Tuesday, June 28, 2011, 144.

28. Nicholas J. Robert, Veronique Diéras, John Glaspy, Adam M. Brufsky, Igor Bondarenko, et al., "RIBBON-1: Randomized, Double-Blind, Placebo-Controlled, Phase III Trial of Chemotherapy with or without Bevacizumab for First-Line Treatment of Human Epidermal Growth Factor Receptor 2-Negative, Locally Recurrent or Metastatic Breast Cancer," *Journal of Clinical Oncology* 29, no. 10 (2011): 1252–1260.

29. "Avastin Approval History," Drugs.com, https://www.drugs.com/history/avastin .html.

30. Michelle Llamas, "Black Box Warnings," *Drugwatch*, April 13, 2020, https://www .drugwatch.com/fda/black-box-warnings/.

31. Llamas, "Black Box Warnings"; Timothy O'Shea, "10 Black Box Warnings Every Pharmacist Should Know," *Pharmacy Times*, March 15, 2016, https://www .pharmacytimes.com/contributor/timothy-o-shea/2016/03/10-black-box-warnings -every-pharmacist-should-know.

32. Pai-Sherf, quoted in "Proposal to Withdraw Approval," part 1, 172.

33. Andrea Anderson, "Demonstrating Discontent," May 21, 1990, *The Scientist*, July 16, 2017, https://www.the-scientist.com/foundations/demonstrating-discontent -may-21-1990-31227.

34. Lewis, "Larry Kramer, Playwright and Outspoken AIDS Activist."

35. Anderson, "Demonstrating Discontent."

36. Erin E. Kepplinger, "FDA's Expedited Approval Mechanisms for New Drug Products," *Biotechnology Law Report* 34, no. 1 (2015): 15–37; George, "The Fight against AIDS Has Shaped How Potential COVID-19 Drugs Will Reach Patients."

37. Kepplinger, "FDA's Expedited Approval Mechanisms for New Drug Products."

38. US FDA, "Guidance for Industry: Expedited Programs for Serious Conditions— Drugs and Biologics, OMB Control Number 0910–0765, May 2014," https://www .fda.gov/media/86377/download.

39. William A. O'Brien, Pamela M. Hartigan, David Martin, James Esinhart, et al., and the Veterans Affairs Cooperative Study Group on AIDS, "Changes in Plasma

HIV-1 RNA and CD4+ Lymphocyte Counts and the Risk of Progression to AIDS," *New England Journal of Medicine* 334 (1996): 426–431.

40. Mikkael Sekeres, *When Blood Breaks Down: Life Lessons from Leukemia* (Cambridge, MA: MIT Press, 2020).

41. Sekeres, *When Blood Breaks Down*.

42. Sekeres, *When Blood Breaks Down*.

43. Sekeres, *When Blood Breaks Down*; for an extended profile on Druker's research and Gleevec, see Terence Monmaney, "A Triumph in the War against Cancer," *Smithsonian*, May 2011, https://www.smithsonianmag.com/science-nature/a-triumph-in-the-war-against-cancer-1784705/; see also M. Deininger, E. Buchdunger, and B. J. Druker, "The Development of Imatinib as a Therapeutic Agent for Chronic Myeloid Leukemia," *Blood* 105 (2005): 2640–2653.

44. Martin H. Cohen, Grant Williams, John R. Johnson, John Duan, Jogarao Gobburu, et al., "Approval Summary for Imatinib Mesylate Capsules in the Treatment of Chronic Myelogenous Leukemia," *Clinical Cancer Research* 8, no. 5 (May 1, 2002): 935–942.

45. S. G. O'Brien, F. Guilhot, R. A. Larson, et al., "Imatinib Compared with Interferon and Low-Dose Cytarabine for Newly Diagnosed Chronic-Phase Chronic Myeloid Leukemia," *New England Journal of Medicine* 348 (2003): 994–1004.

46. E. A. Eisenhauer, P. Therasse. J. Bogaerts, et al., "New Response Evaluation Criteria in Solid Tumours: Revised RECIST Guideline (Version 1.1)," *European Journal of Cancer* 45, no. 2 (2009): 228–247.

47. Eisenhauer et al., "New Response Evaluation Criteria in Solid Tumours."

48. Eisenhauer et al., "New Response Evaluation Criteria in Solid Tumours."

49. Alan K. Burnett, Nigel H. Russell, Ann E. Hunter, Donald Milligan, Steven Knapper, et al., on behalf of the UK National Cancer Research Institute AML Working Group, "Clofarabine Doubles the Response Rate in Older Patients with Acute Myeloid Leukemia but Does Not Improve Survival," *Blood* 122, no. 8 (2013): 1384–1394.

50. F. Stephen Hodi, S. J. O'Day, D. F. McDermott, et al., "Improved Survival with Ipilimumab in Patients with Metastatic Melanoma [published correction appears in *New England Journal of Medicine* 363, no. 13 (September 2010): 1290]," *New England Journal of Medicine* 363, no. 8 (2010): 711–723.

51. US FDA, "Guidance for Industry: Expedited Programs for Serious Conditions."

52. US FDA, "CDER Drug and Biologic Accelerated Approvals Based on a Surrogate Endpoint as of June 30, 2021, https://www.fda.gov/media/151146/download.

53. US FDA, "CDER Drug and Biologic Accelerated Approvals Based on a Surrogate Endpoint as of December 31, 2019, https://www.fda.gov/media/88907/download.

54. CDC, "HIV and AIDS—United States 1981–2000," *Morbidity and Mortality Weekly Reports* 50 (June 1, 2001): 430–434.

55. US FDA, "CDER Drug and Biologic Accelerated Approvals . . . December 31, 2019."

56. US FDA, "CDER Drug and Biologic Accelerated Approvals . . . December 31, 2019.

57. US FDA, "CDER Drug and Biologic Accelerated Approvals . . . December 31, 2019."

58. Abigail Brandel, quoted in "Proposal to Withdraw Approval," part 1, 143.

59. Abigail Brandel, quoted in "Proposal to Withdraw Approval," part 1, 143–144.

60. US FDA, "CDER Drug and Biologic Accelerated Approvals . . . June 30, 2021."

61. US FDA, "CDER Drug and Biologic Accelerated Approvals . . . December 31, 2019."

62. S. L. Spruance, A. T. Pavia, J. W. Mellors, et al., "Clinical Efficacy of Monotherapy with Stavudine Compared with Zidovudine in HIV-Infected, Zidovudine-Experienced Patients: A Randomized, Double-Blind, Controlled Trial," Bristol-Myers Squibb Stavudine/019 Study Group, *Annals of Internal Medicine* 126, no. 5 (2019): 355–363.

## Chapter 8

1. Ronald Piana, "A Leader in Drug Development, Patricia Keegan, MD, Reflects on Making a Difference in Cancer Care," *ASCO Post*, October 10, 2020, https://ascopost.com/issues/october-10-2020/patricia-keegan-reflects-on-making-a-difference-in-cancer-care/.

2. "Proposal to Withdraw Approval for the Breast Cancer Indication for Bevacizumab (Avastin): FDA Public Hearing" (transcript of minutes), part 1, *A Matter of Record*, Tuesday, June 28, 2011, 172, https://www.federalregister.gov/documents/2011/05/11/2011-11539/proposal-to-withdraw-approval-for-the-breast-cancer-indication-for-bevacizumab-hearing.

3. "Proposal to Withdraw Approval," part 1, 173.

4. Patricia Keegan, quoted in "Proposal to Withdraw Approval," part 1, 175.

5. Keegan, citing Eric Winer in "Proposal to Withdraw Approval," part 1, 176.

6. "Proposal to Withdraw Approval," part 1, 177–178.

7. "Proposal to Withdraw Approval," part 1, 178–179.

8. "Proposal to Withdraw Approval," part 1, 180.

9. "Proposal to Withdraw Approval," part 1, 181–182.

10. "Proposal to Withdraw Approval," part 1, 190–191.

11. Keegan, quoted in "Proposal to Withdraw Approval," part 1, 197.

12. Keegan, quoted in "Proposal to Withdraw Approval," part 1, 198.

13. Juliet Preston, "More Change at the FDA as John Jenkins Steps Down," *MedCity News*, December 5, 2016, https://medcitynews.com/2016/12/change-at-fda-as-john-jenkins-steps-down/.

14. "Proposal to Withdraw Approval," part 1, 205–206.

15. John Jenkins, quoted "Proposal to Withdraw Approval," part 1, 206.

16. "Proposal to Withdraw Approval," part 1, 208.

17. Paul Schmidt, quoted in "Proposal to Withdraw Approval," part 1, 213.

18. Schmidt, quoted in "Proposal to Withdraw Approval," part 1, 213–214.

19. Schmidt, quoted in "Proposal to Withdraw Approval," part 1, 214.

20. Schmidt, quoted in "Proposal to Withdraw Approval," part 1, 215.

21. Rick Pazdur, quoted in "Proposal to Withdraw Approval," part 1, 215–216.

22. Schmidt, quoted in "Proposal to Withdraw Approval," part 1, 215–216.

23. Schmidt, quoted in "Proposal to Withdraw Approval," part 1, 220, 221.

24. Schmidt, cited in "Proposal to Withdraw Approval," part 1, 221.

25. Keegan, quoted in "Proposal to Withdraw Approval," part 1, 222.

26. Schmidt, quoted in "Proposal to Withdraw Approval," part 1, 226.

27. Schmidt, quoted in "Proposal to Withdraw Approval," part 1, 229.

28. Keegan, quoted in "Proposal to Withdraw Approval," part 1, 230 (emphasis added).

29. Schmidt, quoted in "Proposal to Withdraw Approval," part 1, 231 (emphasis added).

30. Pazdur, quoted in "Proposal to Withdraw Approval," part 1, 231–232.

31. US FDA, "Summary Minutes of the Oncologic Drugs Advisory Committee," 2007, part 2, 127, https://wayback.archive-it.org/7993/20170404050555/https:/www.fda.gov/ohrms/dockets/ac/07/transcripts/2007-4332t1-part2.pdf.

32. R. M. Stone, S. J. Mandrekar, B. L. Sanford, et al., "Midostaurin Plus Chemotherapy for Acute Myeloid Leukemia with a FLT3 Mutation," *New England Journal of Medicine* 377, no. 5 (August 3, 2017): 454–464.

33. Stone et al., "Midostaurin Plus Chemotherapy for Acute Myeloid Leukemia."

34. Nicholas J. Robert, Veronique Diéras, John Glaspy, Adam M. Brufsky, Igor Bondarenko, et al., "RIBBON-1: Randomized, Double-Blind, Placebo-Controlled, Phase III Trial of Chemotherapy with or without Bevacizumab for First-Line Treatment of Human Epidermal Growth Factor Receptor 2-Negative, Locally Recurrent or Metastatic Breast Cancer," *Journal of Clinical Oncology* 29, no. 10 (2011): 1252–1260.

35. Pazdur, quoted in "Proposal to Withdraw Approval," part 1, 236.

36. Jeff Helterbrand, quoted in "Proposal to Withdraw Approval," part 1, 243.

37. Rajeshwari Sridhara, quoted in "Proposal to Withdraw Approval," part 1, 246.

38. Dr. Seuss, *Green Eggs and Ham* (New York: Beginner Books/Random House, 1960).

39. Helterbrand, quoted in "Proposal to Withdraw Approval," part 1, 248–249.

40. Pazdur, quoted in "Proposal to Withdraw Approval," part 1, 249.

41. Schmidt, quoted in "Proposal to Withdraw Approval," part 1, 260.

42. Pazdur, quoted in "Proposal to Withdraw Approval," part 1, 260.

43. Schmidt, quoted in "Proposal to Withdraw Approval," part 1, 260.

44. Abigail Brandel, quoted in "Proposal to Withdraw Approval," part 1, 262.

45. Schmidt, quoted in "Proposal to Withdraw Approval," part 1, 264.

46. Jenkins, quoted in "Proposal to Withdraw Approval," part 1, 265.

47. Schmidt, quoted in "Proposal to Withdraw Approval," part 1, 265.

48. Jenkins, quoted in "Proposal to Withdraw Approval," part 1, 266–267.

49. Schmidt, quoted in "Proposal to Withdraw Approval," part 1, 268.

50. Keegan, quoted in "Proposal to Withdraw Approval," part 1, 269.

51. Keegan, quoted in "Proposal to Withdraw Approval," part 1, 269–270.

52. Wyndham Wilson, quoted in "Proposal to Withdraw Approval," part 1, 270.

53. Wilson, quoted in "Proposal to Withdraw Approval," part 1, 299–300.

54. National Cancer Institute, "A Story of Discovery: Natural Compound Helps Treat Breast and Ovarian Cancers," https://www.cancer.gov/research/progress/discovery /taxol.

55. Keegan, quoted in "Proposal to Withdraw Approval," part 1, 301.

56. Ralph Freedman, quoted in "Proposal to Withdraw Approval," part 1, 289–290.

57. Keegan, quoted in "Proposal to Withdraw Approval," part 1, 290.

58. Gregory Curt, quoted in "Proposal to Withdraw Approval," part 1, 281.

59. Pazdur, quoted in "Proposal to Withdraw Approval," part 1, 282.

60. Mikkael Sekeres, quoted in "Proposal to Withdraw Approval," part 1, 282–283.

61. Pazdur, quoted in "Proposal to Withdraw Approval," part 1, 283–284.

62. Sekeres, quoted in "Proposal to Withdraw Approval," part 1, 284–285.

63. Pazdur, quoted in "Proposal to Withdraw Approval," part 1, 285.

## Chapter 9

1. Karen Midthun, quoted in "Proposal to Withdraw Approval for the Breast Cancer Indication for Bevacizumab (Avastin): FDA Public Hearing," part 2 (transcript of minutes), *A Matter of Record*, Wednesday, June 29, 2011, 6.

2. Hal Barron, "Judging a Cancer Drug: Avastin's Story," *New York Times*, June 1, 2011, https://www.nytimes.com/2011/06/02/opinion/l02avastin.html.

3. Hal Barron, quoted in "Proposal to Withdraw Approval," part 2, 7.

4. Barron, quoted in "Proposal to Withdraw Approval," part 2, 8–9.

5. Barron, quoted in "Proposal to Withdraw Approval," part 2, 14.

6. Ronald Piana, "Lymphoma Expert and Industry Leader Sandra J. Horning, MD, Pushes the Frontiers of Drug Development and Oncology Research," *ASCO Post*, June 10, 201, https://ascopost.com/issues/june-10-2015-supplement/lymphoma -expert-and-industry-leader-sandra-j-horning-md-pushes-the-frontiers-of-drug -development-and-oncology-research/; "American Society of Clinical Oncology Membership," https://www.asco.org/membership.

7. Sandra Horning, quoted in "Proposal to Withdraw Approval," part 2, 14.

8. Horning, quoted in "Proposal to Withdraw Approval," part 2, 34.

9. Horning, quoted in "Proposal to Withdraw Approval," part 2, 43.

10. Horning, quoted in "Proposal to Withdraw Approval," part 2, 36.

11. Horning, quoted in "Proposal to Withdraw Approval," part 2, 38.

12. Timothy A. Akinyomi, "If You Torture the Data Long Enough, It Will Confess to Anything," Medium.com, December 30, 2019, https://medium.com /@timothyakinyomi/if-you-torture-the-data-long-enough-it-will-confess-to-anything -492786c30169.

13. Horning, quoted in "Proposal to Withdraw Approval," part 2, 43.

14. P. Ranganathan, C. S. Pramesh, and M. Buyse, "Common Pitfalls in Statistical Analysis: The Perils of Multiple Testing," *Perspectives in Clinical Research* 7, no. 2 (2016): 106–107.

15. Ranganathan et al., "Common Pitfalls in Statistical Analysis."

16. Horning, quoted in "Proposal to Withdraw Approval," part 2, 50.

17. Ronald Piana, "On the Frontier of Breast Cancer Research with Joyce A. O'Shaughnessy, MD," *ASCO Post*, October 25, 2018, https://ascopost.com/issues /october-25-2018/on-the-frontier-of-breast-cancer-research-with-joyce-a-o-shaughnessy -md/.

18. Joyce O'Shaughnessy, quoted in "Proposal to Withdraw Approval," part 2, 84, 86.

19. O'Shaughnessy, quoted in "Proposal to Withdraw Approval," part 2, 80.

20. Michael Labson, quoting Robert Temple, in "Proposal to Withdraw Approval," part 2, 92.

21. Labson, quoting Rick Pazdur, in "Proposal to Withdraw Approval," part 2, 93.

22. Labson, "Proposal to Withdraw Approval," part 2, 98.

23. Barron, "Proposal to Withdraw Approval," part 2, 103, 104–105.

24. Carla Cartwright, "Proposal to Withdraw Approval," part 2, 107.

25. "Proposal to Withdraw Approval," part 2, 109–110.

26. Horning, in "Proposal to Withdraw Approval," part 2, 36.

27. John Jenkins, in "Proposal to Withdraw Approval," part 2, 110.

28. Horning, in "Proposal to Withdraw Approval," part 2, 114.

29. Cartwright, "Proposal to Withdraw Approval," part 2, 136.

30. James Reimann, "Proposal to Withdraw Approval," part 2, 136.

31. Julia A. Beaver, Lynn J. Howie, Lorraine Pelosof, et al., "A 25-Year Experience of US Food and Drug Administration Accelerated Approval of Malignant Hematology and Oncology Drugs and Biologics: A Review," *JAMA Oncology* 4, no. 6 (2018): 849–856.

32. Jenkins, "Proposal to Withdraw Approval," part 2, 140.

33. Wilson, "Proposal to Withdraw Approval," part 2, 149–150.

34. Frank Balis, "Proposal to Withdraw Approval," part 2, 159.

35. "Proposal to Withdraw Approval," part 2, 160.

36. "Proposal to Withdraw Approval," part 2, 161.

37. "Proposal to Withdraw Approval," part 2, 178.

38. Mikkael Sekeres, quoted in "Proposal to Withdraw Approval," part 2, 166.

39. Sekeres, quoted in "Proposal to Withdraw Approval," part 2, 166.

40. Reimann, quoted in "Proposal to Withdraw Approval," part 2, 167.

41. Sekeres, quoted in "Proposal to Withdraw Approval," part 2, 168.

42. Freedman, quoted in "Proposal to Withdraw Approval," part 2, 169–170.

43. O'Shaughnessy, quoted in "Proposal to Withdraw Approval," part 2, 170.

44. Freedman, quoted in "Proposal to Withdraw Approval," part 2, 171.

45. Natalie Compagni-Portis, quoted in "Proposal to Withdraw Approval," part 2, 174–175 (emphasis added).

46. Reimann, quoted in "Proposal to Withdraw Approval," part 2, 176.

47. Barron, quoted in "Proposal to Withdraw Approval," part 2, 177–178.

48. Compagni-Portis, quoted in "Proposal to Withdraw Approval," part 2, 179.

49. Horning, quoted in "Proposal to Withdraw Approval," part 2, 180.

50. Midthun, quoted in "Proposal to Withdraw Approval," part 2, 227 (emphasis added).

51. Wilson, quoted in "Proposal to Withdraw Approval," part 2, 228.

52. Sekeres, quoted in "Proposal to Withdraw Approval," part 2, 229.

53. Midthun, quoted in "Proposal to Withdraw Approval," part 2, 230.

54. Logan, quoted in "Proposal to Withdraw Approval," part 2, 237.

55. Midthun, quoted in "Proposal to Withdraw Approval," part 2, 238–239.

56. Compagni-Portis, quoted in "Proposal to Withdraw Approval," part 2, 242, 246 (emphasis added).

57. Compagni-Portis, quoted in "Proposal to Withdraw Approval," part 2, 247.

58. Freedman, quoted in "Proposal to Withdraw Approval," part 2, 266–267.

59. Sekeres, quoted in "Proposal to Withdraw Approval," part 2, 265.

60. Wilson, quoted in "Proposal to Withdraw Approval," part 2, 267–268.

61. "Proposal to Withdraw Approval," part 2, 268.

62. Midthun, quoted in "Proposal to Withdraw Approval," part 2, 268–269, 271.

63. Crystal Hanna, quoted in Andrew Pollack, "Panel Advises FDA to Narrow Its Approval for Avastin," *New York Times*, June 29, 2011.

**Epilogue**

1. US FDA, Docket No. FDA-2010-N-0621, "Proposal to Withdraw Approval for the Breast Cancer Indication for Avastin (Bevacizumab), Decision of the Commissioner," November 18, 2011; "Avastin FDA Approval History," Drugs.com., https://www.drugs.com/history/avastin.html.

2. US FDA, Docket No. FDA-2010-N-0621, 4; US FDA, "Avastin Prescribing Information," https://www.accessdata.fda.gov/drugsatfda_docs/label/2018/125085s323lbl.pdf.

3. US FDA, Docket No. FDA-2010-N-0621, 5.

4. Margaret Hamburg, quoted US FDA, Docket No. FDA-2010-N-0621, November 18, 2011, 5.

5. US FDA, Docket No. FDA-2010-N-0621, 6.

6. US FDA, Docket No. FDA-2010-N-0621, 44; Matthew Herper, "Would Trump's FDA Deregulation Create an Age of Miracles? Don't Bet on It," *Forbes*, March 1, 2017, https://www.forbes.com/sites/matthewherper/2017/03/01/would-trumps-fda-deregulation-create-an-age-of-miracles-dont-bet-on-it/#48219ba53883.

7. US FDA, Docket No. FDA-2010-N-062, 7.

8. Margaret Hamburg, quoted in Andrew Pollack, "Panel Advises FDA to Narrow Its Approval for Avastin," *New York Times*, June 29, 2011.

9. Hamberg, quoted in US FDA, Docket No. FDA-2010-N-0621, 68–69.

10. Kathy D. Miller, Anne O'Neill, William Gradishar, Timothy J. Hobday, Lori J. Goldstein, et al., "Double-Blind Phase III Trial of Adjuvant Chemotherapy with

and without Bevacizumab in Patients With Lymph Node–Positive and High-Risk Lymph Node–Negative Breast Cancer (E5103)," *Journal of Clinical Oncology* 36, no. 25 (September 1, 2018): 2621–2630; Dave Levitan, "Adjuvant Bevacizumab Fails to Help in High-Risk Breast Cancer, *CancerNetwork*, August 1, 2018, https://www .cancernetwork.com/view/adjuvant-bevacizumab-fails-help-high-risk-breast-cancer1.

11. Adam M. Brufsky, Sara Hurvitz, Edith Perez, Raij Swamy, Vincente Valero, et al., "RIBBON-2: A Randomized, Double-Blind, Placebo-Controlled, Phase III Trial Evaluating the Efficacy and Safety of Bevacizumab in Combination with Chemotherapy for Second-Line Treatment of Human Epidermal Growth Factor Receptor 2-Negative Metastatic Breast Cancer," *Journal of Clinical Oncology* 29, no 32 (November 10, 2011): 4286–4293.

12. "Avastin FDA Approval History."

13. Roche, "FY 2010 Results," February 2, 2011, https://www.roche.com/dam /jcr:397f5892-d7fd-46e3-822a-3db037545f23/en/irp110202.pdf.

14. Rob Stein, "FDA Revokes Avastin's approval for Breast Cancer Treatment," *Washington Post*, November 18, 2011, https://www.washingtonpost.com/national /health-science/fda-revokes-avastins-approval-for-breast-cancer-treatment/2011/11 /18/gIQAOTuRYN_story.html.

15. Kyle Blankenship, "Avastin," FiercePharma.com, July 27, 2020, https://www .fiercepharma.com/special-report/top-20-drugs-by-global-sales-2019-avastin.

16. US FDA, "What Is A Biosimilar?," https://www.fda.gov/media/108905/download; US FDA, "Biosimilar Product Information," https://www.fda.gov/drugs/biosimilars /biosimilar-product-information.

17. Sandee LaMotte, "Scott Gottlieb: Conflicts Surround Trumps FDA Pick," CNN.com., April 4, 2017, https://www.cnn.com/2017/04/04/health/fda-gottlieb -background-qualifications/index.html; Herper, "Would Trump's FDA Deregulation Create an Age of Miracles?"

18. Katie Thomas, "FDA Nominee, Paid Millions by Industry, Says He'll Recuse Himself if Needed," *New York Times*, March 29, 2017, https://www.nytimes.com/2017 /03/29/health/fda-nominee-scott-gottlieb-recuse-conflicts.html.

19. Deepak L. Bhatt, David E. Kandzari, William W. O'Neill, Ralph D'Agostino, John M. Flack, et al., for the SYMPLICITY HTN-3 Investigators, "A Controlled Trial of Renal Denervation for Resistant Hypertension," *New England Journal of Medicine* 370 (2014): 1393–1401.

20. Asher Mullard, "2019 FDA Drug Approvals," *Nature Reviews Drug Discovery* 19 (2020): 79–84.

21. Gardiner Harris, "FDA Regulator, Widowed by Cancer, Helps Speed Drug Approval," *New York Times*, January 2, 2016, https://www.nytimes.com/2016/01/03/us/politics/fda-regulator-widowed-by-cancer-helps-speed-drug-approval.html.

22. US Food and Drug Administration, "FDA Approves Voxelotor for Sickle Cell Disease," November 25, 2019, https://www.fda.gov/drugs/resources-information -approved-drugs/fda-approves-voxelotor-sickle-cell-disease.

23. Kathleen M. Mahoney, Gordon J. Freeman, and David F. McDermott, "The Next Immune-Checkpoint Inhibitors: PD-1/PD-L1 Blockade in Melanoma," *Clinical Therapeutics* 37, no. 4 (2015): 764–782.

24. Caroline Robert, Antoni Ribas, Jacob Schachter, Ana Arance, Jean-Jacques Grob, et al., "Pembrolizumab versus Ipilimumab in Advanced Melanoma (KEYNOTE-006): Post-hoc 5-Year Results from an Open-Label, Multicentre, Randomised, Controlled, Phase 3 Study," *Lancet Oncology* 20, no. 9 (2019): 1239.

25. Courtney D. DiNardo, Eytan M. Stein, Stéphane de Botton, Gail J. Roboz, Jessica K. Altman, et al., "Durable Remissions with Ivosidenib in IDH1-Mutated Relapsed or Refractory AML," *New England Journal of Medicine* 378 (2018): 2386–2398.

26. Sergio Amadori, Stefan Suciu, Dominik Selleslag, Franco Aversa, Gianluca Gaidano, et al., "Gemtuzumab Ozogamicin versus Best Supportive Care in Older Patients with Newly Diagnosed Acute Myeloid Leukemia Unsuitable for Intensive Chemotherapy: Results of the Randomized Phase III EORTC-GIMEMA AML-19 Trial," *Journal of Clinical Oncology* 34, no. 9 (March 20, 2016): 972–979.

27. David S. Knopman, David T. Jones, Michael D. Greicius, "Failure to Demonstrate Efficacy of Aducanumab: An Analysis of the EMERGE and ENGAGE Trials as Reported by Biogen, December 2019," *Alzheimer's & Dementia* 17, no. 4 (2021): 696–701; US FDA, "FDA Grants Accelerated Approval for Alzheimer's Drug," https://www.fda.gov/news-events/press-announcements/fda-grants-accelerated-approval -alzheimers-drug.

28. Pam Belluck, Sheila Kaplan and Rebecca Robbins. How an Unproven Alzheimer's Drug Got Approved," *New York Times*, July 19, 2021; Rita Rubin, "Recently Approved Alzheimer Drug Raises Questions That Might Never Be Answered," *JAMA* 326, no. 6 (2021):469–472.

29. US FDA, "FDA Grants Accelerated Approval for Alzheimer's Drug, June 7, 2021, https://www.fda.gov/news-events/press-announcements/fda-grants-accelerated -approval-alzheimers-drug.

30. US FDA, "Right to Try," https://www.fda.gov/patients/learn-about-expanded -access-and-other-treatment-options/right-try; ASCO, "Be Ready for Patient Questions about Right-to-Try and Expanded Access to Investigational Therapies with ASCO

FAQ," *ASCO Connection*, July 11, 2018, https://connection.asco.org/magazine/features/be-ready-patient-questions-about-right-try-and-expanded-access-investigational.

31. Alison Bateman-House, "'Right to Try' Is Law, Now What?" *Health Affairs*, October 25, 2018, https://www.healthaffairs.org/do/10.1377/hblog20181024.111856/full/.

32. Jonathan P. Jarow, Steven Lemery, Kevin Bugin, Sean Khozin, and Richard Moscicki, "Expanded Access of Investigational Drugs: The Experience of the Center of Drug Evaluation and Research Over a 10-Year Period," *Therapeutic Innovation & Regulatory Science* 50, no. 6 (2016): 705–709.

33. US FDA, *Expanded Access Program Report*, May 2018, https://www.fda.gov/media/119971/download.

# Index